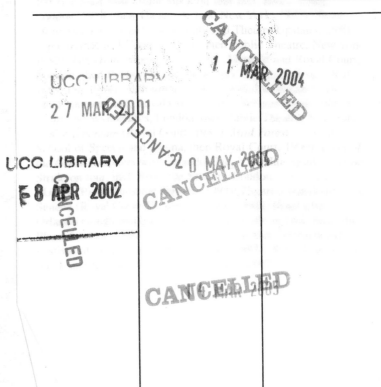

Other works by the same author

Owners

Light Shining in Buckinghamshire (NHB)

Vinegar Tom

Traps (NHB)

Cloud Nine (NHB)

Three More Sleepless Nights

Top Girls

Fen

Softcops

Serious Money

Shorts (NHB)

Hotel (NHB)

This is a Chair (NHB)

Blue Heart (NHB)

CARYL CHURCHILL

Plays: Three

introduced by the author

A Mouthful of Birds
co-author: David Lan

Icecream

Mad Forest

Lives of the Great Poisoners
co-authors: Orlando Gough and Ian Spink

The Skriker

Thyestes
translated from Seneca

NICK HERN BOOKS

London

A Nick Hern Book

Churchill: Plays Three first published in Great Britain in 1998
as a paperback original by Nick Hern Books Limited,
14 Larden Road, London W3 7ST

Front cover photo by Val Rylands

Typeset by Country Setting, Woodchurch, Kent TN26 3TB
Printed in Great Britain by Cox and Wyman, Reading, Berks

A CIP catalogue record for this book is available from the British Library

ISBN 1 85459 342 0

Contents

Introduction

Each of these pieces came about in an entirely different way. *Icecream* is simply a play I wrote. *A Mouthful of Birds*, *Mad Forest* and *Lives of the Great Poisoners* all came from some kind of work with others. *The Skriker*, like *Icecream*, was a solitary piece of work till rehearsal but it took the form it did because of earlier collaborations. *Thyestes* is a translation.

A Mouthful of Birds was a show for Joint Stock, and took Euripides' *Bacchae* as a starting point. Usually with Joint Stock shows there was a gap between workshop and rehearsal when the writer wrote the play, but as we were working with dance as well as words we worked continuously for 12 weeks. For the writers the time still fell into something of the usual structure – roughly the first four weeks were spent by us all looking into possession, violence and other states where people felt beside themselves; then David Lan and I stayed home and wrote, coming in with scenes as they were written; the last few weeks were something like a normal rehearsal. Ian Spink (choreographer) worked with the company continuously, making some material before any text was written, and some to fit specifically into scenes that were written to have dance in them. Though *A Mouthful of Birds* is included in this volume the writing is as much David Lan's as mine, and, as with other Joint Stock shows. it owes a great deal to the company. One can only get a rough idea of the piece by reading it because a large part of it was dance.

After *Icecream* another Joint Stock type play, *Mad Forest*. Mark Wing-Davey, who had worked with Joint Stock, was at the time director of the Central School of Speech and Drama. It was early 1990 and Ceauşescu had been overthrown in December. Mark wanted to take some students to Bucharest to work with students there, and asked if I'd join them and then write something for the Central students' end of year show. Emotions in Bucharest were still raw and the Romanian students and other people we met helped us to understand what Romania had been like under Ceauşescu as well as what happened in December and what was happening while we were there. We learned far more in a short time than anyone could have done alone, and the company's intense involvement made it possible to write the play.

Meanwhile talks had been going on for some time about a piece –
eventually called *Lives of the Great Poisoners* – for Ian Spink's
company Second Stride, with Orlando Gough (composer) and
Antony McDonald (designer), who had both done several Second
Stride shows. We decided that some of the characters would
dance, some sing, some speak. but they could all have a dialogue
in the same scene. so this is another instance where it's hard to
visualise the show from the text alone. Long pieces of dance are
described in a few lines of Ian's stage directions. and sometimes a
few words are the libretto for a long passage of song. The whole
idea of the piece and its structure were worked out with Ian and
Orlando before I wrote any words so it was equally made by us
all. The writer has an unfair advantage because words can easily
be reproduced in a book. Ian's directions should be followed
closely, though the detail will of course be different with each
production. The music of *Poisoners* is integral to the piece.

There's dance and singing in *The Skriker* too, but because of the
way it was written it seems all right that the movement will be
developed differently in each production (though again it is
important to follow the stage directions closely), and even that
different music could be used – though I strongly recommend
Judith Weir's. *The Skriker* is a play I was working on from before
A Mouthful of Birds till after *Poisoners*. Sometimes it seemed like
a social play with lots of characters, other times to be about just a
few people. The solution I found was to have just three speaking
parts, and the rest of the characters played by dancers, so that a
number of stories are told but only one in words. I wrote the
others as stage directions. I decided that the underworld, when
the Skriker takes Josie there, would be a more completely
different world if that scene were an opera, so I wrote it as a
libretto. Judith Weir then wrote the music and during rehearsal
Ian Spink developed the movement from the stage directions. I'd
never have written *The Skriker* that way if I hadn't already worked
on other shows with dancers and singers. It brought together what
had been for me two separate strands of work, plays I worked on
alone and dance/music theatre pieces.

The last play in this volume is a collaboration with a dead writer,
a translation of Seneca's *Thyestes*. It was directed by James
MacDonald, who also directed *Lives of the Great Poisoners*. There
are other overlaps among these pieces – Les Waters and Annie
Smart were the director and designer of both *Mouthful of Birds*
and *Skriker*. Antony McDonald designed *Mad Forest* and
Poisoners.

Caryl Churchill, 1997

A MOUTHFUL OF BIRDS

by Caryl Churchill and David Lan

A Mouthful of Birds was first performed in association with
the Joint Stock Theatre Group at Birmingham Repertory Theatre
on 2 September 1986 and opened at the Royal Court Theatre,
London, on 27 November 1986. The cast was as follows:

LENA, *a mother*	Tricia Kelly
MARCIA, *a switchboard operator*	Dona Croll
DEREK, *unemployed*	Christian Burgess
YVONNE, *an acupuncturist*	Vivienne Rochester
PAUL, *a businessman*	Philippe Giraudeau
DAN, *a vicar*	Stephen Goff
DOREEN, *a secretary*	Amelda Brown
DIONYSOS	Philippe Giraudeau
PENTHEUS, *King of Thebes*	Christian Burgess
AGAVE, *his mother*	Amelda Brown
WOMEN	Dona Croll, Tricia Kelly, Vivienne Rochester
DIONYSOS 2	Stephen Goff

On 11 October, Amelda Brown took over the roles initially
played by Marjorie Yates. Marjorie Yates was a member of the
original workshop company and cast.

Directed by Ian Spink and Les Waters
Designed by Annie Smart
Lighting designed by Rick Fisher

ACT ONE

Part One

1. DIONYSOS dances.

He is played by a man. He wears a white petticoat.

Skinning a Rabbit

LENA *and* ROY.

ROY *is holding a dead white rabbit.*

LENA	(*to audience*). Look at the hole in its stomach. (*To* ROY.) I couldn't possibly.
ROY.	I'll skin it for you.
LENA.	Look at its face.
ROY.	My grandmother used to cook them with prunes.
LENA.	Do you know how to skin it?
ROY.	I've shot rabbits.
LENA.	Look at the hole in its stomach.
ROY.	It's like chicken.
LENA.	It's so white. All right. If you do it all.
ROY.	You soak the prunes.

2. Telephone

MARCIA is *operating a switchboard.*

MARCIA	(*to audience*). In fact I am desperate.
	(*On telephone.*) Continental Lingerie, hold the line.
	Yes, sir? Sir. I am busy.

Continental Lingerie, hold the line.

Yes? Who? Putting you through.

(*West Indian accent.*) You there? . . . so my boss asked me, had l ever been to the Ritz . . . Hang on a minute.

Yes? Look, if this goes on – . It's your firm that suffers. Well, *I* care. I do.

(*West Indian accent.*) You there? . . . so I told him straight. I said, quick as a flash . . .

COLIN *comes in.*

Pause.

Ooh, new trousers? Fit you ever so snug.

COLIN.   My office. Now.

MARCIA.   Get me a cup of tea, be a sweetie.

Continental Lingerie. I'm afraid you can't. He's having a meeting with a lady friend.

COLIN *gestures 'Who?'*

MARCIA *gestures 'You'.*

COLIN *gestures 'Me?'*

MARCIA.   Yes, sir. But he won't want to speak to you. He told me himself he doesn't care what happens to the firm. He's only interested in –

COLIN *goes out.*

MARCIA.   Putting you through. (*West Indian accent.*) You there? . . . I'd have to be desperate to look at him. In fact I am desperate. Even so . . . Oh, hang on.

Continental Lingerie. Putting you through.

3. Weightlifting

DEREK *and two other men are doing weights.*

DEREK   (*to audience*). He thought he wasn't a man without a job.

MAN 1.   How long since you worked?

DEREK.   A while.

MAN 1.   I've never worked.

             Silence.

MAN 2.   I'm going for an interview tomorrow.

MAN 1.   What for?

MAN 2.   They make biscuits.

MAN 1.   Do you know about biscuits?

MAN 2.   Seven years' experience of marketing. First-class
             degree in economics. I've eaten biscuits.

MAN 1.   So we might not be seeing so much of you.

             Pause.

MAN 2.   I've had twenty-three interviews.

             Silence.

DEREK.   Seventeen months.

             Silence.

MAN 2.   Sometimes I think I'll go mad.

DEREK.   No. I don't mind at all any more. I have activities.
             Swimming, karate, jogging, garden, weights.
             There's not enough hours in the day if you put
             your mind to it. My father couldn't. He thought he
             wasn't a man without a job. He died within six
             weeks. But there's no need.

             Silence.

MAN 1.   I can't imagine working.

4. Sleep

YVONNE, *an acupuncturist, is attending to* MR WOOD *who is
lying down. She wears a white coat.*

YVONNE   (*to audience*). What is it makes you so angry?
             (*To* MR WOOD.) Relax your arm. No, relax it.
             All right. Let's start at the top. Back. Relax your
             back. All the way down. There. Now shoulder.
             Let it go. Good. Elbow. Wrist. Fingers. All the
             joints. Let the tension flow away. That's it.

She inserts a needle.

Good. So, Mr Wood, tell me – what is it makes you so angry?

She inserts a needle.

You need to think about it so much? You haven't slept for a week, I give up my lunch break, you come in, your whole body's tense. There must be something winding you up.

She inserts a needle.

Good. Now your neck. Relaaax.

She inserts a needle.

So what is it?

MR WOOD.   Gumminumminumminummi goo goo . . .

YVONNE.   Mr Wood? How can I help you if you fall asleep? Mr Wood!

5. Profit

PAUL *and* MOTHER-IN-LAW *are playing chess.*

PAUL   (*to audience*). That way we make more profit.

MOTHER-IN-LAW. I know you don't like me phoning the office. Mother-in-law.

PAUL.   That's perfectly all right. If it's important.

MOTHER-IN-LAW. June wasn't home and I thought . . . I think I've got your queen.

PAUL.   No.

MOTHER-IN-LAW. Ah.

          Pause.

          So will you be coming to us for the weekend?

PAUL.   If I bring some work.

          She moves.

MOTHER-IN-LAW. Check.

          He moves.

PAUL.   Check.

MOTHER-IN-LAW. Could that be mate?

PAUL.   I think so.

           He picks up the telephone, dials.

           First Berlin, then Boulogne.

           He puts the telephone down.

MOTHER-IN-LAW. What?

PAUL.   Fifty thousand tons of beef. We move them from
           Birmingham first to Berlin then to Boulogne. I was
           working it out.

MOTHER-IN-LAW. Unless my rook – no.

PAUL.   That way we make more profit.

MOTHER-IN-LAW. You're very clever.

6. Angels

DAN, *a vicar. Three* WOMEN *in hats.* WOMAN 1 *has a bag
of jumble.*

DAN   (*to audience*). I don't believe God is necessarily
           male.

WOMAN 1. Where shall I put the jumble?

DAN.   In the vestry.

WOMAN 2. Do you believe in angels?

WOMAN 3. But when it comes to the ordination of women,
           have we your support or not?

DAN.   I don't believe God is necessarily male in the
           conventional . . . But I do think there's a time and
           a place . . . I entirely agree with the bishop when
           he –

WOMAN 2. Do you believe in angels?

DAN.   I'm sorry?

7. Home

DOREEN is *standing some distance from* ED.

DOREEN   (to *audience*). All I wanted was peace and quiet.
          (*To* ED.) I never said I wouldn't come home.

ED.   You didn't say nothing. You just ran, left me sitting
          on the bench like a fool.

DOREEN.   All I wanted was peace and quiet. I found it.

ED.   Sleeping by that canal, on that grass? And to
          scratch me and tear me. What for? I was searching
          five hours. Look, I'm still bleeding. Come here.

DOREEN.   I was happy.

ED.   I warned you what would happen if you ran off
          again.

DOREEN.   What? What will happen? What?

          Pause.

ED.   Well, you had your day out all right.

DOREEN.   Oh I did.

8. Excuses

i.

PAUL   (*on telephone*). I'm sorry I can't make the
          conference. I've sprained my ankle.

MARCIA   (*on telephone*). I can't come in, I've lost my voice.

YVONNE   (*on telephone*). I'm afraid I have to cancel your
          appointment, I've hurt my hand.

DOREEN.   I won't be in today, I'm seeing double.

DEREK.   I can't go swimming this morning, I've got a
          hangover.

DAN.   I really can't do the wedding, I've got earache.

LENA.   I can't come to tea, I've cut my finger.

ii.

DEREK.   I can't come to the pub tonight, my dog's gone
              missing.

LENA.   I can't distribute the leaflets, there's a power cut.

MARCIA.   I can't see you tonight, my car's broken down.

YVONNE.   I can't come to the funeral, the trains have been
              cancelled.

DAN.   I can't visit the old people, my mother's turned up.

DOREEN.   I know it's my turn to collect them but the
              kitchen's flooded.

PAUL.   I can't fly to Rome. My cousin has died.

iii.

LENA.   I can't come in for a perm, my sister's been
              kidnapped.

YVONNE.   I can't go to the disco, the army's closed off the
              street.

DOREEN.   I can't come to dinner, there's a bull in the garden.

DEREK.   I can't play tonight, my house has blown down.

DAN.   I can't see the bishop, the vestry's on fire.

PAUL.   I can't meet the deadline. The chairman's been
              struck by lightning.

MARCIA.   I'll have to see the dentist another time, my aunt's
              gone crazy.

LENA.   So I just stayed in all day.

Part Two

9. Psychic Attack

LENA   (*to audience*). Look at the hole in its stomach.

ROY. LENA. SPIRIT.

The SPIRIT *is seen and heard only by* LENA.
Breakfast time on four successive days.

i.

LENA *sets the table.* ROY *comes in.*

ROY.   So at the light he gets
level again and I don't
look at him but he knows
and I know that one of
us is going to be in
trouble because over the
crossing it's got to be
single lane because
there's cars parked. And
I'm on the outside so
I've every right but I
know / from what he's   SPIRIT. teapot teapot teapot
done already that he's   teapot.
going to cut in if he
possibly can and he
knows that I'm going to
keep him out and with
any luck he'll get
smashed on the parked
cars. I can see without
looking the kind of
person he is and it's a
kind I don't like and
will not put up with, the
whole way he sat there
with his elbow out the
window, / I thought to   elbow out the window
myself I'll have that   elbow out the window
elbow off, I'll have that   elbow out the window
elbow right off. So the

minute the lights change
the other side – *and*
there's a stupid bastard /
crossing the other way
only gets through on the
red – and we're both off
with a hell of a screech
and he's got a slight
edge because pure and
simple it's a faster car,
nothing to do with his
driving, it's a new car,
but I've got my foot
hard down and I not
only get ahead but I
swing out a bit to my
left before I swing in
round the back of the
parked cars / and he's
had to pull away and
he's got to brake hard
and he just catches me
on the bumper and he
hits the island and lucky
for him there's no kiddy
waiting to cross the road.
And I go up the street
and down the next
turning because he's
going to come after me
but I'm off down the
back doubles and I
reckon I showed him.

stupid bastard stupid
bastard stupid bastard

LENA. Do you want some
more toast?

ROY *goes.*

Lena and Spirit – Transformations

*He is a frog. She approaches threateningly as a snake. He seizes
her arm and becomes a lover. She responds but as he embraces
her he becomes an animal and attacks the back of her neck. She
puts him down to crawl and he becomes a train. As he chugs
under the table she blocks the tunnel with a chair and he rolls
out as a threatening bird. She becomes a baby bird asking to be*

fed and he feeds her. As he goes to get more food she becomes
a panther, knocks him to the ground and starts to eat him.
After a moment he leaps up with a fierce roar. She goes into
the next scene.

ii.

LENA *sets the table.* ROY *comes in.*

ROY. Don't forget to phone
your mother

Remind me to get a
light bulb.

LENA. I better go to the
launderette today.

ROY. The plumber's coming
on Thursday

LENA. I think I'll take Sally to
the park.

Can we talk about a
holiday?

Am I putting on weight?

SPIRIT. You're useless. Can't
wipe your own bum.
Useless baby.

You're going to be
unborn. You are unborn.
You're not conceived.
Your parents never met.
Your parents / were
never born. Your parents
were never conceived.
Your grandparents never
met. That's how useless
you are.

Because you don't stand
up to him. He's
disgusting. He fills the
whole / room up.

His hair smells. His
eyes have got yellow in
the corners. His ears
have got hairs on. His
nose has got big pores
and the nostrils are too
big and full of hair and
snot and he snores /
and snorts. His teeth are
yellow. His tongue's
yellow. His mouth tastes
of shit because it's
directly connected to
his arsehole.

ROY.   I'm not made of money
you know.

LENA. Don't forget to get a
lightbulb.

ROY.   Mind you I'd like a
break.

LENA. Sure you don't want
an egg?

The order is to kill the
baby. The order is to
kill the baby. Because
the baby is directly /
connected to him. The
baby is directly con-
nected to you. The baby
is directly connected to
me ./ When you kill the
baby you'll be free of
him. You'll be free of
yourself. You'll be free
of me. That's why
you're going to kill the
baby.

ROY.   No.

*ROY goes. LENA and SPIRIT struggle. LENA finally
gets the SPIRIT down and leaves him lying still as she
goes into the next scene. After a moment he gets up and
goes into the scene.*

iii.

LENA sets the table. ROY comes in.

ROY.   So what I'm going to do
is say to him / straight
out, what about that
twenty pounds you owe
me? Because it's three
weeks, it's over three
weeks, it was the
Sunday after the
Saturday Arsenal beat
Liverpool at home. He
thinks he can let it slide
and I won't do that.
What about that twenty
pounds you owe me?
That's the best way.

SPIRIT. Teapot. Cup. Cup. Is
that a cup? You don't
know do you because
you're useless, you're
not born, you're not
conceived of, this house
was never built.

ROY.   So what was the matter
        with you last night?

LENA.   I don't know what you
        mean.

ROY.   What do you mean
        you don't know what
        I mean?

        *They both start
        speaking at once.*

The universe will go
forward again when you
kill the baby. Then he /
won't fill up all the
space. Then you might
get born. Then I'll stop
talking and go away
because then you'll have
done what you should
and you won't be
useless.

ROY.   Have you gone off me?
        I don't need to stick
        around where I'm not
        wanted.

LENA.   Of course you're
        wanted.

His eyes have got red
lines. His fingernails
have got muck under. /
The hairs in his arse are
stuck together. His
cock's got goo coming
out. His feet are full of
black cracks.

ROY.   Are you trying to tell
        me / there's someone
        else because just tell
        me.

When he breathes it
takes your breath away.

LENA.   There's nobody./ Please
        don't. I love you.

ROY.   Because I'm not
        bothered.

He swallows the air.
That's why you don't
exist.

LENA.   Please don't, I really/
        need you, I do need
        you. Please, come on, /
        I was tired last night.

The solution is to kill the
baby. Hold the baby
under the water.

ROY.   I don't know what
        the idea is./ I think
        you're having me on.

LENA.   I'm not, I'm really –
        Please please please.

ROY.   All right. All right.
        We'll see how we go.

Because you're a baby
and you're unborn and
you aren't even
conceived.

ROY. So what I'm going to
do / is say to him
straight out what about
that twenty pounds you
owe me. Because it's
three weeks.

*He continues speech as
above but silently.*

ROY (*aloud again*). Twenty
pounds you owe me,
that's the best way.

LENA. All right.

You should be sick on
his hair. You should piss
in his tea. You should
rub blood on his teeth.
You should shit on his
eyes. You should hold
the baby under the water.

Then I'll go away. When
you've killed the baby
it's going to be quiet.

The SPIRIT *climbs onto* ROY's *back and pushes him
down onto the table.* LENA *washes a shawl in a baby bath.*

iv.

LENA *returns to the table.*

ROY. So I'll phone up and
book today. I could
really do with a break
myself. I know how
much you've been
wanting to go away.

LENA. I have to talk to you.
I think if you go to the
bathroom. I think
Sally's drowned.

ROY. What did you say?
What did you say?

ROY *keeps repeating
the same gesture and
words.*

LENA. It wasn't me that did it.

ROY. What did you say?

LENA. I thought you'd gone.
You said you'd go
away.

SPIRIT. Teapot teapot teapot
teapot.

You're unborn. His hair smells.

ROY.   What did you say?

LENA.   I poured the teapot and blood came out.

10. Possession

DIONYSOS *appears to* DOREEN.

DOREEN is *possessed by* AGAVE.

AGAVE.   I put my foot against its side and tore out its
              shoulder. I broke open its ribs.

11. Fruit Ballet

Whole company as their main characters.

*This dance consists of a series of movements mainly derived
from eating fruit. It emphasises the sensuous pleasures of eating
and the terrors of being torn up.*

12. Possession

DIONYSOS *appears to* DEREK.

DEREK is *possessed by* PENTHEUS.

DEREK.   She put her foot against my side and tore out my
              shoulder. They broke open my ribs.

13. Baron Sunday

MARCIA   (*to audience*). In fact I am desperate.

              MARCIA's *basement and then* DECIMA's *room in
              north London.*

              In MARCIA's *basement: two chairs (A1 & A2) on
              either side of a table, a third chair (A3) a short
              way behind and to the side of one of the others.*

              *A repeat of this arrangement of tables and chair
              stands to the left – B1, B2, B3.*

i.

Table A has a white table cloth and a small glass vase of flowers.

MARCIA, *a Trinidadian medium in her mid-thirties, sits on chair A1.*

On A2, opposite MARCIA, *sits* DECIMA *a younger Trinidadian woman.*

SYBIL, *a spirit from the white upper-middle classes, sits on chair B3.*

When MARCIA *speaks as the spirit, she uses a very deep voice.*

DECIMA.   Who are you?

          Pause.

DECIMA.   If you don' say something soon, Marcia, I'm gonna ask my money back. Who are you?

          Pause.

          Ok. I got shoppin' a do, I got my mama's laundry, I got plenty, plenty.

          Pause.

DECIMA.   Why'd you make me give you all a' my ten p's? Listen, m'dear, the truth is I saved those ten p's for the launderette. I don' know what got into me to give you all a' them. You hear me? Marcia? Give me back my ten p's, I'll go down the launderette an' come try again nex' week. It ain' no shame if you can' do it one time. Marcia, girl? You hear me?

MARCIA.   Baron Sunday.

DECIMA.   You said?

MARCIA.   This is Baron Sunday talkin' to you. Ask.

DECIMA.   Where is the bracelet was stole from me?

          Pause.

MARCIA.   In purgatory.

DECIMA.   You said? My bracelet? Purgatory? What for? It weren't worth hardly nothing. C'mon, Marce. Give me the ten p's, let me get on down the launderette.

MARCIA.   The one who thiefed the bracelet, that's the one's
           in purgatory. The penalty to break god's law –
           hm – death.

DECIMA.   And the bracelet?

MARCIA.   Ha ha ha ha.

DECIMA.   I love that bracelet. Uncle Short Plank sent it all
           the way for me.

MARCIA.   Ha ha ha ha ha.

SYBIL.   You can't tell her where it is. Can you?

           Pause.

MARCIA.   Where is it? Where? (*Own voice.*) Go down the
           launderette. Try again nex' week.

           DECIMA *goes out.*

ii.

MARCIA *stands and moves towards table B. She hesitates,
retreats to A1, sits.*

SYBIL.   You come to this place. Why not? You try to pack
           your powers in your knapsack. They're fond of
           you. They like to help. They come. They stay
           awhile. They go. Of course they do. What are you
           left with? What? But you have such skill.
           Experience. Technique. I've been waiting and
           waiting.

MARCIA   (*own voice*). Who are you?

           Pause.

MARCIA   (*with defiance*). Baron Sunday betrayed his spirit.
           All the people saw his black deceit. Every day the
           bucket goes to the well, one day the bottom falls
           out. (*In agony.*) Aaahh! Eeyaaghooouugh!

           She writhes in pain.

           As MARCIA *writhes in agony,* SYBIL *leaves her
           table and slowly approaches* MARCIA's. *She
           moves only while* MARCIA *wails.*

MARCIA.   When they caught him at his business they
           hounded him out a' his birthplace. For two years
           he carried on his practice round about Port
           Antonio. Then it happened all over again just the
           same. Aaaah!

           *She writhes, falls and pulls the vase and tablecloth
           off the table.*

SYBIL.   Pick it up.

           Pause.

MARCIA.   Eeyaaghooouugh!

SYBIL.   There *is*.

MARCIA.   No!

SYBIL.   Room. For me. There is.

           Pause.

MARCIA.   They knocked him about, cut out his tongue. He
           went home. He died. They buried him like a dog.

SYBIL.   Pick – it – up.

           MARCIA *picks up the table and resets the vase,
           flowers and cloth. She sits. The pain has gone.*

iii.

MARGARET, *white, middle-class, comes on and sits on A2.*

MARGARET. She said an evil spirit is angry with me. She said
           she could break the spell. She couldn't. Now I'm
           desperate. Is it a spell that causes damp? All the
           methods I've found for casting off spells have no
           effect whatsoever. And I've looked up damp as
           well. It's not in anything. I've spent hundreds. And
           builders aren't cheap. As you know.

MARCIA   (*deep voice*). Baron Sunday.

MARGARET. Yes. Yes, I heard you, dear. Can you help me or
           not? You see, in the past I believe there was a West
           Indian family . . . When we bought it we had the
           place stripped, of course, top to toe. Even so –

MARCIA.   Blood.

MARGARET. Yes?

MARCIA. Of a mongoose.

SYBIL. I don't believe it.

MARGARET. I've tried that. Not exactly with a mongoose. Could that be why?

Pause. MARCIA *is hyper-ventilating loudly.*

MARCIA. Baron Sunday.

As she speaks, SYBIL *arrives at A3 and sits.*

SYBIL. Damp proofing. Tell her. Don't skimp. Gypsum, sand, proper chemicals. Tell her.

MARGARET. My dear. I'm sure hyper-ventilation *is* a valuable aid but – are you quite sure you're all right?

iv.

MARCIA is *laying table B with cloth, cutlery and plates.*

SYBIL *sits on A1.*

SYBIL. Voodoo. Juju. Tomtom. You want to stay in this basement forever? Voodoo, juju, tomtom – you will.

MARCIA. I'm gonna need that chair.

MARCIA *goes on laying the table.*

SYBIL. Didn't I tell you? Tap the teaspoon three times on the back of your hand before you lay it down. That's how it's done in this country. Go on.

MARCIA. This is my things! I got Jojo an' Big Bonus and all the family comin'. I'm gonna need all the chairs.

SYBIL. Go on!

MARCIA *taps a teaspoon three times on the back of her hand before laying it down.*

MARCIA. I don' want you here.

SYBIL. Good. Now, the knife. The knife must always be pressed against the forehead. It keeps it honed sharp. Try.

Pause.

MARCIA *pulls up the sides of the cloth into a bundle with cutlery and crockery inside. She holds it over her shoulder.*

MARCIA.   What's your name?

SYBIL.   Today? The princess.

MARCIA.   I get on good with Baron Sunday. I don't want no princess.

SYBIL.   Put everything back on the table like I told you. Go on.

v.

SYBIL *sitting at A1.*

MARCIA *and* DECIMA *in* DECIMA's *room.*

MARCIA.   I think it's time I went back home. I talked to my mother. She agrees. She says this place is workin' on me an' workin' on me. I don't know how she knows the things she knows. She just knows. I am bein' worked on. I don't intend to stay at home forever. But for me to go is good, you think so? My doctor said I'm just not feeling right in myself. She understands me. I got to go back home and find myself. I lost myself. I don't know where.

DECIMA.   How's ol' Baron Sunday?

MARCIA.   Oh, my head is painin' me.

DECIMA.   I got a message for that ol' Baron.

MARCIA.   It's painin'. You don' care 'bout that?

DECIMA.   Your head? It's bad?

MARCIA.   Bad?

DECIMA.   I'll go get a aspirin for you.

DECIMA *goes out.*

SYBIL.   The musicologist's booked for half past three. *He* won't be late.

DECIMA *comes in with an aspirin and a glass of water. She hands them to* MARCIA.

DECIMA.   You tell the Baron I found my bracelet. I'm gonna get a refund of all my ten p's?

As DECIMA *speaks,* MARCIA *holds the aspirin in her left fist and makes a circle round it with the glass of water in her right hand. She does this five times.*

DECIMA.   You feelin' all right, girl?

MARCIA.   Some people live here and live here. They never learn nothin'.

vi.

MARCIA *on A1,* SYBIL *on A3,* CURZON, *a white musicologist, on A2.*

MARCIA *is hyper-ventilating but not loudly. She tries to speak. No words come out.*

CURZON *writes as* SYBIL *speaks.*

SYBIL   (*different voice, German accent*). Quaver G, semi-quaver F, quaver E, semi-quaver D –

CURZON.   D or D sharp?

SYBIL.   D! D natural! Vot you tink I'm writink? Gypsy dances?

MARCIA *tries to speak. No words come out.*

SYBIL *pulls her chair down next to* MARCIA's.

MARCIA *cries out in agony. No sound is heard.*

SYBIL.   Demi-quavers E and F, quaver G and G again. Got it?

CURZON.   Got it.

SYBIL.   Now the second theme.

CURZON *turns the page of his notebook, his pencil poised to write.*

vii.

SYBIL *on A1*, MARGARET *on A2*, MARCIA *on B3*.

SYBIL   (MARCIA*'s voice, West Indian accent*). I been
             away back home. That's why it took so long to
             answer your letter. I wanted to go back home. But
             I found I got no spirit for my ol' home. I got
             nothin' for it at all. You wan' talk to the spirit?

MARGARET. Baron Sunday? Yes please.

SYBIL.   Baron who? No. I left him.

MARGARET. Then – ?

SYBIL.   You want to put your money down or not? I got
             one, believe me. I got one just for you.

14. Possession

DIONYSOS 1 *and* 2 *dance destructively.*

DEREK *is possessed by* PENTHEUS.

PENTHEUS. This is my city. I love it, leave it alone. Kill the
          god!

15. Dancing

DIONYSOS *passes* DAN *as he enters, then goes out.*

DAN   (*to audience*). I don't believe god is necessarily
             male.

i.

Towards the back, a male and a female PRISON OFFICER *are
sitting together at a table. Towards the front, a* WOMAN *is
sitting on a chair wearing a hat.*

DAN, *the vicar, dances to her.*

*This dance is precisely the dance that the woman in the chair
longs for. Watching it she dies of pleasure.*

After a few moments of DAN*'s dance, the* PRISON OFFICERS
start to speak.

FEMALE PRISON OFFICER. All right, a mistake's a mistake.
But – this. No, you're kidding me.

MALE PRISON OFFICER. It wasn't our mistake.

FEMALE PRISON OFFICER. You admitted him.

MALE PRISON OFFICER. Her.

FEMALE PRISON OFFICER. Her.

MALE PRISON OFFICER. It was him when we admitted her.
I can guarantee that.

FEMALE PRISON OFFICER. Guarantee?

MALE PRISON OFFICER. You want a cup of coffee?
Guarantee!

FEMALE PRISON OFFICER. You tell me it's Tuesday,
I'm going to write down Easter Sunday, that
I guarantee.

MALE PRISON OFFICER. I'm asking, you want coffee?

FEMALE PRISON OFFICER. I don't touch it. Heart.

The MALE PRISON OFFICER *starts making
coffee.*

MALE PRISON OFFICER. I didn't put my finger up. If that's
what it takes to guarantee, you're right, I can't
guarantee.

FEMALE PRISON OFFICER. You said when she came in here
she was a he. Have I got it correct?

MALE PRISON OFFICER. What are you trying to say to me?
You'll take him –

FEMALE PRISON OFFICER. Her.

MALE PRISON OFFICER. – or you won't take him? Her! The
governor's waiting.

FEMALE PRISON OFFICER. He's a convicted multiple killer.
He comes into your place a man. Now they want
to transfer him from your place to mine. Pour me
that coffee. My nerves, they can't stand it. Be
straight with me, Tommy. What the hell's going on?

The WOMAN *on the chair has died.*

DAN *stops dancing and hauls out the body.*

ii.

A MAN sits on the chair wearing the hat.

The MALE PRISON OFFICER extracts from a large file various pieces of paper. He reads from one. The difficulty he has with reading produces a flat, matter-of-fact tone. Often he stumbles. When he loses interest in a passage, he skips.

MALE PRISON OFFICER. 'My plan was that they should all be good deaths. Clean, effortless, without tension or pain. To die of pleasure, like a young boy slipping through the mirror of a mountain stream. These are the deaths the earth needs to grow strong. We have asked too much of the earth. We take from her everything that is good. What do we give back? Lives that end in hatred and agony. Our rejected, our despised. So why should the rain . . .'

DAN speaks to the MAN on the chair.

DAN. Hi. I'm Dan. Don't think I'm pushy. Uh, you know how it is. You see someone attractive at the other end of the bar. But you're shy. I'm not shy. What would you like? What would you really like? I can get you anything you like.

The MAN on the chair looks at DAN intrigued.

DAN dances to him.

MALE PRISON OFFICER. '. . . From the age of seventeen I studied theology at the university of Saint Cecille outside Brussels. One summer I worked in a vineyard near Antwerp. The grapes were stillborn. The vineyard failed. O cowards! Embrace the earth willingly! Why don't you? How can she do you harm? Press your throats against her boulders. Rip them. Why not, if that is what she wants? What has she ever refused you? . . .'

'. . . They will say I have tried to play god. I have not. God makes and destroys. I make and destroy nothing. I do man's work. I transform.'

'Fools! You ransack the guts of the earth – '

I can't make out this bit. Call this handwriting?
You wouldn't think he'd been educated at all. You
want to hear any more of this?

The MAN *in the chair dies.*

DAN *stops dancing and hauls out the body.*

iii.

A WOMAN *sits on the chair wearing the hat.*

DAN *puts his head in her lap and talks to her.*

DAN.   I want to be milked from the udder of a cow.
        I'd like a pine tree to grow inside me. I want to
        rest the tips of my fingers on the peaks of two
        mountains so my muscles tear. I want to burn.
        And you?

        DAN *dances briefly to her.*

        The WOMAN *dies.*

        DAN *stops dancing and hauls out the body.*

iv.

The two PRISON OFFICERS *are sitting in different positions
at the table drinking coffee.*

On the chair is the hat.

DAN *dances to it.*

FEMALE PRISON OFFICER. You must have been killing
                yourself. Did you know what you were letting me
                in for? Pass the sugar. I find my girls lying in the
                corridors, the workshops, the latrines. Dead.
                Untouched. Beautiful. I know she done it – all
                of them. Ask me how. Ask me.

MALE PRISON OFFICER. How?

FEMALE PRISON OFFICER. That's what I say – capital
                punishment. Finish her off – quick smart! But they
                won't. I have to look after my girls. You know
                what I done? Ask me.

MALE PRISON OFFICER. What?

FEMALE PRISON OFFICER. What could I do? I let her go.

> *They go on drinking their coffee.*
>
> DAN *continues dancing to the chair.*
>
> DAN *finishes and goes.*

16. Possession

DIONYSOS *appears to* DOREEN *and* DEREK.

DOREEN *is possessed by* AGAVE, DEREK *by* PENTHEUS.

PENTHEUS. Mother! Why have the women left the city?

AGAVE.   I'm happy. Leave us alone.

PENTHEUS. I'm hungry.

> AGAVE *laughs with joy.*

PENTHEUS. I'll fill the woods with blood.

17. Pig

PAUL   (*to audience*). That way we make more profit.

i.

PAUL, *a businessman in a suit, is presenting a report to colleagues.*

Meanwhile the PIG *is dancing. The* COLLEAGUES *don't notice the dance.* PAUL's *attention sometimes goes to it against his will but mainly he is concentrated on what he is doing.*

PAUL.   Page 103 refers back pages 78 and 22. Tables
            E and F correlate in major areas though not as
            regards beef surplus requirements for Benelux
            countries. Reliable figures are still unavailable. The
            improvement in UK exports remains steady, as you
            will see in my conclusions, but – and here there is,
            I agree, room for discussion – no substantial
            acceleration will occur until tariffs are genuinely
            equalised between all trading partners. The details
            of what is required as a matter of urgency are
            found in Appendix E paragraphs 42 to 67.

I hope you will find my conclusions realistic and acceptable. If benefits are to be widespread, duties must remain low. That is uncontested. But the attractions of higher priced European pork, beef and lamb for our own internal domestic markets must be increased if established commercial avenues are to be kept open, standards maintained and profitability stabilised. Turin may wish to go her own way. She will find she cannot. The reasons I hope are now clear.

ii.

PAUL *and* COLLEAGUE.

PIG *continues dancing through beginning of this but comes to an end and goes off without* PAUL *noticing.*

COLL.   Brilliant report.

PAUL.   Thank you.

COLL.   I only had a slight problem with section 6.2.

PAUL.   We must talk about it.

COLL.   And the column of figures at the top of page 52, I'm probably confused but they don't seem to correlate with the March-April statistics for Belgium.

PAUL.   That's an interesting point.

COLL.   And one other thing, when it says twenty-four million here, I can't for the life of me see where it comes from.

PAUL.   Tomorrow morning?

COLL.   Certainly, no hurry, say ten o'clock? You look as if you could use a drink.

PAUL.   Thank you, no. I have an appointment.

PAUL *turns towards the* PIG *but he's gone.*

iii.

PAUL *drinking with a* FRIEND.

PAUL.   I've never noticed pigs before.

FRIEND.   If you drive past a pig farm you notice the smell.

PAUL.   But really they are very clean animals.

FRIEND.   They lie about in the mud. Filthy pig.

PAUL.   It depends how they're kept. Sometimes they lie in mud to get cool. That must be nice.

FRIEND.   Nice?

PAUL.   Like a swimming pool or a sauna. All together in a jacuzzi.

FRIEND.   In mud?

PAUL.   Women put mud packs on their faces. Children like it. There's a tribe in New Guinea who put mud – No? No. Anyway they don't go in the mud very much. They are very clean. They don't smell if they're kept properly.

FRIEND.   So you're off to Italy next week?

PAUL.   And anyway it's not such a bad smell. No, no I can't get away at the moment.

FRIEND.   I thought you'd booked a villa.

PAUL.   Yes, but no, I can't, unfortunately, no. I can't leave just now.

FRIEND.   I'm off to Spain myself.

PAUL.   They are also very intelligent, did you know that?

FRIEND.   Sorry?

PAUL.   Pigs. Are very intelligent. Like a dog. More than a dog.

FRIEND.   Really?

PAUL.   Yes, you can train them. I was reading about it. Somebody lived with a pig in his house. You can housetrain a pig. It comes when you call its name.

FRIEND.   Applesauce!

PAUL.   It could sleep on the end of your bed.

FRIEND.   Bring your slippers and lick your face.

PAUL.   They are quite affectionate. If they know you. And in Moscow they have them in the circus, they do the trapeze. They are not fat.

FRIEND.   Of course they're fat. Fat pig. / Pig ignorant.

PAUL.   They are not fat. They are fattened. They are made fat. We could be fat.

FRIEND.   Some of us are.

PAUL.   There you are.

FRIEND.   But pigs are fat.

PAUL.   They are not fat. If a pig has exercise it isn't fat. It's solid but it's strong. Pigs are very strong. They are quite dangerous.

FRIEND.   Wild boar of course. Kill them with a pack of dogs.

PAUL.   They have tusks. They can kill the dogs. But even your domestic pig can be dangerous. They have a huge bite. Have you looked at their mouths? They've eaten babies. They can bite through metal. And at the same time they are so gentle. You can stroke their ears. Their ears have blue veins.

FRIEND.   Silk purse out of a sow's ear.

PAUL.   I prefer the ear. Really.

FRIEND.   Since when were you a pig fan then?

PAUL.   I went to a pig farm last week.

FRIEND.   I've been to a pig farm.

PAUL.   Yes, I've often done it, of course. But I'd never noticed a pig before. There was one pig I noticed. Once I started looking at him . . . I tried to look at them all again as so many hundred pigs, so many kilos.

FRIEND.   As exports.

PAUL.   Yes, as percentages. But I came back to this pig.

FRIEND.	I'm fond of animals myself. Everyone is, basically. It's recreation, a pet.
PAUL.	Yes.

iv.

PAUL *dances with the* PIG, *tenderly.*

v.

PAUL *and his wife,* JUNE. *She is eating fruit.*

JUNE.	So can we go on the 23rd?
PAUL.	I don't know.
JUNE.	We have to make plans.
PAUL.	Make the booking. You can always go without me.
JUNE.	I just might go without you.
PAUL.	No of course. I'll come. Make the booking. That's fine.
JUNE.	How was your day.
PAUL.	Good, a good day. Long meeting.
JUNE.	Did you go to your pig farm again?
PAUL.	Yes, I think so. Yes, I did, of course.
JUNE.	You really like that pig, don't you?
PAUL.	It's amusing.
JUNE.	Do you want to get a piglet as a pet? We could try it. People keep snakes and eagles, I could probably cope with a pig.
PAUL.	No, no, I don't want to. Thank you.
JUNE.	If you'd like it.
PAUL.	It's not any pig.
JUNE.	How do you mean?
PAUL.	It's that pig. I like that pig.

JUNE.   Why?

PAUL.   It's just – Can I explain this to you, please. You
           look at him, you just – You don't want to do
           anything else. His shape is cut in the air. You feel
           completely – there is nothing else to be said. There
           he is – and . . .

JUNE.   Are you in love with this pig?

PAUL.   Of course not.

JUNE.   You sound like it.

PAUL.   I'm fond of it, yes, people get fond of animals
           don't they, this is usual, people have animals they
           are fond of. People leave money to cats. They have
           tombstones for dogs. I am interested in the pig,
           that's all.

JUNE.   So you don't mind leaving him to go on holiday?

PAUL.   That's nothing to do with the pig. I'm very busy.

JUNE.   So we can go away and leave the pig?

PAUL.   Of course.

JUNE.   I'm only teasing. You're so funny.

vi.

PAUL *and the* PIG *dance, dangerously.*

vii.

A COLLEAGUE *is reading a report to* PAUL *and another*
COLLEAGUE. *Meanwhile the* PIG *is wrapped in clingfilm.*
It is now dead meat.

COLL.   In the second column we have the agricultural
           levies for financial year 1986. Belgium 186 billion,
           Denmark 7 billion, Italy 313 billion, 300 thousand,
           Germany 187½ billion, Germany 26 billion . . .

           She stops and looks at PAUL *who is smiling to*
           himself.

> Germany 187½ billion, Greece 26 billion, France 96 billion, Spain – .

PAUL.   I'm sorry. I'm just so happy.

viii.

PAUL *and* FRIEND.

PAUL.   I telephoned. They said they were going to be slaughtered that afternoon. I said I would buy my pig. They said which pig, I didn't know, I said I would come at once. I got in the car. It's a two-hour drive. I go there sometimes at night just to stand in the yard, it's an hour and a half at night but during the day it's two hours. There was a traffic jam on the motorway, there'd been an accident. I had to be there by twelve, I arrived at twelve-thirty, they'd sent them off to the abattoir. I drove to the abattoir. It's hard to drive when you're crying.

ix.

PAUL *tears up the documents and scatters them. He rips his jacket off and knocks over the furniture.*

PAUL *takes the dead pig and lays it on the ground.*

He takes off the clingfilm. The PIG *comes out alive.*

PAUL *and the* PIG *dance, tenderly, dangerously, joyfully.*

18. Extreme Happiness

Whole COMPANY *as their main characters.*

This dance consists of memories of moments of extreme happiness.

After a while all the members of the COMPANY *find themselves in a waterfall. They dash in and out, they stand letting the stream pour down on their backs – a moment of severe physical pleasure.*

In the midst of this, the four WOMEN *become possessed by* AGAVE *and the spirits of three* BACCHANTS.

DOREEN *is possessed by* AGAVE.

AGAVE.   Why are my feet cut and blistered? I've been running all night.

MARCIA *is possessed by a* BACCHANT.

BACCHANT 1. Honey in my hair!

YVONNE *is possessed by a* BACCHANT.

BACCHANT 2 (*of the waterfall*). It's wine!

LENA *is possessed by a* BACCHANT.

BACCHANT 3. Salt and sweet. I can feel its heart throb!

Interval.

ACT TWO

19. Herculine Barbin

DIONYSOS *appears to* DEREK *and stays throughout the scene.*

DEREK *is exercising with weights.*

DEREK   (*to audience*). He thought he wasn't a man without
a job.

> HERCULINE BARBIN *enters. She is played by a*
> *woman but dressed in the clothes of a Frenchman*
> *of the nineteenth century.*

> *While she talks she gives* DEREK *objects from her*
> *past which she takes from a small suitcase.*

HERCULINE. Couldn't I have stayed with her? No one was
stopping us, I was the one who – and afterwards
it would even have been legal, she still loved me
then, I must have lost my mind for a while. Blame
her mother, (*Gives a book.*) refusing to notice,
have some apricot tart children, my daughter's
dearest friend, a daughter to me, goodbye dear
daughter, goodbye. Why didn't I keep hold of
those hands? Blame yourself, kill yourself.

Abel Barbin, suicide, they'll find the body of a
man in the morning, no one will doubt it. Was
I really Herculine Barbin, playing by the sea,
starting school at the convent, nobody doubted
I was a girl. Hermaphrodite, the doctors were
fascinated. how to define this body, does it
fascinate you, it doesn't fascinate me, let it die.

Where are the girls I loved? They go on not
appearing every minute, sometimes it eases, often
what I am saying often it eases completely, oh it's
not like it was I can have a good – an eyelid, the
fall of a skirt, a startling tenderness at the next
table, and gone again, all my loves and Sara, Sara
and the air, you don't notice your breath till
something stops it.

I had schools, I had nuns, I had girls I loved even
only a little, no, wholly each time but more and –
Lea, so old. seventeen, I was twelve, leaning on
me in the garden, I took her a pretty crucifix at
night, (*Gives a rose.*) Mother Superior made me
cry. Was I really a lady's maid, undressing
Clothilde, combing her hair, it was my job, she
got married, no one worried about my body, my
periods would come in time.

Hair on my face and arms, cut it with scissors,
worse; I kissed Thecla on the mouth. Clever with
books, clumsy at sewing, lightning struck, leapt
out of bed naked into the nun's arms, feelings of
shame I didn't understand. Sinking in sand (*Gives
scissors and a comb.*) up to our knees, laughing,
three in a bed, they took off their skirts and tucked
up their petticoats, the water splashed high, I was
the only one who stayed on the beach.

Where it led, to Sara, I wouldn't let her get dressed
without me, stroked her hair, kissed her neck, she
put my hand aside and gazed in amazement.
Mysterious pains, (*Gives crucifix.*) she took me
into her bed to comfort me, god, Sara was mine,
romantic words, Sara is mine, nobody knew, this
lasted a long time, the children watched, her hair
fell down. In the middle of class she would smile
at me.

The pains, the doctor, I screamed, he could hardly
speak, but still he didn't stop us, her mother didn't,
nobody would admit, I did it myself in the
vacation, did I have to? The bishop, very kind, his
own doctor, yes I should be declared a man, (*Gives
the lace shawl.*) the documents, Sara's grief, have
some tart dear daughter, couldn't I have asked to
marry her, goodbye dear daughter, how to hold my
body as a man.

Soon less jeering, job in the railroad, long time
with no job, sit in the cafés and see who loves
who, at least I'm not a man like the men I see.
(*Gives the petticoat.*) Maybe waiter's assistant on
ship to America, what to do, everyone thought it
must be something good to take me so far away.

Into the unknown, like now, breathing in fumes,
soon dead, how to get back, all the girls' bodies,
Sara's body, my girl's body, all lost, couldn't you
have stayed?

*DEREK holds all the objects and has dressed
himself in the shawl and petticoat. He sits in the
chair and becomes HERCULINE.*

*She stands beside him and takes the objects from
him and packs them into her suitcase.*

DEREK.   Couldn't I have stayed with her? No one was
stopping us, I was the one who – and afterwards
it would even have been legal, she still loved me
then, I must have lost my mind for a while. Blame
her mother, refusing to notice, have some apricot
tart children, my daughter's dearest friend, a
daughter to me, goodbye dear daughter, goodbye.
Why didn't I keep hold of those hands? Blame
yourself, kill yourself.

Abel Barbin, suicide, they'll find the body of
a man in the morning, no one will doubt it. Was
I really Herculine Barbin, playing by the sea,
starting school at the convent, nobody doubted
I was a girl. Hermaphrodite, the doctors were
fascinated, how to define this body, does it
fascinate you, it doesn't fascinate me, let it die.

HERCULINE. What's the matter? Be happy. You know I love
you.

DEREK.   Where are the girls I loved? They go on not
appearing every minute, sometimes it eases, often
what am I saying often it eases completely, oh it's
not like it was I can have a good – an eyelid, / the
fall of a

HERCULINE. Lea, I love you.

DEREK.   skirt, a startling tenderness at the next table, and
gone again, (*Takes away the rose.*) all my loves
and Sara, Sara and the air, you don't notice your
breath till something stops it.

I had schools, I had nuns, I had girls I loved even
only a little, no, wholly each time but more and –

Lea, so old, seventeen, I was twelve, leaning on me in the garden, I took her a pretty crucifix at night, Mother Superior made me cry. Was I really a lady's maid, undressing Clothilde, combing her hair, it was my job, she got married, no one worried about my body, my periods would come in time.

HERCULINE. May you be happy later, poor child.

DEREK.   Hair on my face and arms, cut it with scissors, worse; / (*Takes the book.*)

HERCULINE. I'm sorry to hurt you, once more, nearly over.

DEREK.   I kissed Thecla on the mouth. Clever with books, clumsy at sewing, lightning struck, leapt out of bed naked into the nun's arms, feelings of shame I didn't understand. Sinking in sand up to our knees, / (*Takes the scissors and comb.*)

HERCULINE. Modesty, morality and the respect you owe a religious house.

DEREK.   laughing, three in a bed, they took off their skirts and tucked up their petticoats, the water splashed high, I was the only one who stayed on the beach. Where it led, to Sara, /

HERCULINE. Herculine! come in the water.

DEREK.   I wouldn't let her get dressed without me, stroked her hair, kissed her neck, she put my hand aside and gazed in amazement. Mysterious pains, she took me into her bed to comfort me, god, Sara was mine, romantic words, Sara is mine, (*Takes the crucifix.*) nobody knew, this lasted a long time, the children watched, her hair fell down. In the middle of class she would smile at me.

HERCULINE. I've made you an apricot tart.

DEREK.   The pains, the doctor, I screamed, he could hardly speak, but still he didn't stop us, her mother didn't, nobody would admit, I did it myself in the vacation, did I have to? The bishop, very kind, his own doctor, yes I should be declared a man, the documents, Sara's grief, have some tart dear daughter, couldn't I have asked to marry her, goodbye dear daughter, / (*Takes the lace shawl.*)

HERCULINE. Goodbye, dear daughter.

DEREK.   how to hold my body as a man.

Soon less jeering, job in the railroad, long time with no job, sit in the cafés and see who loves who, at least I'm not a man like the men I see. Maybe waiter's assistant on ship to America, what to do, everyone thought it must be something good to take me so far away.

Into the unknown, like now, breathing in fumes, soon dead, how to get back, all the girls' bodies, (*Takes the petticoat.*) Sara's body, my girl's body, all lost,

HERCULINE *starts to go.*

DEREK.   couldn't you have stayed?

HERCULINE *turns back and kisses him on the neck.*

20. Possession

DIONYSOS *approaches* DEREK.

DEREK *is possessed by* PENTHEUS.

PENTHEUS. Send the soldiers to fetch the women. I want to kill them. I want to see them. I'll go to the mountain.

21. Gold Shoes

YVONNE's *room.*

DIONYSOS *passes through* YVONNE's *room and goes out.*

YVONNE   (*to audience*). What is it makes you so angry?

In another room YVONNE'S MOTHER *sits crocheting.* YVONNE, *a woman in her late twenties, comes in wearing a white housecoat. She sits on the bed, leans over, letting her head down between her knees. She sits up, breathes out. Her manner is listless, distracted.*

YVONNE.   A – apple. B? Butterfly. C? C – dammit.

She leans back, looks around the room.

C, C – what can I see?

She is still.

In the distance – a scrap of music plays three or four bars and stops.

Ma? Ma, are you there?

A – advocaat. B? Brandy? C? Cognac. D? D, D – Sweet Jesus, get it out of your . . . mind! D, D – what can I – ? Ma! Ma, I'm not going out, ma. You hear me? I swear to you. I am no more going out of this house – . Drambuie! Got it. Right, that's it. Now E!

She is in pain.

Oh! I can't bear – can't bear . . .

She gets up, takes off her housecoat. She wears a light cotton dress underneath. She stands with her housecoat over her arm.

Um – ladies and gentlemen – no. Friends, my name is Yvonne, I – am – . I am an – .

She stops, thinks, lies on the bed.

Ma?

She starts to rise from the bed. As she lifts herself away from the bed the music returns, the same few bars – deafeningly loud.

During the music enter two WOMEN (WOMAN A and WOMAN B). They sit drinking and leafing through fashion magazines. Both WOMEN are dressed in smart evening clothes. WOMAN A wears a red dress, WOMAN B wears turquoise. Both wear gold shoes.

When the music ends, YVONNE goes out.

She comes in wearing her white housecoat. As before she sits on the bed, leans over letting her head down between her knees. She sits up, breathes out. Her manner is listless, distracted.

YVONNE.   A – apple. B? Butterfly. C? Caramel. D? Doughnut. E? Envelope.

She leans back, looks around the room.

Wilson – you taught me something bad with your alcohol alphabet. I'll wipe my brain clean. F? Frascati. Damn.

She sits up.

I am not! I am not!

She goes over to her mother.

You really got nothing hidden in this whole house? I don't believe it.

I'm not going out. Tonight I've got to – . So don't ask me to go out for, buy you – whatever. I can't do that now. The roads at this time of the evening? It's not that. That's not it. That's over. I don't feel like that about roads, roads and cars, cars and drivers any more. To cross roads at night . . . Stand on the pavement, the cars are coming for me, trying to . . . I know they're not trying to crush me . . . You want something, ask Wilson. (*Calls.*) Wilson!

MOTHER.   He's gone out.

YVONNE.   I'll go to the meeting but I won't go tonight. I can't bear to sit there – ladies . . . my name, Yvonne . . . alcoholic. I'm not an alcoholic. Anyway, tonight I've got to paint the window frame.

She goes back to her bed.

F. Done it. G? Gloss paint.

She gets up, takes off her housecoat, finds a pot of paint and a paint brush. She goes out of the room and reappears with a pair of paint-bespattered dungarees. She kicks off her shoes, slips off her dress. She is wearing a slip underneath. She opens a cupboard. Out falls a pair of gold shoes.

The music returns.

WOMAN A *greets* WOMAN B *with a bright cheery wave.*

WOMAN A. Good time?

WOMAN B. Very pleasant.

> *They go on drinking.*
>
> YVONNE *picks up the gold shoes and looks at them.*
>
> *She pulls on the dungarees.*
>
> *She puts on the gold shoes.*
>
> *The dungarees fall to the ground and she is dressed exactly like* WOMAN A.
>
> *The volume of the music rises.*
>
> YVONNE *dances. She ends up on the bed in despair.*
>
> *The music fades.*
>
> MOTHER *waves at the* TWO WOMEN.

MOTHER. You should see our Yvonne. What a beauty. What a peach.

> *The music stops.*

You should see our Yvonne. What a pity. Life's a bitch. (*To* YVONNE.) You said you weren't going out.

YVONNE. No.

MOTHER. So why you dressed up for a party? Yvonne? Someone's having a party? You going out, yes or no? You losing control of yourself again? Don't look to me for help. You've worn me out, out, out. I'm finished with your crying, your howling. You want to go out with your smart friends, go out. You got a thought in your head to cut me? Yvonne? I'm not one of your patients for you to stick needles in. You going to cut me again? I'm cut to pieces. Your father cut me there. Doctor – there. That crazy boy at the church cut me here. You cut me there, there, there.

> *She shows the places.*

YVONNE. I –

> YVONNE *rushes out and comes in immediately wearing the white housecoat.*

A – apple. B? Butterfly. C? C dammit. C, C – what can I see? (*In anguish.*) I never cut you!

MOTHER.   Then what's this. And what's this? I don't give you what you're asking, you cut me. You're cutting me up bit by bit like a pig – you know that? Go in that room. Do as you told me. Paint the window frame. Yvonne? You never lied to me. Tell me what it is.

YVONNE.   Just one.

MOTHER *exhales deeply.*

She produces a bottle of gin and puts it on the table.

YVONNE.   Oh yes. G for gin.

She drinks.

She takes off the housecoat. YVONNE*'s dress is now yellow.*

WOMAN A *and* WOMAN B *come into* YVONNE*'s room and sit on the bed. She fills their glasses and her own. They all drink.*

The music returns.

YVONNE *and the two* WOMEN *dance. After a moment,* YVONNE *retches and pulls away from them. The* WOMEN *offer her another drink. She rushes to her bed and kicks off her shoes.*

The music stops.

The TWO WOMEN *return to their places and go on drinking.*

YVONNE.   A – apple. B – butterfly. C – caramel. D – dough-nut. E – envelope. F? Fire. G?

She pulls her dungarees over her clothes, picks up the paint and brush and starts painting the window frame.

After a moment, she puts down the brush and picks up the gold shoes. She examines them closely, then puts them on.

YVONNE.   G for gold shoes.

She goes on painting the window frame.

22. The Dressing of Pentheus

In this dance, DEREK *is possessed by* PENTHEUS *and is dressed as a woman by* DIONYSOS 1 *and* DIONYSOS 2.

At first PENTHEUS *attacks* DIONYSOS 1 *and* 2. T*hey elude him as though it were a game and transform his aggression into acceptance. They dress him in their own clothes so that he is dressed as a woman.*

PENTHEUS.   Do I look like my mother?

23. Hot Summer

DIONYSOS *passes* DOREEN *as she enters. He goes out.*

DOREEN   (*to the audience*). All I wanted was peace and quiet.

Each in a different room:

MRS BLAIR *is listening to the radio quietly in the room above* DOREEN.

LIL *is reading a newspaper.*

TONY *is chopping vegetables.*

EVANS *is drinking heavily.*

SUSY *is massaging* DOREEN*'s neck and shoulders while* DOREEN *talks.*

I don't know which bit of me it's in. My head aches but if you ask me where it's not so much my head, it's more my neck. Or behind my eyes, there's something behind – My shoulders are a mass of knots, anywhere you touch on my shoulders is where the trouble is. Here, there's a spot here, I can't quite – My whole spine if you went down it. There's a pain in my stomach I get if I don't eat and another I get after I've eaten, and another, it's not in the stomach – I don't know where all your tubes are but there's definitely something. And the pain in my shoulders and hips goes right down, my elbows are stiff, my knees seize up, my fingers crack, my toes throb – so from head to foot. Anywhere you touched me would hurt. And that's not even the worst. It's not so much as if I'm going to vomit but every bit of me is nauseated, my left foot wants to vomit, my blood – I'm completely full of this awful sickness.

SUSY *finishes the massage. She kisses the top of* DOREEN*'s head and goes to the room she shares with* LIL. LIL *starts quietly reading from the paper. Soon what she is reading is lost beneath the sound of the radios.*

TONY *and* EVANS *continue as before.*

LIL.   'An unemployed Liverpool man was found guilty yesterday of the murder of his wife and two children aged 9 and 4. Michael Burns, 38, told police, "God asked me to send them to him." A neighbour summoned by Burns found the bodies in a bedroom and bathroom. They had been stabbed repeatedly. Burns was described in court as "a quiet friendly man who never raised his voice".

'A Turkish villager left prison to find his former girlfriend had married another man. He had been imprisoned for abducting the girl and returned to his village to discover she had married. He shot or knifed to death nine people he met as he searched for her.

'The Victoria line was out of action for two hours last night after a woman, 35, grabbed a stranger and pushed him in front of an approaching train. The victim, a man of 40, died instantly.

'A Manchester woman, 22, who said she feared demons would possess her baby daughter was found not guilty of the child's murder by reason of insanity. The two-month-old girl dressed in pink was found buried in a park with her mouth full of leaves.

An eighteen-year-old typist pleaded guilty to murdering her flatmate by stabbing her with a carving knife while she slept. She told police, "I just got the knife and went and did it. It seemed important at the time. I didn't have anything against her."

'Police in Los Angeles are looking for a strangler who has raped and killed twelve women in recent months. Their naked bodies have been found on hillsides and in rivers. Their ages range from 13 to 51. Women have been advised not to go out alone after dark and to close all ground floor doors and windows.

'Three youths are being held in Adelaide without bail on charges of having stabbed a man fifty times, poured turpentine into his wounds and cut him to pieces with a butcher's knife. The body of the victim, 42, was found in a black rubbish bag in a neighbour's back yard.

'A fifteen-year-old girl was admitted to hospital yesterday with third degree burns to her face after pouring petrol on her hair and setting light to it.

'Housewife Cindy Johnson, 36, of Little Rock Arkansaw yesterday shot and killed her husband and two of her three children and then killed herself. She used a rifle the family kept to protect themselves from intruders. One of her daughters, Ellen, 17, escaped by jumping from a bedroom window. The youngest child, Luke, 6, was playing outside when his mother called him in and shot him in the kitchen.'

Soon after LIL *has started reading,* DOREEN *turns her radio on.*

MRS BLAIR *turns her radio up.*

DOREEN *turns her radio up.*

MRS BLAIR *turns her radio up and thumps.*

DOREEN *turns her radio up, thumps and shouts.*

MRS BLAIR *turns her radio up, thumps, shouts, and bangs saucepans.*

DOREEN *turns her radio up, thumps, shouts, bangs saucepans and knocks a chair over.*

MRS BLAIR *turns her radio up, thumps, shouts, bangs saucepans and knocks a chair over and smashes crockery.*

DOREEN *turns her radio up, thumps, shouts, bangs saucepans and knocks a chair over, smashes crockery and shakes out a roll of carpet.*

*Both radios are now at full volume, both playing
different things. It is impossible to hear anything,
but LIL keeps reading aloud.*

MRS BLAIR *continues thumping and shouting.*

DOREEN *rolls up the carpet and unrolls it again.*

*Suddenly both rush out of their rooms shouting.
They meet.* DOREEN *slashes* MRS BLAIR *in the
face with a knife.* MRS BLAIR *stands there with
blood coming out of her face.* DOREEN *pulls her
down onto the floor and rolls her up in the carpet.*
DOREEN *pulls the end of the carpet so* MRS
BLAIR *is rolled out.* DOREEN *turns off the radio,
both radios go off.*

Silence except that LIL *is still reading from the
newspaper. Everyone else is still doing what they
were doing.*

While LIL *is still reading* MRS BLAIR *goes back
to her room and turns the radio on quietly.*

Once the radio is on, LIL *stops reading aloud and*
SUSY *goes back to* DOREEN'*s room.* SUSY *now
keeps some distance from* DOREEN.

SUSY.   We'll go on a coach from Victoria. It only takes an
           hour. We'll get back in the evening about eight.

DOREEN.   I've been up since five.

SUSY.   Won't you come though? We can get a boat and go
           on the river. It won't be so hot.

DOREEN.   I don't need sleep anymore. I don't need food.

SUSY.   And your back's better.

DOREEN.   What's wrong with my back?

SUSY.   Nothing, that's good.

DOREEN.   There's nothing at all wrong with my back or any
           other part of me. Do you know that?

SUSY.   Yes.

DOREEN.   Good.

SUSY.   So would you like to come for a day out? It's cool
           on the river. It's one thing always makes me happy,

being in a boat and putting your hand in the water. It makes you feel better.

DOREEN.   I don't need a boat. I don't need water. I don't need you coming in here trying to make me better. What? What's better? What?

SUSY.   I thought you might like it.

DOREEN.   You better get out of the room.

SUSY goes back to the room she shares with LIL. MRS BLAIR *still listens to the radio and* EVANS *still drinks.*

TONY *comes to* DOREEN's *room.*

TONY.   Hi, we've seen each other in the hall, my name's Tony. I'm sorry to bother you but I wonder if you could let me have a teabag? I forgot I was out of tea when I went –

DOREEN.   You come in a room where I'm perfectly peaceful. How do I know what you are? Teabag? You could be going to put a sack over my head. You could have a knife but I have a knife so think again. / My sister lives with a man who

TONY.   Look I only –

DOREEN.   poured boiling water over her and she thinks it's her fault.

TONY.   Lady, I don't need this.

DOREEN.   Anyone can do it. There's nothing can't be used as a weapon. Chair. String. A cup of hot tea.

TONY.   You are a crazy, you know that? Suck my cock. It's a hot night. Now. Let's just –

TONY *goes.*

DOREEN.   Tear you up.

TONY *goes back to his room. He starts to eat what he prepared.*

DOREEN *bites her arm.*

SUSY *comes back to* DOREEN's *room. She still keeps her distance but less far than before.*

DOREEN.   Once you start fighting you don't stop. There's two
           ways you end up. One's with six warders on top of
           you. They drag you so your head bangs on each
           step. You keep fighting till they stick a needle in
           and you're glad to be gone out of it. The other way
           you end up is by yourself. I've done weeks on end.
           All you've got left is your own piss and shit. A lot
           of women cut themselves. I've a friend who
           swallowed glass. I don't want to.

           Silence.

           SUSY *starts massaging* DOREEN's *feet.*

           LIL *comes to* DOREEN's *room but keeps her
           distance.*

SUSY.   There are people who can stare at walls and bring
           them down.

DOREEN.   What have you been taking?

SUSY.   I think I made a cup fall off the table.

DOREEN.   By what?

SUSY.   By looking at it. We could try and blow that light.

DOREEN.   You're not strong enough. You're a butterfly.

SUSY.   I'm getting stronger. Will we try?

DOREEN.   Have we really got nothing better to do than this?

           *The three of them try to blow the light bulb of a
           lamp by concentrating on it. Silence for some time.
           Nothing happens.*

DOREEN.   I'm just going red in the face.

SUSY.   One of these days.

           TONY *comes into the room.*

TONY.   Hi. I was just wondering if any of you guys have
           got some salad cream –

DOREEN.   No.

           DOREEN's *'No' is quiet but it bounces* TONY *off
           the walls.*

SUSY.   You can do it.

DOREEN.   Yes.

> *She puts out her hand and the lamp comes through the air into it.*

> DOREEN, SUSY *and* LIL *keep repeating yes and laughing. Objects keep flying across the room.*

24. The Death of Pentheus

DEREK, *still dressed as he was by* DIONYSOS, *is possessed by* PENTHEUS.

PENTHEUS. Kill the god! Kill the god! Kill the god!

> PENTHEUS *is brought by* DIONYSOS *into a dance of the whole company in which moments of extreme happiness and of violence from earlier parts of the play are repeated.*

> *Apart from* DEREK, *all the other actors are dressed in the clothes of their main characters.* PENTHEUS *is torn to pieces by* DOREEN *who is possessed by* AGAVE *and the other* WOMEN *who are possessed by* BACCHANTS.

> PAUL/DIONYSOS *and* DAN/DIONYSOS *watch.*

> *When* PENTHEUS *is dead,* AGAVE *and the* BACCHANTS *become quiet and realise what they have done.*

AGAVE.   I broke open his ribs. I tore off his head.

> *She gathers his limbs together.*

> LENA, YVONNE *and* MARCIA *get up and start to go.*

AGAVE.   Where are you going?

LENA.   Home.

MARCIA.   I'm late for work.

YVONNE.   I have to look after someone.

AGAVE.   There's nothing for me there. There never was. I'm staying here.

> *The* WOMEN *turn back and stay.*

Part Three

25. Old people

LENA.   Every day is a struggle but that's all right. Old
           people are very tiring. I'm not squeamish, I used to
           be, couldn't kill a rabbit, I deal with sick and shit
           every day. I'm not frightened of anything, I walk
           alone at night, throw him over my shoulder if
           I have to. Some of the old ladies know me, some
           of them don't know anyone. You can get fond of
           them. You tuck them up like babies. Every day is
           a struggle because I haven't forgotten anything.
           I remember I enjoyed doing it. It's nice to make
           someone alive and it's nice to make someone dead.
           Either way. That power is what I like best in the
           world. The struggle is every day not to use it.

26. Meat

YVONNE.   Many people are surprised to see a woman behind
           this counter. They look round the shop. Where's
           the butcher? I smile, show my teeth. I spend all
           day sawing and hacking. I have a feel for the
           strengths of a body. All the men know it. They ask
           me: slit here or slit there? I close my eyes. Feel.
           Slit there. When I was young I'd dream. I'd wake
           and forget. Now I sleep, wake, I'm here. Half of
           kidneys, pound of stewing. Chop chop!

27. Desert

DAN.   Can you believe this was all sand? The most
           beautiful garden I know is an oasis, high walls
           round it, peaches, nectarines, figs, the gardener
           makes sweet syrups from violets and roses. These
           fields don't compare. But if you'd seen it before.
           I can't tell you what a day it was when I woke up
           and saw the first green.

28. Sea

MARCIA.   My boat is twenty foot long, twelve foot wide, too
           small to sail far out. Longing cannot carry over
           water so a short way from the land is far enough.
           Alone I need nothing. What I want I order with my
           radio. Hearing voices gives me pain but to test my
           strength sometimes is good. If I go ashore they'll
           ask my name. I could tell them – oh, what I could
           tell them. Horror. What for? At sea, at night the air
           is silent. I listen. I hear nothing. I am full of joy.
           Of course, the rocks speak. That's quite different.
           Most days I sleep. My wish is that I'll never wake
           to see the sky without a star.

29. Drinking

PAUL.   When you stop being in love the day is very
           empty. It's not just the one you loved who isn't
           exciting any more, nothing is exciting. Nothing is
           even bearable. So it wasn't till then that I left my
           wife and my job. I can't stand small pleasures.
           If there's nothing there's room for something to
           come. Sometimes on my third scotch I'd wonder
           if now . . . so I continued with the scotch. Days
           are quite long when you sit in the street but it's
           important not to do anything. It may not be love
           next time. You can't tell what it's going to be.
           You're lucky if once in your life. So I stay ready.

30. Body

DEREK.   My breasts aren't big but I like them. My waist
           isn't small but it makes me smile. My shoulders
           are still strong. And my new shape is the least of it.
           I smell light and sweet. I come into a room, who
           has been here? Me. My skin used to wrap me up,
           now it lets the world in. Was I this all the time?
           I've almost forgotten the man who possessed
           this body. I can't remember what he used to
           be frightened of. I'm in love with a lion-tamer
           from Kabul. Every day when I wake up, I'm
           comfortable.

31. Birds

DOREEN.   I can find no rest. My head is filled with horrible
          images. I can't say I actually see them, it's more
          that I feel them. It seems that my mouth is full of
          birds which I crunch between my teeth. Their
          feathers, their blood and broken bones are choking
          me. I carry on my work as a secretary.

32. **DIONYSOS** *dances*.

ICECREAM

Characters

LANCE,
VERA, *husband and wife, American, around 40*
PHIL,
JAQ, *brother and sister, English, twenties*
MAN IN DEVON
SHRINK
COLLEAGUE
FELLOW GUEST
DRUNK WOMAN
HITCHER
HITCHER'S MOTHER
PROFESSOR
SOUTH AMERICAN WOMAN PASSENGER

The first ten scenes are set in the UK during a summer in the late eighties, the second ten in the US the following year.

Icecream was first performed at the Royal Court Theatre on 6 April 1989. The cast was as follows:

LANCE	Philip Jackson
VERA	Carole Hayman
PHIL	David Thewlis
JAQ	Saskia Reeves
MAN IN DEVON, SHRINK, FELLOW GUEST, HITCHER, PROFESSOR	Allan Corduner
WAITRESS, DRUNK WOMAN, HITCHER'S MOTHER, SOUTH AMERICAN WOMAN PASSENGER	Gillian Hanna

Directed by Max Stafford-Clark
Designed by Peter Hartwell
Costumes designed by Jennifer Cook
Lighting by Christopher Toulmin
Sound by Bryan Bowen

I   UK

1. Road to the Isles

LANCE *and* VERA *in car. They are singing.*

LANCE *and* VERA.

> The far coo-oolins are putting love on me
> As step I with my something to the road
> The dadeda dedadeda dedadeda away
> As step I with the sunlight for my load.
> And by something and by something and by
> > something I will go
> And never something dadedadeda
> And something and dedadeda and something
> > in my step
>
> And I'll never something something of the isles.

They laugh.

LANCE.

> Speed bonny boat
> Like a bird on the wing
> Over the sea to Skye

VERA.   You're really flat.

He stops.

VERA.   Sorry.

LANCE.   No, you're right.

VERA.   Oh come on.

Pause.

She sings.

> Why don't we go walking together
> Out beyond the valley of trees
> Out where there's a hillside of heather
> Curtsying gently in the breeze.
> That's what I'd like to do
> See the heather but with you.

It's a pity no one remembered her though.

LANCE. My great grandmother was a very obscure woman.

VERA. Drowning yourself in a well isn't obscure.

LANCE. They were probably all at it.

Pause.

LANCE. What was that from?

VERA. Brigadoon.

LANCE. You've got such a great memory.

2. Castle

LANCE *is turning round looking up at ceiling.* VERA *has a guide book.*

LANCE. What have we got that's old?

VERA. Sofa. Freezer.

LANCE. Nothing old. Just plenty worn out. No history.

VERA. It's twelfth century up the end and thirteenth on top.

LANCE. Eight hundred years. Whahey!

VERA. I've been touching the walls to try and believe it.

LANCE. We think the nineteenth century is history. We had wilderness and aboriginal people. For the British the nineteenth century is just now, they hardly notice it's gone. For them history is this castle. Aboriginal is before 1066. No, even that's history, they had Alfred and the cakes. Aboriginal is Stonehenge.

Pause. VERA *licks her fingers.*

VERA. We do too have history.

LANCE. Indians have their oral traditions. We can't claim a share in that.

VERA. Everyone has ancestors.

LANCE. Yes indeed and this is where they came from. So to that extent this is our history.

VERA. Your history.

LANCE.   If it's mine it's yours. Like a joint bank account. They would all be our children's ancestors.

VERA.   My history's in Russia and Germany and god knows where.

LANCE.   Not in America anyhow because America's too damn recent.

Pause.

Do you want an icecream? Do you want an ice CREAM?

Pause.

What nobody knows isn't history.

VERA.   Just because someone doesn't know who their grandparents are doesn't make them not exist. Everyone comes from something.

LANCE.   That's evolution. I'm talking about history.

3. Cottage

LANCE *and* VERA *outside a cottage in Devon.* MAN *carrying chest of drawers.*

VERA.   If only we'd come to Devon first.

LANCE.   Do you know who's inherited the cottage?

MAN.   It were rented. They were waiting for her to die.

LANCE.   So what happens to it now?

MAN.   Holidays.

LANCE.   You don't know if there were any relatives mentioned in the will?

VERA.   We're not after her money. We're researching my husband's family tree.

LANCE.   Miss Glade was a cousin on his mother's side of my maternal grandfather. But I liked to think of her as Greataunt Dora.

MAN.   She didn't have any money to be after.

VERA.   Did you know her well?

MAN.   I used to do her garden when I was a boy. She had
           a sharp tongue but she'd give me a biscuit.

LANCE.   That's wonderful.

VERA.   Rose Cottage, Lance.

LANCE.   Maybe we could buy the chest of drawers.

4. Flat

LANCE *and* VERA *with* PHIL *in his flat in east London.*

LANCE.   So great aunt Dora was my great /

PHIL.   was your greatgrandfather's –

LANCE.   grandmother's brother's daughter – mother's, great
           / grandmother's –

PHIL.   – mother's, right,

LANCE.   she was my greatgrand*mother's* brother's daughter
           and your greatgrand / *father's*

PHIL.   father's

LANCE.   brother's daughter.

PHIL.   So they were both / the brothers, the brother and
           sister of –

LANCE.   So looking at it another way they were the brother
           and sister of Dora's father, who was Albert. So
           there's / Henry, Albert and

PHIL.   Albert, Henry. . .

LANCE.   Mavis, / a sister and two brothers, the

PHIL.   Mavis, that's good.

LANCE.   children of William and Jane who was born,
           William was born in eighteen ten, we're going back
           one hundred and eighty years, and he was a
           shoemaker in York and Dora's / grandfather.

PHIL.   That's my great . . .

LANCE.   Your great *great* grandfather, because your great-grandfather was Henry, who had five children / one of whom –

PHIL.   And who went to America?

LANCE.   Wait, let me, / one of those five children was

VERA.   Lance's grandfather.

LANCE.   your grandmother – yes my grandfather, that's Thomas, who was the son of Mavis and Frank who drank himself to death, Thomas sailed from Bristol in nineteen oh two and settled / in Michigan.

PHIL.   And made his fortune.

LANCE.   No, unfortunately I would say no.

PHIL.   Are you frightened of dogs?

VERA.   No, that's fine, I, no, German shepherds, it's stupid, / I know he won't –

PHIL.   No, you're right to be frightened, that's what he's for, a deterrent, I count on it, scares the shit – some people just put up a sign in the window but I do actually have one because I think people find you out and then they really go for you.

VERA.   So is he very fierce?

PHIL.   No, you could put a baby on his plate.

VERA.   But if someone attacked you?

PHIL.   I hope so or what's the point of the food bill?

LANCE.   So your grandmother, did you say Madge?

PHIL.   I think it was Madge. Unless it was Elsie. Let's go for Madge.

LANCE.   So Madge and Thomas and Dora, that's Thomas who went to America, were all first cousins. And Thomas was my mother's father and Madge was your father's mother / so they

PHIL.   father's, yes

LANCE.   were second cousins, second cousins, yes, and that makes you and me one down from that is third cousins.

PHIL.   Is that how it works? what about removed? /
           Cousin once –

LANCE.   No. that's if you take say Dora and your father,
           if you go another generation / up or down you
           get . . .

PHIL.   So we're third cousins and you're (*To* VERA.) my
           third cousin in law. / I don't even know

VERA.   I guess.

PHIL.   my first cousins.

LANCE.   Are you not in touch / with a great many relatives?

VERA.   Or maybe just plain cousins because what's
           Lance's is mine, I mean third, third cousins.

PHIL.   Sorry, what?

VERA.   Nothing, sorry.

LANCE.   With other relatives, are you in touch with – ?

PHIL.   I have a sister. She's out.

LANCE.   And your parents?

PHIL.   Both alas deceased.

VERA.   I'm sorry.

PHIL.   No, well, a long time.

LANCE.   So what about aunts and uncles?

PHIL.   I had a loony uncle in Brighton but he shot
           himself. That was on my mother's side.

VERA.   Do you not like family?

PHIL.   I quite fancy Americans.

LANCE.   Well I'm certainly very glad we found you. It's a
           great thrill for us.

           Pause.

PHIL.   Shall we go for a curry?

5. Pub

LANCE *and* VERA *drinking with* PHIL *and* JAQ.

JAQ.   Paper round, busker, Tesco, toy factory, jeans shop,
      Woolworth, winebar, van driver, pavement artist,
      singer with a rock group, photographer's assistant,
      office cleaner, primary school teacher, drug pusher,
      vet's receptionist, journalist, cleaning chickens,
      hospital orderly, gardener, carpenter, my friend's
      dress shop, traffic warden, tourist guide,
      hypnotherapist, motorbike messenger, frozen peas,
      stall in the market, plumber's mate, computer
      programmer, translator, escapologist, and five
      secretarial.

VERA.   You make me feel so boring.

JAQ.   Whereas Phil never worked / – never had a job

PHIL.   Ah.

JAQ.   in his life, never had to get up / in the

PHIL.   I do always get up.

JAQ.   morning, never had to get up.

VERA.   I do get bored but it doesn't occur to me to just –
      not that being a dental assistant is as boring as it
      might sound because if you keep abreast of the
      new technology, it's a different world / almost
      from when I started.

PHIL.   I can't stand pain.

VERA.   You wouldn't *feel* any pain with us.

PHIL.   There's the one like a road drill and the one like a
      jet plane and that's not two things I want / in my
      mouth.

LANCE. I did a great many jobs working my way through
      college but that's some time back. I worked as a
      lumberjack in Oregon.

PHIL.   Now Oregon –

JAQ.   The Oregon Trail.

PHIL.   The idea of Oregon, the word, just the word
      Oregon really thrills me. Say some more things.

LANCE.	Say –
PHIL.	Like butter pecan icecream.
VERA.	Apple pie.
PHIL.	Apple pie's not American.
VERA.	It is to us.
PHIL.	With ice cream it is.
VERA.	No with ICEcream.
LANCE.	A drug store. A soda when you're a kid / with the icecream floating.
JAQ.	Old Cadillacs. Cactus. Long straight roads.
VERA.	Yellow cabs.
PHIL.	Yellow cabs.
VERA.	Preachers on TV.
PHIL.	Preachers.
LANCE.	Hamburgers, / hotdogs.
PHIL.	Hamburgers are disgusting, we have them here thank you very much, so much American filth here, I completely loathe the United States of America.
LANCE.	I'm sorry to hear that.
PHIL.	Turn on the TV and it's American cops blowing each other through walls, this is happening all over the world. People have their own walls, they have their own policemen, they have their own guns, they have their own deaths, thank you very much. No wonder America is paranoid, you export all this filth you think someone's going to throw it back at you. Did you know the Contras think the Americans won in Vietnam because of Rambo?
LANCE.	I'm somewhat of a dove myself / but –
VERA.	If it's foreign policy, / if we're talking about
PHIL.	It's the essential nature of –
VERA.	the country in the world here, then England's / no better.

JAQ.   No one's defending England.

VERA.   The Falklands.

LANCE.   The British Empire, you can't –

PHIL.   The British and American empires.

LANCE.   There you are.

VERA.   The pot calling the kettle.

PHIL.   The slave trade. / Ireland.

VERA.   Slaves, slavery, both –

LANCE.   Ireland. Ireland.

VERA.   They are both major powers, England has been,
            America is, and it's hard, there is a responsibility,
            it's a hard position, you're up there to be knocked
            down, it's, I do feel sorry for the decision makers.
            No, they're both terrible countries, I guess. But
            America did stand for, at one time, when England
            was, it did stand, my people came, it must have
            stood for, a long time ago of course. No, they are
            both . . .

JAQ.   You read about Ancient Rome.

VERA.   Yes, you read where they threw the Christians to
            the lions.

JAQ.   And what will they think / when they read about
            us?

VERA.   Yes, what will they say about us?

LANCE.   But Great Britain is one thing. England is
            something else. And Scotland. Wales. Ireland.

JAQ.   No. Ireland is something / else again.

PHIL.   Something *else*.

LANCE.   You can't help loving England. The green fields.
            The accents. The pubs. / I mean people

VERA.   Pubs are so great.

LANCE.   are violent and stupid, that's all. It's just life.

JAQ.   That's shit.

VERA.   That's so negative, Lance.

LANCE.   No, it's positive. Life as in life goes on.

PHIL.   Yes, I have to admit there is still the butter pecan.
           Rocky road. Mocha. Blueberries and cream.
           Peppermint stick. / Black

VERA.   Peppermint stick yes, candy canes at Christmas on
           the tree, that's another . . .

PHIL.   cherry. Daiquiri. / Chocolate fudge.

LANCE.   Rum and raisin.

JAQ.   Key lime.

PHIL.   That and the movies.

           Then PHIL notices someone in the pub.

LANCE.   Movies, if we're talking movies – you OK?

PHIL.   Don't look now but see that man over there, /

LANCE.   Which one?

PHIL.   don't look, the ugly one, the fat –

JAQ.   Don't start / anything.

PHIL.   Start, I'm not starting, let him start, he's already /
           started.

LANCE.   The one in the jacket?

JAQ.   No, the shirt, the blue –

VERA.   What's he done?

PHIL.   If you want to see evil, / if you want to see

JAQ.   Phil.

PHIL.   evil that should be wiped out, just look, / just

JAQ.   Phil.

PHIL.   get him in your mind, just take care, if he's seen
           you with me you won't be safe / at night, just take
           it from me.

VERA.   Why, what?

LANCE.   What's he do, this guy?

JAQ.   Phil.

PHIL.   Don't you hate him?

JAQ.   Yes.

PHIL.   Well then.

6. Kiss

The flat. VERA *and* PHIL *kiss.*

VERA.   This is a mistake.

PHIL.   OK.

VERA.   It didn't happen.

PHIL.   No problem.

VERA.   Some people do this, I don't, I never did do this,
            not just because of Aids, even when I was young
            and it was practically compulsory I was never
            particularly . . . it's been a relief to me that
            monogamy is fashionable because it was always
            my secret / preference.

PHIL.   Secret vice?

VERA.   No that's right, chastity, fidelity was my secret
            vice, I thought it meant I was frigid / or

PHIL.   I don't think you are.

VERA.   anyway rigid – well I'm not, but I thought I didn't
            have an appetite for life and adventure or I was
            insecure, I guess I may be insecure but then some
            of the most flamboyantly sexual people I've known
            have also been the most flamboyantly insecure so
            I don't know. I must be insecure right now or
            I wouldn't be talking so much.

PHIL.   It wouldn't be fair to Lance.

VERA.   It wouldn't – look I'm not even remotely
            considering. Lance adores you like I don't know
            I'd say like a son but the age difference is hardly,
            like a brother maybe, a long lost /

PHIL.   Cousin.

VERA.   brother, well yes cousin is it after all, kissing
cousins, but Lance just is crazy about you and so
am 1 which is all that was. I guess you feel drawn
to your own flesh and blood which is after all why
the incest taboo, you don't taboo things nobody
wants to do, you don't taboo kissing the furniture.
Not that the relationship is within the proscribed
whatsits. And anyway you're not my flesh and
blood only Lance's which is kind of the same
thing but of course it's not. When I think of my
European ancestors I see this long row of women
picking cabbages.

PHIL.   Is that what they did?

VERA.   I've no idea, it's a cliché, I guess I think in clichés
all the time. It's depressing but then I think hell,
clichés are just what's true, what millions of people
have already realised is true. Like proverbs are
true. A stitch in time does in fact save nine.

PHIL.   Too many cooks do spoil the broth.

VERA.   The early bird does catch the worm.

PHIL.   Many hands do make light work. Many cooks do
make light broth.

They laugh.

PHIL.   Two is company and three is a crowd.

VERA.   There you are.

PHIL.   I think you're very nice.

VERA.   Good. I hope that's good?

PHIL.   It is good. I'm not at all nice. I get angry.

VERA.   You have good reason.

PHIL.   I didn't say without reason. I have bloody good
reason, don't worry.

VERA.   That man sounds just horrible.

PHIL.   I'll probably kill him.

VERA.   Don't talk like that.

PHIL.   Don't talk, all right I won't *talk*.

VERA.   You're angry now. Don't be angry with me.

PHIL.   The trouble with relations is they're irritating.
             Nothing personal. They are irritating.

VERA.   Irritating does feel personal.

PHIL.   Not *you*, *Vera*, but being related.

VERA.   I kind of like it.

PHIL.   That must be nice for you.

             Pause.

VERA.   Well, there we are.

             Pause.

PHIL.   I like your ears. People will have mentioned your
             eyes.

             Pause.

VERA.   I love you. I just want to say that. I don't mean
             anything by it. Lance loves you too, I know he
             does. That's one more reason why I couldn't
             possibly, so it's all right to say it. You won't feel
             it's an overture. People feel being loved is a
             pressure, they like it better if you don't care, I used
             to notice that in the days when I felt I had to and
             one of the reasons I didn't take to it was I always
             did care when I shouldn't have. But this is quite
             different. Lance and I both love you. And Jaq too,
             we love Jaq. But somehow we particularly . . .
             I just wanted to get that out of the way.

PHIL.   I need you.

VERA.   We would do anything for you. I would die. Do I
             speak in clichés? I *would* die.

7. Body

The flat.

Body on the floor under a blanket. LANCE, VERA, PHIL, JAQ.

LANCE.   This is ridiculous.

PHIL.   He shouldn't have come in here.

JAQ.   You shouldn't have let him in.

PHIL.   You shouldn't have / asked him here.

JAQ.   I didn't, he said he had to see me, I told him you wouldn't / let him in.

PHIL.   That was asking.

JAQ.   I thought you wouldn't let him in.

LANCE.   This is unbelievable.

PHIL.   It was self-defence.

JAQ.   I didn't know you had a gun. / Where did you get it?

PHIL.   He barges in here. Of course you knew I had a gun. Who are you planning to lie to?

LANCE.   We must get the police.

PHIL.   Are we planning to lie to the police?

LANCE.   This is just so . . .

JAQ.   It wasn't self-defence.

PHIL.   There are witnesses that it was self-defence.

LANCE.   What do you get for murder in this country?

    Pause.

VERA.   Maybe he isn't dead.

    Pause.

LANCE.   I don't like the idea of committing perjury. I don't think I'd be very good at it. And Vera's extremely truthful, she gets a funny look round the mouth if she's even just modifying the truth.

JAQ.   You'll need a good lawyer.

LANCE.   No, we're witnesses not – no, yes, I guess you're, yes, we could be held as accessories, the whole thing could snowball and would they keep us in the country till they – I have to be back home by Labour Day.

PHIL.   But you've got to say, you've got to / help, you –

LANCE.   I came here for a vacation.

Pause.

LANCE.   You going to prison isn't going to bring him back.

Pause.

PHIL.   I think we should just dump him in Epping Forest.

LANCE.   Where's that?

JAQ.   Not far. It's nice. It's a nice forest.

8. Breakfast

LANCE *and* VERA *at breakfast in hotel.*

LANCE.   I can't eat this.

VERA.   It's an English breakfast.

LANCE.   I can't eat it.

VERA.   We've paid for it anyway. Bed and Breakfast. They don't give you a discount.

LANCE.   If I've paid for it the money's gone. Start from there. Do I want this greasy muck? / No. I

VERA.   Hush.

LANCE.   would pay double not to have to eat it.

VERA.   I think it's delicious. It's only the egg is kind of greasy, they fried it too fast, that's why it has those little bobbles / where the fat's burst –

LANCE.   You eat it. You eat it.

VERA.   I can't eat two breakfasts.

LANCE.   I can't eat any breakfast.

VERA.   You'll be hungry at lunch.

Pause

It's not economic.

Pause.

It looks suspicious. We have to act natural. People will remember you didn't . . .

Pause.

Give me your mushroom. And the tomato.

He does. He picks up the newspaper and reads. She eats.

Pause.

VERA.   So what's new?

LANCE.   Things aren't getting too much farther in the middle east.

VERA.   Good.

Pause. He puts the paper down.

Don't cry. Don't cry.

Pause.

Do you feel ill? Do you have a temperature? Do you want to go lie down?

9. Walk

LANCE *and* VERA *in the country with a map.*

LANCE.   Do you think he's insane?

VERA.   What *is* insane?

LANCE.   If he didn't know what he was doing.

VERA.   Are *we* insane?

LANCE.   I was insane / not to call the police.

VERA.   But not *insane.* If we're not insane and he is, he'd get off / and we'd go to prison.

LANCE.	Not *off*, a mental hospital isn't my idea of off, Broadmoor / is hardly –
VERA.	I don't think he *is* insane like Broadmoor, isn't that mass murderers and I don't know werewolves or you know what I mean isn't that for weirdos / and I don't think he is,
LANCE.	And isn't he –
VERA.	I think he's a psychopath, / which means he
LANCE.	I think all these terms –
VERA.	knows what he's doing but he doesn't care, a psychopath / does mean something,
LANCE.	I don't think these terms –
VERA.	it's not like schizophrenic / which –
LANCE.	Schizophrenic does mean something.
VERA.	OK, it means *something* but there's a lot of debate about like is it your family or is it chemical and is it a positive thing / or a
LANCE.	Not nowadays, it's not positive nowadays.
VERA.	sickness or adapting to a sick environment / which we all have to –
LANCE.	I think this is hippy thinking.
VERA.	Well I don't think he is that, I think he's a psychopath / which means you can't do
LANCE.	I think he's a shit.
VERA.	anything for them, they just don't feel the consequences of their actions, I mean more than most people, we can all get *over* the consequences, I do think we can and should, I think it's our duty / to get over it.
LANCE.	It might be our duty not to.
VERA.	No, because we didn't do it, he did it, if we'd *done* it it might be different, but whatever, I think you have to be positive and somehow assimilate / the experience –
LANCE.	I think he's a shit.

VERA.   Yes, sure he's a shit, a psychopath *is* a shit.

LANCE.   He manipulated us, I wouldn't be surprised he planned the whole thing so he'd have us to help him, / he knew he could count on us

VERA.   That would be premeditated.

LANCE.   because we're his family. So it was premeditated.

VERA.   It could have been. If you're a psychopath / you –

LANCE.   If you're a shit.

VERA.   I thought he was beautiful at first. He looks like a weasel.

Pause.

LANCE.   And the girl, what about her?

VERA.   I suppose she is his sister?

LANCE.   What? Why not?

VERA.   I don't know anything about them any more.

LANCE.   Now she's a weirdo.

Pause.

VERA.   We came up here to get away from it. Why don't we look at the map?

LANCE.   Because we know where we are. We follow the footpath.

VERA.   I like to see on the map. And I'm not sure we do follow the footpath because look, we should have turned off here / down that other –

LANCE.   Where was that?

VERA.   By the field with the bull.

LANCE.   I'm not going through a field with a bull.

VERA.   They *have* bulls in English fields, they don't hurt you.

LANCE.   We can get round here by this path, look, it brings us back. Shall we do that? Look. I thought you were the one who liked maps.

VERA.   Ok, we'll do that.

LANCE. But look.

VERA. I don't care.

Pause

VERA. What do you think they're saying about us?

LANCE. They're probably laughing.

VERA. No, I think they're grateful. We make them feel secure.

Pause.

We could go to the police in Chipping Camden.

LANCE. You don't go to the police about your own family.

VERA. That isn't necessarily so.

Pause.

LANCE. I think he's crazy. He has a crazy look.

VERA. Maybe it runs in the family.

LANCE. You think I look crazy?

VERA. It was a joke.

LANCE. I think I am. I think I'm crazy now. I think this has driven me crazy.

VERA. Let's walk, we don't feel so bad.

Pause.

LANCE. I think his hand moved. In the forest. I think his hand moved a leaf. If he wasn't dead then, it wasn't too late *then* when I thought it was too late, if only I'd realised, if only I'd dared, but now it really is too late.

VERA. He was dead, it was too late then. But it's not too late now / to –

LANCE. It is too late now.

Pause.

VERA. I like her, I really feel sorry for her.

LANCE. Is *she* insane?

10. Quarrel

All four at the flat. PHIL asleep. The others sitting about. Long silence.

JAQ.   You could go to the zoo.

VERA.   I've seen animals.

JAQ.   But every zoo's / different.

VERA.   I don't like animals in cages. I don't like animals.

JAQ.   You've been to the Tower? You've been to
            Madame Tussaud's?

            Pause.

            You could go in a boat up the river.

            Pause.

VERA.   *You* could go on a boat up the river. Do you want
            to? No, neither do I. I'm in terror. How do I go on
            a boat? I can't read a magazine. I can't go five
            minutes without UH this horrible thing hits inside
            me, *that happened*, what do you do with that, go
            on a boat? In the country we got in a panic, that's
            why we came back, do you think we *wanted* to see
            you, we had to see you that's all, because it's less
            horrible, the grass was so green it was threatening,
            the trees you felt someone was going to jump out,
            you felt the *tree* was going to jump out, and at
            least here we're *facing* . . .

            Silence.

LANCE.   When you belong somewhere you don't need to
            rush round seeing things all the time, you don't
            have to be a tourist, you're a visitor sure but you
            stay a while, you have family here you can sit
            down and do nothing all day, it's great.

            Silence.

JAQ.   Nothing in the Gazette.

LANCE.   What we really need is the Epping Gazette. Do
            they have an Epping Gazette?

            Pause.

PHIL *wakes suddenly,* VERA *is startled then realises.*

PHIL.   Uh.

VERA.   What? Oh.

PHIL.   I was dreaming, I dreamt . . . there was this . . . we
           were all . . . then it changed and . . . it was
           extraordinary because . . . and then I . . . the
           answer, the answer was orange. I wish you
           wouldn't wake me up.

JAQ.   We didn't wake you up, / you just –

PHIL.   I'm awake aren't I?

VERA.   You woke yourself up.

PHIL.   No one can sleep with all these people in the room.

LANCE.   Go in the bedroom.

PHIL.   Who lives here? Do you think you're at home?
           Why don't you get off my back? Why don't you
           go back to a hotel and / have a holiday?

LANCE.   Because we've no money because we lent you /
           five hundred pounds.

PHIL.   So you think you've bought me, you can live in
           my flat, wake me up from my dream, typical
           American think you can take the place over, think
           people like you, nobody likes you, / you are very

LANCE.   You have killed a man. / You have killed.

JAQ.   We know that. Do you have to

PHIL.   boring, very patronising, / very insincere, very
           ugly, very selfcentred –

VERA.   It's you you're describing, it's a game where

JAQ.   tell us that? You sit about suffering, you make it
           your *problem.*

VERA.   you get people to describe / what they most

PHIL.   Why don't you go home?

LANCE.   What about our money? / We're going home on
           Friday.

PHIL.   You've plenty of money.

LANCE.   We do not have money.

VERA.   don't like and it's always what *they're* – You think
            it's not a problem?

JAQ.   You're so important.

II US

1. Shrink

VERA *lying on couch,* SHRINK *sitting at her triad.*

VERA.   I'd lost a child and I was looking for it in a chest
of drawers. I was going through these drawers
pulling out sweaters and I found some kittens,
there were kittens everywhere but I still hadn't
found the child and I hadn't been looking after the
kittens so they were dying, I kept putting them in
the water in the sink and all I had at the end was
socks, not even a pair, just odd socks.

Pause.

Then there was a body on the floor and it was me
and as I looked at it it moved, I was terrified, it
meant it was about to be the end of the world.

Pause.

There's not having had a child of course is the lost
child. And the child in me I've lost. Odd socks is
perfect. And I do feel dead and I do feel I'm going
to be judged.

Pause.

My descendants are dead because they're never
going to exist and my ancestors are dead partly
because everyone's ancestors are dead but because
they were killed, so many of them were killed, and
sometimes I can feel that and some times I can't.
If I think of my father and try to think of a boy of
six in Russia seeing his mother cut open from her
breast to her stomach . . . it's embarrassing, why,
because he never mentioned it, my mother said it
at his funeral and wouldn't talk about it again.
I see her naked which is wrong. She would have
been wearing . . . I give up, I turn it into a Russian
doll. And my mother was got out of Germany so
she never saw anything, but her parents, her two

sisters, her little brother, all *gone,* how would you understand that if you hadn't seen them for months anyway? She wouldn't speak either. She wanted me to be happy.

Pause.

There's something I'm not telling you.

Pause.

When I was in England someone was killed. I was there in the room, I'd never seen anyone dead. One minute he was – . And I joined in, I helped bury him in a wood at night, we put the dead leaves over, we ran all round in the dead leaves so they'd all be churned up so nobody – . And nobody ever did find him. Didn't he have a family? Didn't someone care if he was dead?

Pause.

I'm telling you something true, that wasn't a dream.

SHRINK.   You feel guilt for the deaths in your family because you are a survivor. You and your parents buried them with silence.

VERA *sits up and faces him.*

VERA.   Go for the police. I'm a murderer.

He doesn't react. She lies down.

SHRINK.   The child is lost but your dead body is coming back to life. You are frightened by the day of judgment because it means living with the consequences of your actions, which you feel include these deaths. Your past self should be in a drawer where you can find it but it has split into many defenceless creatures dying of neglect. You are letting yourself die as an expiation, and similarly killing your children by not allowing them to live. The water is to drown the kittens but also to wash them clean. They turn into part of your everyday life. The man in the wood is your dead ancestors, your unborn children and the part of yourself you fear to have discovered. When you ask me to go for the police you are asking me to discover this self and help you to face the consequences. Which is what I am trying to do now.

Pause.

The man in the wood is also me.

2. Bar

LANCE *and a* COLLEAGUE *in a bar.*

COLL.   So sales are down, this is seasonal. The guy should know it's seasonal, he has access to the figures, or what kind of a hell job is he doing?

        Pause.

        I mean it's seasonal.

LANCE.   It is, it's the time of year.

COLL.   That's what I'm saying. But does he see that?

        Silence.

LANCE.   What's the worst thing you ever did?

COLL.   Well now, two years back, the figures really took a dip / and that was in –

LANCE.   No, I don't mean sales, I mean in your life.

COLL.   The worst? The worst thing that happened to me / was when that fire –

LANCE.   No, the worst thing you did. You did it. Not it happened. You did. Something.

COLL.   The worst thing I did.

LANCE.   Yes.

COLL.   Why what's the worst thing you did?

LANCE.   You first.

COLL.   OK. Well I haven't told anyone this, OK. It's about five years ago. The kids were in camp, my wife's mother was sick so she'd – you get the picture. All

alone in a hot summer. So one weekend I lit out,
I was I don't even know where, some small town
I stopped for a soda. There's a girl in the drug-
store, real hair, maybe not all that special, I don't
know. We just looked at each other and hey. We
didn't even say very much, just hi, that kind of
stuff. We get in my car and drive off down some
track she told me and we come to a river, and we
take all our clothes off and first of all we swim in
the river, and afterwards we throw ourselves down
on the grass, soaking wet, and we do it all afternoon, and on till it gets dark, we just keep on
doing it.

LANCE. And then?

COLL. That's it, what do you think? We picked ourselves
up around midnight and I explained I had to get
home and she said she did too.

LANCE. She wanted to do it? You didn't, I mean, / if it was
rape I –

COLL. What are you saying? Didn't I tell you? / What do
you think I am?

LANCE. Ok ok I'm sorry. And when you / left –

COLL. For Chrissakes.

COLL. Ok I'm sorry, ok? And when you left her she
wasn't upset?

COLL. She was in the same situation as me, her old man
was out of town.

LANCE. That was the worst thing?

COLL. It sure was.

LANCE. Made you feel bad?

COLL. Made me feel real bad. I'd never cheated on
Marianne before.

LANCE. Did you ever tell her?

COLL. No now hey don't you ever let on to Marianne.
I thought did I ought to tell her and then I thought

hell it only make her unhappy. It was all over, it wasn't somebody I was ever going to see. It was in another state. But I did feel bad for a while there. Every now and again there we'd be and it'd hit me.

LANCE.   But you liked it too?

COLL.   Oh sure, I liked it. I liked it a lot.

Pause.

So what's your worst thing?

Pause.

Come on, don't pull out on me. What you been up to behind Vera's back?

Pause.

You won't tell Vera what I told you. In case she might mention.

LANCE.   Yes, that's it, there was a girl in England. Vera never knew anything about it. We drove out to a forest, one night. I bumped into a tree because I couldn't see. There were dead leaves all over the ground. We ran round in the leaves.

COLL.   What she look like the girl?

Pause.

You don't even want to talk about it, huh, you feel that bad?

Pause.

Come on, guy, these things happen. It was in another country.

3. Passport Control

PHIL *and* JAQ *in the* (*unseen*) *passport control queue. Hand-baggage, passports. Now and then they shuffle forward.*

JAQ.   Do you think this is the right place to be? It's such a long queue.

PHIL.   Look / over there.

JAQ.	There might be a quicker – I don't recognise any of these people. Where are the people from our plane?
PHIL.	Look.
JAQ.	What?
PHIL.	It's a policeman.
JAQ.	So?
PHIL.	It's an actual American cop with a gun. Look at that holster. We're actually in America, you realise that?
JAQ.	That's the couple with the baby, they were on our flight.
PHIL.	Did you see that?
JAQ.	What?
PHIL.	That man with the glasses – look – / he's gone
JAQ.	What?
PHIL.	back, he got shouted at because he didn't wait behind the line.
JAQ.	What line?
PHIL.	Look, the line. You mustn't cross the line while you're waiting your turn. / He got shouted –
JAQ.	In case you rush the passport control.
PHIL.	Yes, in case you break into America.
JAQ.	But anyway the cop would shoot / you down.
PHIL.	In a hail of bullets.
JAQ.	Look at that one, in the third / booth.
PHIL.	Which one, / the passenger?
JAQ.	The official, the passport / one.
PHIL.	Yes, what about him?
JAQ.	I don't know, he just looks American.
PHIL.	He does, he looks really American.
JAQ.	That's because we're in America.
PHIL.	We are. That's where we are.

4. Party

LANCE, VERA, JAQ *and* FELLOW GUEST *at a party.*

GUEST.   If you're going to Arizona to see the Grand
         Canyon, you want to see Indians. You want to
         go to the caves where there's like whole cities
         in caves from hundreds of years ago – you ever
         do that?

JAQ.   No, / I never –

GUEST.   You want to do that. You should all go together.
         We don't see enough of this beautiful country of
         ours. Stuck here, this suburb, this could be
         anyplace, don't you think? This isn't what you
         came to the United States for, is it? Now is it?

JAQ.   I came to see my cousins but / I do –

GUEST.   But, exactly, but.

JAQ.   I do, it's true of course, I do / want to see far

GUEST.   Of course you do. This is dullsville.

JAQ.   more of the country, we thought we'd hire a car
         and just set off / and drive

GUEST.   That's right.

JAQ.   right across / out west and then

GUEST.   That's right.

JAQ.   down south.

GUEST.   That's right, you want to see the size of it, you
         want to experience – hey, Lance, you going with
         your cousin, / show her round?

LANCE.   No, unfortunately, no, I can't, / I can't take a
         vacation right now.

GUEST.   You ought to go. Vera, you going?

VERA.   No, I don't / think –

GUEST.   What's the matter with you people? I'll go with
         you, ok? Show you a good time. You want to see
         Yosemite National Park.

JAQ.   I want to see everything. / I want to see New

GUEST.   That's right.

JAQ.   York and New Orleans and the Rocky Mountains and the Everglades and the Grand Canyon / and

GUEST.   And the caves, the Hopi Indians,

JAQ.   Disneyland / and Hollywood –

LANCE.   Not Disneyland, / Disneyland is sick.

VERA.   You'll be bored, / you'll be disappointed.

GUEST.   Are you a tourist or are you a traveller? / I will

JAQ.   No, I do, I do want to go to Disneyland.

GUEST.   show you adventure. No you don't, I will make out an itinerary –

Interrupted by PHIL *and a* WOMAN, *both drunk, their arms round each other.*

DRUNK.   Phil's a killer, would you have guessed that? He's just been telling me how in London he killed some guy who broke / into his apartment.

GUEST.   Is this true ?

PHIL.   Of course / it's true.

GUEST.   Hey, did you know this? What did you do? /

DRUNK.   He shot him.

PHIL.   I shot him.

GUEST.   Did you know this? / Just like that?

LANCE.   Yes.

PHIL.   He was a villain. He was our landlord and he was a villain / and he was extorting

DRUNK.   I've never met a killer before.

PHIL.   money from us / and he was a known villain.

GUEST.   So when was this? / You never told me this.*

LANCE.   Last summer.   PHIL. *He was a very evil man. I don't like evil.

VERA.   August.

GUEST.   When you were there?

VERA.	Yes we were in the apartment.	DRUNK. I don't. I don't like evil.
GUEST.	You were *there, /* right *there?*	PHIL. Exterminate.
LANCE.	Yes, we saw it.	DRUNK. Absolutely
GUEST.	and you, did you know – you *saw /* this, this is amazing, so	exterminate.
VERA.	Yes.	
GUEST.	what happened, so what did you do, / what did you feel?	
VERA.	We buried him in the forest.	PHIL. Blew him away. DRUNK. Blew him away.
GUEST.	You what?	
LANCE.	Yes, we / buried –	
JAQ.	We buried him / in a forest.	
VERA.	We dug a hole.	
DRUNK.	Isn't this great?	
GUEST.	And is it a secret?	
PHIL.	Not any more.	
GUEST.	And weren't you frightened?	
JAQ.	Not / very.*	
VERA.	Yes, I was, I was terrified.	
GUEST.	*You're a heroine I can tell, / you're the heroine type.	
LANCE.	I thought his hand moved, / yes I thought I	
DRUNK.	Aah.	
LANCE.	saw his hand move.	
VERA.	And when they showed up, when you showed up on the doorstep / I thought	
GUEST.	They just showed up without warning, these murderers just –	
VERA.	holy shit / but	

JAQ.   You weren't very glad / to see us.

VERA.   We weren't.

LANCE.   We didn't let on, / we were polite.

PHIL.   You hated / seeing us.

VERA.   Not / *you*, we didn't hate –

DRUNK.   You saw the dead man's *hand move?*

LANCE.   But there's nothing, when they told us there'd been
            nothing / in the papers then we felt* such relief
            whahey!

JAQ.   No police, / nothing.   VERA. *Then we felt glad
                                            to see you because
DRUNK.   You got away with it   we love you.

PHIL.   We did, / I guess we did.

GUEST.   You got away with murder. My god. Some
            adventure. Wow. Is this true? Jee-zus.

            They are all laughing and shouting.

5. Hospital

LANCE, VERA *and* JAQ *sitting on a bench.* VERA*'s arm
round* JAQ.

LANCE.   Nurse. Excuse me.

            *The nurse (unseen) passes without stopping.
            Silence.*

LANCE.   So he just stepped out.

VERA.   Was he looking the wrong way?

LANCE.   If he looked the wrong way and stepped out / and
            the car –

JAQ.   I didn't see, / I said I didn't see him step out,

VERA.   She didn't see him step out.

JAQ.   I saw the car hit him.

LANCE.   And it threw him / in the air.

JAQ.   It threw him forward and sideways.

LANCE.   Sideways which was lucky / so he wasn't under the wheels.

VERA.   Though he might have been thrown under another car if there'd been one so that was lucky.

JAQ.   The driver said he just stepped out / in front

VERA.   Made out it was *his* fault.

JAQ.   of him but the car / was going too fast.

LANCE.   Had the driver been drinking?

VERA.   They've always been drinking / in most accidents.

LANCE.   We don't know that yet but we will find it out.

            Pause.

JAQ.   I'm not so worried about the broken / bones, it's his head.

VERA.   Broken limbs can always be fixed, it's only if there's a head / injury.

LANCE.   We know there is / a head injury.

VERA.   Only if there's a serious / head injury.

LANCE.   Obviously, / that's what we're waiting to find out.

JAQ.   Or some internal . . .

            Long silence.

LANCE.   Excuse me. Nurse.

            Again the (unseen) nurse doesn't stop.
            Very long silence.

6. Car

JAQ *driving with a* HITCHER.

JAQ.   Where you heading?

HITCHER.   Just fifteen miles up the road.

            Pause.

You often pick up hitchers at night?

JAQ.   Sometimes.

HITCHER.   You should be careful. A nice girl like you
            something could happen.

JAQ.   If it does.

HITCHER.   That's not a good attitude.

            Pause.

            Maybe that is a good attitude. You are putting your
            trust in the Lord.

JAQ.   No, I don't believe in the Lord.

HITCHER.   I'm sorry to hear that.

            Pause.

            If you're not putting your trust in Him you are
            inviting disaster. I'm not saying you deserve it.
            But there's nothing to stop it. You are an attractive
            young woman. That is an incitement. You shouldn't
            go about leading people into temptation. / On the
            last day the Lord will say –

JAQ.   I'm not. I'm giving you a lift. Do you want a lift?

HITCHER.   How do you mean a lift?

JAQ.   A ride in the car.

HITCHER.   I do want a ride, yes please. You certainly give a
            lift to my spirit. I was wondering if it had some
            other meaning I didn't get, some kind of invitation.

            Pause.

            You from out of state?

JAQ.   Yes, England.

HITCHER.   You give people rides in England?

JAQ.   I haven't got a car.

            Pause.

HITCHER.   Don't misunderstand me, I am not being led into
            temptation because I put my trust in the Lord. Five
            years ago it would have been a different matter.

But now I've been born again you could take all
your clothes off if you want / and I wouldn't harm
a hair

JAQ   I don't want.

HITCHER.   of your head, no of course you don't, I wasn't
meaning that.

Pause.

JAQ.   I stole this car.

HITCHER.   I'm sorry to hear that.

JAQ.   My brother died yesterday.

HITCHER.   My, I'm sorry to hear that. Did he die in the Lord?

JAQ.   No.

HITCHER.   You don't know what was going on in his mind.
He may have repented and welcomed the Lord into
his heart and not told anyone, and may now be in
the bosom of Jesus.

JAQ.   He was hit by a car. He never regained
consciousness.

HITCHER.   It may have flashed through his mind in a split
second.

Pause.

In about half a mile, I'll tell you when, if you drop
me there, and I'll just walk up the track.

Pause.

Do you want to come to my house and have a cup
of coffee and a piece of pie with my mother?

7. Coffee

JAQ *having coffee with the* HITCHER *and his* MOTHER.

MOTHER.   We were sitting right up on the roof. Don't ask me
why, I was four years old. I don't know if they
thought the world would end by flood and we'd
be safe up there a bit longer, I don't think they

thought it out too good. I remember I had to go to the bathroom and my ma held me out off of the roof. And it got to sunset and everybody was saying hallelujah. I don't remember us climbing back down though that's what must have happened. What I do know is the next day was my best friend's party and my mother had been going to make me a new dress out of some beautiful blue stuff, and then she'd decided not to because the party wasn't going to be till after the end of the world so she said there was no point. And the party went ahead after all, and I had my old pink dress and I was real mad at my ma.

JAQ.   But you still think the world's going to end?

MOTHER.   I know for a fact it's going to end, it's just people have trouble working out exactly when. You know it's going to rain, you see the big clouds piling up, you don't know at what exact minute, maybe you take the washing in and it blows over. Now Hank and I have a disagreement about this. He thinks it's going to end sometime / in the next couple of years.

HITCHER.   I'm not the only person thinks that. There's thousands getting ready all over the country.

MOTHER.   And they don't mean *end* either because they're laying in supplies, like sacks of flour and cans of food / and guns –

HITCHER.   Because we're going to survive.

MOTHER.   Seems like sitting on the roof to me and hoping the flood water / won't get you.

HITCHER.   It's going to be fire not water, it's going to be nuclear, and the Lord will save the righteous but only if they have the good sense to prepare themself / because God is no damn fool.

MOTHER.   There's no sense preparing except in your heart, that's where you have to prepare, and you won't need baked beans when you have manna and no amount of guns are going to help you / get to heaven.

HITCHER.   Yes because there will be desperate people trying
           to survive / who are not meant to survive.

MOTHER.   Then let the Lord deal with it himself. Don't you
           agree with me? Tell him you think he's a silly boy
           wasting his money / stocking up for heaven.

JAQ.   I don't think getting all that food and weapons / is
           going to –

HITCHER.   So what do you think? You think I should sit here
           and wait till it happens and get incinerated / like
           any sinner?

JAQ.   I don't think the world's about to end.

HITCHER.   That just shows you don't know, / and will be one
           of the first to go which I'm sorry to hear.

MOTHER.   That's right, it's not going to end till the year two
           thousand, and then it will end in the proper way,
           with no need for cans or grenades because Jesus /
           will come and judge both

HITCHER.   The year two thousand is meaningless.

MOTHER.   the quick and the dead.

HITCHER.   Do you agree with that? No she doesn't, because
           why should it end in two thousand just because
           that's a round number some people made up, if we
           didn't count in tens it wouldn't sound / like an
           interesting year.

JAQ.   If we didn't count from when Jesus / was born.

MOTHER.   No we have to count / from –

JAQ.   Not everyone does, there are other years, like
           Muslims or Jews can't count their years / from –

HITCHER.   You a Jew? You telling me you're a Jew? / You a
           Muslim?

JAQ.   No but or Hindus or Buddhists in India they can't
           think it's two thousand.

HITCHER.   They accept / what we call it, it's going to be,

MOTHER.   It isn't two thousand yet.

HITCHER.   she means going / to be –

MOTHER.   Of course it's going to be two thousand.

HITCHER.   They accept like English is the international
            language, it is the international year, everyone in
            the world / is going to know it's two

JAQ.   I'm not sure they are.

HITCHER.   thousand when it *is* two thousand only it won't
            ever *be* because that doesn't mean the world is
            going to end / then because

MOTHER.   There's no arguing with children.

HITCHER.   it's just a number, / you don't understand

MOTHER.   It's a millennial number.

HITCHER.   what I'm saying you're not living / in the modern
            world.

MOTHER.   You'll see, that's all.

HITCHER.   I won't see because two thousand will never come
            because it will happen before that. Then the years
            will start over, we'll count forward from there, one
            two / three –

MOTHER.   You'll get to around nine, which will be two
            thousand / and then you'll see.

HITCHER.   It will already have happened, we'll already be
            saved.

MOTHER.   Let's ask our guest to decide between us.

JAQ.   I don't think either of you, I don't think the world,
            I mean it could do just by chance, I mean by
            the way things are going it could happen, by a
            nuclear – or the way things – if we don't – I don't
            know much about it, about the greenhouse and
            the ozone, but people are beginning – so it could
            be – if it's not too late, but anyway no, I don't
            believe the world is going to end either of your
            ways.

            Pause.

HITCHER.   I'm sorry to hear that.

MOTHER.   Don't you want to meet your brother? Don't you
            want him to rise up from his grave in the year two

thousand? How long do you want to wait? What
do you think's going to happen?

JAQ.   I don't know.

HITCHER. Yes, if you're so smart, what do you think's going
          to happen?

8. View

JAQ *and* PROFESSOR *having a picnic high above a lake.*

PROF.   My wife died of cancer last year and that seemed
          to me very unjust. She didn't smoke. She wasn't
          sexually promiscuous. She didn't eat fatty foods.
          She didn't repress her aggressions. You think why,
          why me? She got very angry.

JAQ.   Who with?

PROF.   With God. With me. With the doctors. With me,
          for chrissake, I didn't give her cancer. *I* thought
          why me, just as much, why my wife? Why no sex,
          why no cheerful conversation, why should I be
          plunged into this hideous world of hospitals and
          hysterical emotion? Because my wife did not make
          what is called a good death. It's expected, there's
          a very high standard set nowadays of what you're
          supposed to be like if you're terminally ill and
          my wife did not measure up. She didn't develop
          spiritually and become an inspiration to her
          friends. She became a monster. She left her friends
          shitscared.

          Pause.

JAQ.   I think Americans are happier than the English.

PROF.   Do you have some explanation of that
          phenomenon?

JAQ.   Or if they're not they think they should be, they
          think they have a right, / while the

PROF.   It's in the constitution, pursuit of happiness.

JAQ.   English feel more comfortable if it rains every
          day / in August.

PROF.   So would this be because of the respective history of the two nations?

Pause.

JAQ.   This view, that lake down there, no one's ever heard of it, but we'd say a lake, a lake district, it's a different scale.

PROF.   So are you suggesting the psychology is geographical?

Pause.

JAQ.   I'm happy now because I feel I'm in a road movie and everyone I meet is these interesting characters.

PROF.   Do I come into that category?

JAQ.   No, you're sort of normal, as it goes.

PROF.   I guess I am. I guess professors are kind of dull in any country.

Pause.

JAQ.   So now your wife's dead do you still expect to be happy?

PROF.   I am more determined than ever to be happy. Anything I want, I consider I have a right to it now after what fate has subjected me to. I think the universe owes me one.

Pause.

JAQ.   What was your wife's name?

PROF.   Why do you ask?

JAQ.   Curiosity.

PROF.   Beth, she was called Beth. Ok? You wouldn't have liked her.

Pause.

JAQ.   So does it work, being determined to be happy?

PROF.   I go for what I want and I invariably get it.

JAQ.   How? such as what?

PROF.   To take an example. I'm going to get what I want now.

JAQ.	How do you mean?
PROF.	Take off your shirt.
JAQ.	Sorry?
PROF.	Take off your shirt, bitch, let's see what you've got.

9. Ticket

LANCE *and* VERA *at their house with* JAQ.

VERA.	A thousand dollars?
JAQ.	Dollars, not even pounds, a thousand dollars / isn't a lot of money.
VERA.	Why should we give you / a thousand dollars?
LANCE.	Don't discuss it.
JAQ.	Because I've got no money left and you / have got –
VERA.	You stole our car.
JAQ.	I brought it back.
VERA.	In what / condition? *
LANCE.	Don't discuss it. We are not giving you any money.
JAQ.	*Give me a thousand dollars and I'll have it serviced.
	Pause.
JAQ.	I want to go home.
LANCE.	Then get work, you don't have a green card there are places be glad to give you work less than the going – you can stand on your own two – . The hell with it, her brother died.
JAQ.	I don't like asking.
LANCE.	No, it's ok, you're family, what the hell.
VERA.	The car if you'd only asked, / of course you
JAQ.	Yes, I'm sorry.

VERA.   could, it's not surprising we got mad, we got
         worried, / not a word in six weeks,

JAQ.   Yes, I'm sorry.

VERA.   you don't have to be sorry, I'm just saying.

LANCE.   Are you ok to go home and be on your own?

VERA.   Yes, why don't you stay with us till you get
         over . . . ?

JAQ.   No, because one of the people I met, he was a
         university professor, we were having a picnic up
         above a lake, and we were near the edge of where
         it sloped down sort of fell quite steeply down to
         the lake, because the view was really spectacular,
         and I gave him a push / because he was going to
         attack me,

LANCE.   Hey.

JAQ.   he was / starting to

LANCE.   What are you saying?

JAQ.   attack me, / I gave him quite a hard push and

VERA.   How do you mean, attack?

JAQ.   he / went over backwards and lost his balance

LANCE.   You pushed him over the edge? Was he hurt or
         what?

JAQ.   and slipped down the first part and I thought he'd
         get hold of a tree / but he went right over.

VERA.   My god, oh my, oh . . . That is just . . . isn't that
         just the most . . .

         Pause.

LANCE.   Right over and what? all the way down to the lake
         are you saying? and what? / Did he

VERA.   So what led up to this, what exactly did he . . . ?

LANCE.   drown in the lake? / Did you climb down

JAQ.   I expect . . .

LANCE.   and look? Did you / get the police?

JAQ.   So I'd better go home.

Pause.

LANCE.   What the hell are you telling us? you telling us you
            killed him? you killed him and drove off, you
            drove off, you go round killing people, you think
            you can go round killing, / you can

VERA.   Was it self-defence? It was self-defence.

LANCE.   just go home? / What are you saying? Did

JAQ.   I didn't know him.

LANCE.   anyone see you?

JAQ.   No, there was no one / about.

LANCE.   Did anyone get the number of the car / as you

VERA.   Oh my god.

LANCE.   drove off? / Or earlier if you stopped for gas

JAQ.   No, there wasn't anyone.

LANCE.   or you stopped for a coke, / where did you

JAQ.   No.

LANCE.   meet the guy? someone's going to be able to
            connect you with him, when they find him, /
            someone's going to know who he is.

VERA.   A professor of what?

JAQ.   I don't know, I think history, / something –

VERA.   Where was this? what university / was he a
            professor at?

LANCE.   What the hell does it matter what subject what
            university, he'll be found, / he'll be identified,

JAQ.   It's a very remote lake.

LANCE.   what do you know about remote, nothing's remote,
            did you hike a hundred miles to this lake? There
            will be fishermen, there will be children
            swimming, / he will

JAQ.   It's getting cold now, there might not be –

LANCE. be found, he will be found, and even if it's next year or the year after, even if he's totally decomposed there will be documents, there will be teeth for god's sake, / even if he's a

VERA.   Yes, teeth are completely individual.

LANCE. skeleton even if it's when we're old they'll raise him up out of the lake / and –

VERA.   But by then they won't remember her talking to him.

LANCE. By when by when, this could be in twenty years or it could be next / week.

VERA.   So why don't we go to the police now, because we just had our car stolen, and Jaq tells them it was self-defence / and your brother was run

JAQ.   No, I'm not going to.

VERA.   over and you were in shock, I do think we'd better do that.

JAQ.   No, I'm not going to.

VERA.   And why?

LANCE. Because of in England, she'd tell about the forest, / we're too implicated, we're too far, we can't possibly get –

VERA.   No because she'd be in worse trouble and that's her own country, they couldn't get us for that, they'd have to / extradite –

JAQ.   Why don't I just go home?

LANCE. You are some kind of monster, I opened my heart. Are you my family? your brother, you're both, I was so happy to find – You are nothing to do with me, I won't be involved / in – You sicken, inhuman, how

VERA.   It's better if she goes home before anything . . .

LANCE. can you sit, vile, you are – . Hate you hate you, how – ?

JAQ.   Yes, you better give me the money straight away so I can get my ticket.

LANCE.   It doesn't cost a thousand dollars / to get a ticket to
                London.

JAQ.   All right, just get the ticket, I don't care.

10. Airport

JAQ *and a* SOUTH AMERICAN WOMAN PASSENGER *in the
departure lounge.*

WOMAN.   The flight is the shortest part. I arrive at night and
                sleep at the airport and at half past six I get on a
                bus. Twelve hours on the bus and I stay with some
                friends who have a bar. In the morning I get on the
                boat and it arrives in the afternoon. Everyone will
                come in the evening to hear how my grandfather
                died. We could only afford one person to come
                and see him.

JAQ.   How did he die?

WOMAN.   Very well.

                Silence.

                I don't like airports.

JAQ.   I thought I didn't but I do. There's everything you
                need. Food, toilets. Books. Alcohol.

WOMAN.   Do you like flying?

JAQ.   I like seeing everything get smaller.

WOMAN.   You can have the window, I'll have the aisle.

JAQ.   We're not on the same flight.

                Silence.

WOMAN.   My grandfather breathed and stopped, breathed
                and stopped. Then I saw there was a butterfly in
                the room. When it went out of the window my
                grandfather breathed and stopped and didn't
                breathe again. What do you think?

JAQ.   I think it was a coincidence.

WOMAN.   I know how to think it was a coincidence. I went to
                university in Chicago. But I know how else to
                think of it.

JAQ.   I *know* how else to think of it but I don't.

             Silence.

WOMAN.   Change your flight.

JAQ.   I'm not going to the same / place. I'm going –

WOMAN.   Change your destination.

JAQ.   I don't think you can do that, swap your ticket.

WOMAN.   Have you tried?

JAQ.   It would cost more and I can't afford it.

WOMAN.   How much more?

JAQ.   Can you afford it?

WOMAN.   I don't know till you find out.

             Pause.

JAQ.   I want to be at home and have a cup or tea.

WOMAN.   Go and find out. I love you already. Go and find
             out.

MAD FOREST

On the plain where Bucharest now stands there used to
be 'a large forest crossed by small muddy streams . . .
It could only be crossed on foot and was impenetrable
for the foreigner who did not know the paths . . . The
horsemen of the steppe were compelled to go round it,
and this difficulty, which irked them so, is shown by
the name . . . Teleorman – Mad Forest.'

A Concise History of Romania
Otetea and MacKenzie

Production Note

Since the play goes from the difficulty of saying anything to
everyone talking, don't be afraid of long silences. For instance,
in Scene One, the silence before Bogdan turns up the music was
a good fifteen seconds in our production. Short scenes like 13
and 15 need to be given their weight. Don't add additional
dialogue (for instance in queues, party or arrival in country)
except in III 6 where 'etc' means there can be other things
shouted by the spectators.

The queue scenes and execution scene should have as many
people as are available. In the execution scene it is the violence
of the spectators which is the main focus rather than the
execution itself.

We didn't use a prop rat. The Vampire was not dressed as a
vampire.

In Part II (December) the language of the different characters
varies with how well they speak English, and this should be
reflected in their accents.

In the hospital and party scenes it is particularly important that
the short scenes within them are not run together and that time
has clearly passed.

Music. As in the text, the music after the opening poem becomes
the music on the Vladu radio. It's not essential to do what we
did with the music, but it may be helpful to know that at the end
of the wedding we used a hymn to the Ceauşescus and continued
the music till everyone was in place for the beginning of
December; at the end of December the whole company sang a
verse from 'Wake up Romania' in Romanian, which then merged
with a recording of it; we had music at the beginning of Part III.
The party music in III.8 should be western euro-pop. The dance
music should be the lambada – this is not an arbitrary choice, it
was the popular dance at the time. The nightmare scene and the
very end of the play probably need sound.

Words for the poem at the beginning and words and music for
'Wake up Romania' can be got from Casarotto Ramsay.

Caryl Churchill and Mark Wing-Davey, March 1991

Mad Forest was first staged by students in their final year of training at the Central School of Speech and Drama, London, on 25 June 1990 with the cast as follows. It was subsequently performed at the National Theatre, Bucharest, from 17 September, and opened at the Royal Court Theatre, London, on 9 October 1990 with the same cast.

VLADU FAMILY

BOGDAN, *an electrician*	David MacCreedy
IRINA, *a tramdriver*	Lucy Cohu
Their children:	
LUCIA, *a primary school teacher*	Nicola Gibson
FLORINA, *a nurse*	Victoria Alcock
GABRIEL, *an engineer*	David Mestecky
RODICA, *Gabriel's wife*	Sarah Ball
WAYNE, *Lucia's bridegroom*	Gordon Anderson
GRANDFATHER, *Bogdan's father*	Iain Hake
GRANDMOTHER, *Bogdan's mother*	Sarah Ball
OLD AUNT, *Bogdan's aunt*	Iain Hake

ANTONESCU FAMILY

MIHAI, *an architect*	Gordon Anderson
FLAVIA, *a teacher*	Sarah Ball
RADU, *an art student, their son*	Mark Heal
GRANDMOTHER, *Flavia's grandmother, who is dead*	
	Lucy Cohu

IANOŞ	Philip Glenister
SECURITATE MAN	Iain Hake
DOCTOR	Joseph Bennett
PRIEST	Iain Hake
ANGEL	Joseph Bennett
VAMPIRE	Iain Hake
DOG	Gordon Anderson
SOMEONE WITH SORE THROAT	Iain Hake
PATIENT	Joseph Bennett
TWO SOLDIERS	Iain Hake, Joseph Bennett

TOMA, *aged 8*	David MacCreedy
GHOST	Joseph Bennett
WAITER	Joseph Bennett
PAINTER	Philip Glenister
GIRL STUDENT	Lucy Cohu
TWO BOY STUDENTS	Joseph Bennett, David MacCreedy
TRANSLATOR	Gordon Anderson
BULLDOZER DRIVER	David Mestecky
SECURITATE OFFICER	Mark Heal
SOLDIER	Iain Hake
STUDENT DOCTOR	Nicola Gibson
FLOWERSELLER	Victoria Alcock
HOUSEPAINTER	Sarah Ball

PEOPLE IN QUEUES AND WEDDING GUESTS
plaayed by members of the company

Directed by Mark Wing-Davey
Designed by Antony McDonald
Lighting Design Nigel H. Morgan

Bucharest Workshop Group

Victoria Alcock, Sarah Ball, Joseph Bennett, Caryl Churchill,
Lucy Cohu, Nicola Gibson, Iain Hake, Mark Heal,
David MacCreedy, Antony McDonald, David Mestecky,
Nigel H. Morgan, Indra Ove, Mark Wing-Davey,
Jason Woodford.

Special thanks to

The staff and pupils of the Institutul de Arta Teatrala si
Cinematografica, I.L. Caragiale, Bucharest; and all the
Romanians who helped both groups in Bucharest.

I LUCIA'S WEDDING

The company recite, smiling, a poem in Romanian in praise of Elena Ceauşescu.

Stirring Romanian music.

Each scene is announced by one of the company reading from a phrasebook as if an English tourist, first in Romanian, then in English, and again in Romanian.

1. Lucia are patru ouă. Lucia has four eggs.

Music continues. BOGDAN *and* IRINA VLADU *sit in silence, smoking Romanian cigarettes.*

BOGDAN *turns up the music on the radio very loud. He sits looking at* IRINA.

IRINA *puts her head close to* BOGDAN's *and talks quickly and quietly, to convince him.*

He argues back, she insists, he gets angry. We can't hear anything they say.

They stop talking and sit with the music blaring. BOGDAN *is about to speak when* FLORINA *and* LUCIA *come in, laughing.*

They stop laughing and look at BOGDAN *and* IRINA.

IRINA *turns the radio down low.*

LUCIA *produces four eggs with a flourish.* IRINA *kisses her.*

BOGDAN *ignores her.*

LUCIA *produces a packet of American cigarettes.*

FLORINA *laughs.*

LUCIA *opens the cigarettes and offers them to* IRINA. *She hesitates, then puts out her cigarette and takes one.* FLORINA *takes one.*

BOGDAN *ignores them.*

LUCIA *offers a cigarette to* BOGDAN, *he shakes his head.*

LUCIA *takes a cigarette. They sit smoking.*

BOGDAN *finishes his cigarette. He sits without smoking. Then he takes a cigarette.*

LUCIA *and* FLORINA *laugh.*

BOGDAN *picks up an egg and breaks it on the floor.*

IRINA *gathers the other eggs to safety.*

LUCIA *and* FLORINA *keep still.*

IRINA *turns the radio up loud and is about to say something.*

BOGDAN *turns the radio completely off.* IRINA *ignores him and smokes.*

FLORINA *gets a cup and spoon and scrapes up what she can of the egg off the floor.*

LUCIA *keeps still.*

2. Cine are un chibrit? Who has a match?

ANTONESCU *family, noticeably better off than the* VLADUS. MIHAI *thinking and making notes,* FLAVIA *correcting exercise books,* RADU *drawing. They sit in silence for some time. When they talk they don't look up from what they're doing.*

MIHAI.   He came today.

FLAVIA.   That's exciting.

RADU.   Did he make you change it?

MIHAI.   He had a very interesting recommendation. The arch should be this much higher.

RADU.   And the columns?

MIHAI.   We will make an improvement to the spacing of the columns.

FLAVIA.   That sounds good.

They go on working.

The lights go out. They are resigned, almost indifferent.

RADU *takes a match and lights a candle.*

They sit in candlelight in silence.

RADU. I don't see why.

FLAVIA. We've said no.

RADU. If I leave it a year or two till after the wedding, I / could –

FLAVIA. No.

RADU. It's not her fault if her sister –

MIHAI. The whole family. No. Out of the question.

Pause.

There are plenty of other girls, Radu.

They sit in silence.

The lights come on.

FLAVIA *blows out the candle and snuffs it with her fingers.*

They all start reading again.

RADU. So is that the third time he's made you change it?

MIHAI *doesn't reply. They go on working.*

3. Ea are o scrisoare din Statele Unite.
She has a letter from the United States.

LUCIA *is reading an airmail letter, smiling. She kisses the letter. She puts it away.* FLORINA *comes in from work.*

LUCIA. Tired?

Pause. FLORINA *is taking off her shoes.*

I'm sorry.

FLORINA *smiles and shrugs.*

LUCIA. No but all of you . . . because of me and Wayne.

FLORINA. You love him.

LUCIA *takes out the letter and offers it to* FLORINA.

FLORINA *hesitates.* LUCIA *insists.*

FLORINA *reads the letter, she is serious.* LUCIA *watches her.*

FLORINA *gives the letter back.*

LUCIA.   And Radu? Have you seen him lately?

FLORINA *shrugs.*

4. Elevii ascultă lecția. The pupils listen to the lesson.

FLAVIA *speaks loudly and confidently to her pupils.*

FLAVIA.   Today we are going to learn about a life dedicated to the happiness of the people and noble ideas of socialism.

The new history of the motherland is like a great river with its fundamental starting point in the biography of our general secretary, the president of the republic, Comrade Nicolae Ceaușescu, and it flows through the open spaces of the important dates and problems of contemporary humanity. Because it's evident to everybody that linked to the personality of this great son of the nation is everything in the country that is most durable and harmonious, the huge transformations taking place in all areas of activity, the ever more vigorous and ascendant path towards the highest stages of progress and civilisation. He is the founder of the country. More, he is the founder of man. For everything is being built for the sublime development of man and country, for their material and spiritual wellbeing.

He started his revolutionary activity in the earliest years of his adolescence in conditions of danger and illegality, therefore his life and struggle cannot be detached from the most burning moments of the people's fight against fascism and war to achieve the ideals of freedom and aspirations of justice and progress.

We will learn the biography under four headings.

1. village of his birth and prison

2. revolution

3. leadership

4. the great personality of Comrade Nicolae Ceauşescu.

5. Cumpărăm carne. We are buying meat.

RADU *is in a queue of people with shopping bags. They stand a long time in silence.*

Someone leaves a bag with a bottle in it to mark the place and goes.

They go on standing.

RADU *whispers loudly.*

RADU.   Down with Ceauşescu.

> *The woman in front of him starts to look round, then pretends she hasn't heard. The man behind pretends he hasn't heard and casually steps slightly away from* RADU.

> *Two people towards the head of the queue look round and* RADU *looks round as if wondering who spoke. They go on queueing.*

6. Doi oameni stau la soare. Two men are sitting in the sun.

BOGDAN *and a* SECURITATE MAN.

SECURITATE. Do you love your country?

> BOGDAN *nods.*

> And how do you show it?

> *Pause.*

> You love your country, how do you show it?

BOGDAN *is about to speak. He stops. He is about to speak.*

You encourage your daughter to marry an American.

BOGDAN.   No.

SECURITATE.   She defies you?

Silence.

Your daughter was trained as a primary school teacher, she can no longer be employed. Romania has wasted resources that could have benefited a young woman with a sense of duty.

Silence.

I understand your wife works as a tram driver and has recently been transferred to a depot in the south of the city which doubles the time she has to travel to work. You are an electrician, you have been a foreman for some time but alas no longer. Your son is an engineer and is so far doing well. Your other daughter is a nurse. So far there is nothing against her except her sister.

Pause.

I'm sure you are eager to show that your family are patriots.

Silence. BOGDAN *looks away.*

When they know your daughter wants to marry an American, people may confide their own shameful secrets. They may mistakenly think you are someone who has sympathy with foreign regimes. Your other children may make undesirable friends who think you're prepared to listen to what they say. They will be right. You will listen.

Pause. BOGDAN *is about to say something but doesn't.*

What?

Pause.

Your colleagues will know you have been demoted and will wrongly suppose that you are short of

money. As a patriot you may not have noticed
how anyone out of favour attracts the friendship
of irresponsible bitter people who feel slighted.
Be friendly.

Pause.

What a beautiful day. What a beautiful country.

Silence. BOGDAN *looks at him.*

You will make a report once a week.

7. Ascultaţi? Are you listening?

LUCIA *and a* DOCTOR. *While they talk the* DOCTOR *writes
on a piece of paper, pushes it over to* LUCIA, *who writes a
reply, and he writes again.*

DOCTOR.   You're a slut. You've brought this on yourself. The
            only thing to be said in its favour is that one more
            child is one more worker.

LUCIA.   Yes, I realise that.

DOCTOR.   There is no abortion in Romania. I am shocked
            that you even think of it. I am appalled that you
            dare suggest I might commit this crime.

LUCIA.   Yes, I'm sorry.

            LUCIA *gives the doctor an envelope thick with
            money and some more money.*

DOCTOR.   Can you get married?

LUCIA.   Yes.

DOCTOR.   Good. Get married.

            The DOCTOR *writes again,* LUCIA *nods.*

DOCTOR.   I can do nothing for you. Goodbye.

            LUCIA *smiles. She makes her face serious again.*

LUCIA.   Goodbye.

8. Sticla cu vin este pe masă.
The bottle of wine is on the table.

RADU, GABRIEL *and* IANOŞ with *a bottle of wine. They are in public so they keep their voices down.*

IANOŞ.   He died and went to heaven and St Peter says, God
            wants a word with you. So he goes in to see God
            and God says, 'I hear you think you're greater than
            me.' And he says, 'Yes, I am.' And God says,
            'Right, who made the sun?' 'You did.' 'Who made
            the stars?' 'You did.' 'Who made the earth?' 'You
            did.' 'Who made all the people and all the animals
            and all the trees and all the / plants and –

RADU.   And all the wine.

IANOŞ.   And everything?' And he said, 'You did, God.' And
            God says, 'Then how can you possibly be greater
            than me?' And he says, 'All these things, what did
            you make them from?' And God said, 'Chaos, I
            made it all out of Chaos.' 'There you are,' he said,
            'I made chaos.'

RADU.   A cosmonaut leaves a message for his wife. 'Gone
            to Mars, back in two weeks.' Two weeks later he
            comes back and his wife has left him a message.
            'Gone shopping, don't know when I'll be back.'

GABRIEL.   A man wants a car and he saves up his money and
            at last he's able to buy a Trabant. He's very proud
            of it. And he's driving along in his little Trabant
            and he stops at the traffic lights and bang, a car
            crashes into the back of it. So he leaps out very
            angry, and it's a black car with a short number-
            plate, but he's so angry he doesn't care and he
            starts banging on the bonnet. Then a big dumper
            truck stops behind the black car and the driver gets
            out and he takes a crowbar and he starts smashing
            the back of the black car. And the Securitate man
            gets out of his battered black car and he says to the
            truck driver, 'What's going on? I can understand
            him being upset because I hit his car, but what's
            the matter with you?' And the driver says, 'Sorry,
            I thought it had started.'

9. Cerul este albastru. The sky is blue.

An ANGEL *and a* PRIEST.

ANGEL.   Don't be ashamed. When people come into church
          they are free. Even if they know there are
          Securitate in church with them. Even if some
          churches are demolished, so long as there are some
          churches standing. Even if you say Ceauşescu,
          Ceauşescu, because the Romanian church is a
          church of freedom. Not outer freedom of course
          but inner freedom.

          Silence. The PRIEST *sits gazing at* the ANGEL.

PRIEST.   This is so sweet, like looking at the colour blue,
          like looking at the sky when you're a child lying
          on your back, you stare out at the blue but you're
          going in, further and further in away from the
          world, that's what it's like knowing I can talk to
          you. Someone says something, you say something
          back, you're called to a police station, that
          happened to my brother. So it's not safe to go out
          to people and when you can't go out sometimes
          you find you can't go in, I'm afraid to go inside
          myself, perhaps there's nothing there, I just keep
          still. But I can talk to you, no one's ever known an
          angel work for the Securitate, I go out into the blue
          and I sink down and down inside myself, and yes
          then I am free inside, I can fly about in that blue,
          that is what the church can give people, they can
          fly about inside in that blue.

ANGEL.   So when the Romanian church writes a letter to the
          other Christian churches apologising for not taking
          a stand / against –

PRIEST.   Don't talk about it. I'd just managed to forget.

ANGEL.   Don't be ashamed. There was no need for them to
          write the letter because there's no question of
          taking a stand, it's not the job of the church / to –

PRIEST.   Everyone will think we're cowards.

ANGEL.   No no no. Flying about in the blue.

PRIEST.   Yes. Yes.

Pause.

You've never been political?

ANGEL.   Very little. The Iron Guard used to be rather
          charming and called themselves the League of the
          Archangel Michael and carried my picture about.
          They had lovely processions. So I dabbled.

PRIEST.   But they were fascists.

ANGEL.   They were mystical.

PRIEST.   The Iron Guard threw Jews out of windows in '37,
          my father remembers it. He shouted and they beat
          him up.

ANGEL.   Politics, you see. Their politics weren't very
          pleasant. I try to keep clear of the political side.
          You should do the same.

          Pause.

PRIEST.   I don't trust you any more.

ANGEL.   That's a pity. Who else can you trust?

          Pause.

          Would you rather feel ashamed?

          Pause.

          Or are you going to take some kind of action,
          surely not?

          Silence.

PRIEST.   Comfort me.

10. Acesta este fratele nostru. This is our brother.

BOGDAN, IRINA, LUCIA, FLORINA, *sitting in the dark with
candles.* IRINA *is sewing* LUCIA*'s wedding dress.* GABRIEL
arrives, excited.

GABRIEL.   Something happened today. / They came to

IRINA.   Wait.

IRINA *moves to turn on the radio, then remembers it isn't working.*

GABRIEL. the office yesterday and gave us their usual pep talk and at the end one of them took me aside / and said we'd like to see you

IRINA. Wait.

GABRIEL. tomorrow. So I knew what that meant, they were going to ask me / to do something for

IRINA. Wait, stop, there's no power.

GABRIEL. them. I prayed all night I'd be strong enough to say no, I was so afraid I'd be persuaded, / I've never been brave. So I went in and they said . . .

IRINA. Gaby, stop, be quiet.

FLORINA. No, what if they do hear it, they know what they did.

GABRIEL. And they said, 'What is patriotism?' I said, 'It's doing all you can, working as hard as possible.' And they said, / 'We thought you might

BOGDAN. Gabriel.

FLORINA. No, let him.

IRINA *puts her hands over her ears. But after a while she starts to listen again.*

GABRIEL. not understand patriotism because your sister and this and this, but if you're a patriot you'll want to help us. And I said, 'Of course I'd like to help you,' and then I actually remembered, listen to this, 'As Comrade Ceauşescu says, "For each and every citizen work is an honorary fundamental duty. Each of us should demonstrate high professional probity, competence, creativity, devotion and passion in our work." And because I'm a patriot I work so hard that I can't think about anything else, I wouldn't be able to listen to what my colleagues talk about because I have to concentrate. I work right through the lunch hour.' And I stuck to it and they couldn't do anything. And I'm so happy because I've put myself on the other side, I hardly knew there was one. They made me promise never

to tell anyone they'd asked me, and they made me
sign something, I didn't care by then, I'd won, so
I signed it, not my wife or my parents, it said that
specifically because they know what the first thing
is you'd do, and of course I'm doing it because I
don't care, I'm going straight home to Rodica to
tell her, I'm so happy, and I've come to share it
with you because I knew you'd be proud of me.

IRINA.   But you signed. You shouldn't tell us. I didn't hear.

FLORINA *kisses* GABRIEL.

FLORINA.   But Radu's right to keep away from us.

Pause.

BOGDAN.   You're a good boy.

GABRIEL.   I was shaking. The first thing when I went in they
said –

BOGDAN *holds up his hand and* GABRIEL *stops.*

Pause.

LUCIA.   What if I don't get my passport?

11. Uite! Look!

A SOLDIER *and a* WAITER *stand smoking in the street.*
Suddenly one of them shouts 'Rat!' and they chase it. RADU,
IANOȘ *and* GABRIEL *pass and join in. The rat is kicked about*
like a football. Then RADU, IANOȘ *and* GABRIEL *go on their*
way and the SOLDIER *and the* WAITER *go back to smoking.*

12. Eu o vizitez pe nepoata mea.
I am visiting my granddaughter.

FLAVIA *and* MIHAI *sitting silently over their work.* FLAVIA'S
GRANDMOTHER, *who is dead. She is an elegant woman in*
her 50s.

GRANDMOTHER. Flavia, your life will soon be over. You're
nearly as old as I was when you were a little girl.

You thought I was old then but you don't think
you're old.

FLAVIA. Yes I do. I look at my children's friends and I
know I'm old.

GRANDMOTHER. No, you still think your life hasn't started.
You think it's ahead.

FLAVIA. Everyone feels like that.

GRANDMOTHER. How do you know? Who do you talk to?
Your closest friend is your grandmother and I'm
dead, Flavia, don't forget that or you really will
be mad.

FLAVIA. You want me to live in the past? I do, I remember
being six years old in the mountains, isn't that
what old people do?

GRANDMOTHER. You remember being a child, Flavia,
because you're childish. You remember expecting
a treat.

FLAVIA. Isn't that good? Imagine still having hope at my
age. I admire myself.

GRANDMOTHER. You're pretending this isn't your life. You
think it's going to happen some other time. When
you're dead you'll realise you were alive now.
When I was your age the war was starting. I
welcomed the Nazis because I thought they'd
protect us from the Russians and I welcomed the
Communists because I thought they'd protect us
from the Germans. I had no principles. My
husband was killed. But at least I knew that was
what happened to me. There were things I did.
I did them. Or sometimes I did nothing. It was
me doing nothing.

Silence.

FLAVIA. Mihai.

MIHAI. Mm?

FLAVIA. Do you ever think . . . if you think of something
you'll do . . . do you ever think you'll be young
when you do it? Do you think I'll do that next time
I'm twenty? Not really exactly think it because of

course it doesn't make sense but almost . . . not
exactly think it but . . .

MIHAI *shakes his head and goes back to his work.*

FLAVIA.   Yes, my life is over.

GRANDMOTHER. I didn't say that.

FLAVIA.   I don't envy the young, there's nothing ahead for
them either. I'm nearer dying and that's fine.

GRANDMOTHER. You're not used to listening. What did I say?

Pause.

FLAVIA.   But nobody's living. You can't blame me.

GRANDMOTHER. You'd better start.

FLAVIA.   No, Granny, it would hurt.

GRANDMOTHER. Well.

Silence.

FLAVIA.   Mihai.

MIHAI *goes on working.*

Mihai.

He looks up. Silence.

13. Ce oră este? What's the time?

LUCIA *and* IANOŞ *standing in silence with their arms round
each other.*

She looks at her watch, he puts his hand over it.

They go on standing.

14. Unde este troleibuzul? Where is the trolleybus?

People waiting for a bus, including RADU.

FLORINA *joins the queue. She doesn't see him.*

He sees her. He looks away.

She sees him without him noticing, she looks away.

He looks at her again, they see each other and greet each other awkwardly. They look away.

RADU *goes up to her.*

RADU.   How are you?

FLORINA.   Fine.

RADU.   And your family?

FLORINA.   Fine, and yours?

RADU.   So when's Lucia's wedding?

FLORINA.   You know when it is.

            They stand apart waiting for the bus.

15. Pe Irina o doare capul. Irina has a headache.

LUCIA is *trying on her wedding dress, helped by* IRINA.

16. Lucia are o coroană de aur. Lucia has a golden crown.

The wedding. LUCIA *and* WAYNE *are being married by the* PRIEST. BOGDAN, IRINA, FLORINA, GABRIEL *and* RODICA. *Other guests.*

Two wedding crowns. The PRIEST *crosses* WAYNE *with a crown, saying:*

PRIEST.   The servant of God Wayne is crowned for the
             handmaid of God Lucia, in the name of the father,
             and of the son, and of the holy spirit.

ALL   (*sing*). Amen.

             This is repeated three times, then the PRIEST *puts
             the crown on* WAYNE's *head. He crosses* LUCIA
             with a crown saying:

PRIEST.   The handmaid of God Lucia is crowned for the
           servant of God Wayne, in the name of the father,
           and of the son, and of the holy spirit.

ALL   (*sing*). Amen.

           This is repeated three times, then the PRIEST *puts
           the crown on* LUCIA's *head.*

           Music.

II DECEMBER

None of the characters in this section are the characters in the play that began in Part I. They are all Romanians speaking to us in English with Romanian accents. Each behaves as if the others are not there and each is the only one telling what happened.

PAINTER. My name is Valentin Bărbat, I am a painter, I hope to go to the Art Institute. I like to paint horses. Other things too but I like horses. On December 20 my girlfriend got a call, go to the Palace Square. People were wearing black armbands for Timişoara. There was plenty of people but no courage. Nothing happened that day and we went home.

GIRL STUDENT. My name's Natalia Moraru, I'm a student. On the 21 of December I had a row with my mother at breakfast about something trivial and I went out in a rage. There was nothing unusual, some old men talking, a few plainclothes policemen, they think they're clever but everyone knows who they are because of their squashed faces.

TRANSLATOR. I'm Dimitru Constantinescu, I work as a translator in a translation agency. On the 21st we were listening to the radio in the office to hear Ceauşescu's speech. It was frightfully predictable. People had been brought from factories and institutes on buses and he wanted their approval for putting down what he called the hooligans in Timişoara. Then suddenly we heard boos and the radio went dead. So we knew something had happened. We were awfully startled. Everyone was shaking.

BOY STUDENT 1. My name is Cornel Drăgan, I am a student and I watch the speech on TV. The TV went dead, I was sure at last something happens so I go out to see.

GIRL STUDENT. I went into a shop and heard something had been organised by Ceaușescu and the roads were blocked by traffic. I thought I'd walk to the People's Palace.

BULLDOZER DRIVER. My name is Ilie Barbu. I can work many machines. I work in all the country to build hospitals and schools. Always build, never pull down. In December I work at the People's Palace, I drive a bulldozer. There are always many Securitate and today they make us scared because they are scared.

BOY STUDENT 1. I see people running away and I try to stop them to ask what is happening but nobody has courage to talk. At last someone says, Let's hope it has started.

BOY STUDENT 2. Well, I'm Stefan Rusu, in fact I come from Craiova, I only live in Bucharest since September to study. On the 21 no one in our zone knew what was going on. My uncle had just come back from Iran so my sister and I went to meet him and my mother. In the Callea Vittoria I saw Securitate who were upset, they were whispering. Well in fact Securitate have come to me when I was working and asked me to write reports on my colleagues. I agreed because I would get a passport and go to America, but I never wrote anything bad to get someone in trouble. Nobody knew I did this with Securitate. Now I could see the Securitate in the street were scared. Cars were breaking the rules and driving the wrong way up the road. We went to the Intercontinental Hotel but we were not allowed to have a meal. We were whispering, my mother told us she had been in the square and heard people booing.

STUDENT 1. I got to the square and people are shouting against Ceaușescu, shouting 'Today in Timișoara, tomorrow in all the country'. I look at their lips to believe they say it. I see a friend and at first I don't know him, his face has changed, and when he looks at me I know my face is changed also.

DOCTOR.   My name is Ileana Chiriţa. I'm a student doctor,
           I come to this hospital from school, we must get
           six months' practical. The 21 was a normal day on
           duty, I didn't know anything.

GIRL STUDENT. On my way to the People's Palace I saw
           people queueing for a new thriller that had just
           been published, so as I was feeling guilty about my
           mother I decided to try and buy one, thrillers are
           her favourite books. So I queued to get the book,
           and at about one o'clock I went home.

BULLDOZER DRIVER. I leave work to get my son from
           school and I don't go back to work, I go to the
           Palace Square.

STUDENT 1. There were two camps, army and people, but
           nobody shooting. Some workers from the People's
           Palace come with construction material to make
           barricades. More and more people come, we are
           pushed together.

DOCTOR.   On my way home in the afternoon there was a
           woman crying because she lost her handbag, the
           other women comfort her saying, 'It could be
           worse, people were crushed and lost their shoes,
           don't cry for such a small thing.'

SECURITATE. Claudiu Brad, I am an officer in Securitate. In
           everything I did I think I was right, including the
           21. I went to military high school because I like
           uniforms. My family has no money for me to study
           but I did well. I went to the Officers School of
           Securitate and got in the external department,
           which is best, the worst ones go in the fire service.
           Nobody knows I am in Securitate except one
           friend I have since I am three years old. I have no
           other friends but I like women and recruit them
           sometimes with clothes. On December 21 I am
           taking the pulse of the street in plain clothes with a
           walkie-talkie hidden. My district is Rossetti Place.
           I report every three hours if the crowd move their
           position, how could they be made calm, what they
           want.

SOLDIER   My name is Gheorghe Marin. I am in the army
           from September. My mother is in house, my father
           mechanic in railway. December I am near the
           airport. They say Hungarians come from Hungary
           into Romania, we must shoot them. They give us
           four magazines. Before, we work in the fields, we
           have one lessons to shoot. 21 we are in trenches,
           we have spades to dig. We wait something, we
           don't know what. We don't know Ceauşescu speak,
           we don't know what happen in Bucharest.

GIRL STUDENT. I'd planned to go to see a film with a friend
           but in the afternoon my father said I must ring up
           and pretend to be ill, then my friend rang and said
           that she is ill. I wanted to go out and my father
           said I couldn't go alone. I thought of an excuse –
           we had to have some bread, so we went out
           together. There were a lot of people moving from
           Union Place towards University Place and I heard
           someone shout, 'Down with the Dictator.' I was
           very confused. This was opposed to the policy of
           the leading forces. A man came up and asked what
           was happening but my father pulled me away
           because he realised the man was a provoker who
           starts arguments and then reports the people who
           get involved. My father insisted we go home, I said
           he was a coward and began to cry. He said if he
           was single he would behave differently.

BULLDOZER DRIVER In the square there is much army and
           tanks. My son is six years old, I am scared for him.
           I take him home and we watch what happens on
           TV with my wife and daughter.

STUDENT 2. About five o'clock we heard people shouting 'Jos
           Ceauşescu.' My uncle wanted to go home to Cluj.
           Walking back I noticed it was 99 per cent young
           people in the square with police and soldiers near
           them and I thought 'That's the end for them.' At
           home we tried to avoid the topic and get it out of
           our minds.

STUDENT 1. There are vans bringing drink and I tell people not
           to drink because Securitate wants to get us drunk
           so we look bad. In the evening we tried to make a
           barricade in Rosetti Place. We set fire to a truck.

SECURITATE. There are barricades and cars burning in my
district, I report it. Later the army shoot the people
and drive tanks in them. I go off duty.

HOUSEPAINTER. My name is Margareta Antoniu, my work is
a housepainter. I paint the windows on the big
apartment blocks. I come back to work just now
because I have a baby. The 21, the evening, I come
home from a village with my children and my
husband says it is happening. We expect it because
of Timişoara. He hear tanks and shooting like an
earthquake. We are happy someone fight for our
people.

DOCTOR.   My husband was away to visit his parents and
I felt lonely. My mother phoned and warned me
to stay home and said, 'Listen to the cassette' –
this is our code for Radio Free Europe.

FLOWERSELLER. My name is Cornelia Dediliuc. I am a
flowerseller, 22 years. Three children, 7, 4 and 2.
I have a great pain because my mother die three
weeks. My husband is very good, we meet when
I am 14, before him I know only school and home.
Before I tell you December I tell you something
before in my family. My son who is 4 is 2, we live
in a small room, I cook, I go out and my child pull
off the hot water and hurt very bad. I come in and
see, I have my big child 5 my hands on his neck
because he not take care. Now I have illness, I
have headache, and sometimes I don't know what
I do. When the revolution start I am home with my
children. The shooting is very big. I hold my
children and stay there.

PAINTER.   When we heard shooting we went out, and we
stayed near the Intercontinental Hotel till nearly
midnight. I had an empty soul. I didn't know who
I was.

STUDENT 1. They shot tracer bullets with the real bullets to
show they were shooting high. At first people don't
believe they will shoot in the crowd again after
Timişoara.

PAINTER.   I saw a tank drive into the crowd, a man's head
was crushed. When people were killed like that
more people came in front of the tanks.

FLOWERSELLER. My husband come home scared, he has seen dead people. I say him please not to go out again because the children.

GIRL STUDENT. At about 11 my family began to argue so I went to my room. I heard shooting and called my father. He wouldn't let me open the shutter but through the crack I saw a wounded army officer running across the street screaming.

PAINTER. It's enough to see one person dead to get empty of feeling.

FLOWERSELLER. But I sleep and he goes out. I can't see something because the window of the apartment is not that way but I hear the shooting.

STUDENT 2. My mother, sister and I all slept in the same room that night because we were scared.

DOCTOR. The block of flats was very quiet. Lights were on very late. I could hear other people listening to the radio.

GIRL STUDENT. I sat up till four in the morning. I wanted to go out but my father had locked the door and hidden the key.

STUDENT 1. At four in the morning I telephone my mother and tell her peoples are being killed.

PAINTER. That night it seems it must be all over. I hope it will go on tomorrow but don't know how.

SECURITATE. In the night the army cleaned the blood off the streets and painted the walls and put tar on the ground where there were stains from the blood so everything was clean.

STUDENT 1. At six in the morning there is new tar on the road but I see blood and something that is a piece of skin. Someone puts down a white cloth on the blood and peoples throw money, flowers, candles, that is the beginning of the shrines.

DOCTOR. On my way to work on the morning of the 22 there were broken windows and people washing the street.

BULLDOZER DRIVER. On the 22 I go back to work. I am afraid I am in trouble with Securitate because I leave work the day before but nobody says nothing.

DOCTOR.   At the hospital no one knew what had happened but there were 14 dead and 19 wounded. There were two kinds of wounds, normal bullet wounds and bullets that explode when they strike something and break bones in little pieces, there is no way of repairing them.

HOUSEPAINTER. About 7 o'clock I take a shower. I hear a noise in the street. I look out, I see thousands of workers from the Industrial Platforms. I am wet, I have no clothes, I stay to watch. They are more and more, two three kilometres. Now I know Ceauşescu is finish.

DOCTOR.   At about 8 I saw out of the window people going towards University Square holding flags. They pass a church and suddenly they all knelt down in silence. My colleagues began to say, He will fall. An old doctor, 64 years old, climbed to a dangerous place to get down Ceauşescu's picture and we all cheered. We heard on the radio the General in charge of the Army had killed himself and been announced a traitor. We kept treating patients and running back to the radio.

STUDENT 2. We heard that the General committed suicide and there was a state of emergency declared. I thought everything is lost.

GIRL STUDENT. I insisted we go out. My father dressed like a bride taking a long time.

FLOWERSELLER. I go to the market to get food and many people are going to the centre. I watch them go by. I am sorry I get married so young.

TRANSLATOR. I went to work as usual but there was only one colleague in my office. We heard shots so we went out. I've noticed in films people scatter away from gunfire but here people came out saying, 'What's that?' People were shouting, 'Come with us', so we went in the courtyard and shouted too.

GIRL STUDENT. We hadn't gone far when we saw a crowd of people with banners with Jos Ceauşescu, shouting, 'Come and join us.' They were low class men so we didn't know if we could trust them. I suggested we cross the road so no one could say we were with them.

TRANSLATOR. I heard people shouting, 'Down with Ceauşescu', for the first time. It was a wonderful feeling to say those words, Jos Ceauşescu.

GIRL STUDENT. Suddenly there was a huge crowd with young people. For the first time I saw the flag with the hole cut out of it. I began to cry, I felt ashamed I hadn't done anything. My father agreed to go on but not with the crowd.

STUDENT 2. Then I saw students singing with flags with holes in them and I thought, Surely this is the end. I walked on the pavement beside them, quickly looking to the side for an escape route like a wild animal.

TRANSLATOR. I had promised my wife to take care. We were walking towards the tanks and I was in a funk. But when you're with other people you keep walking on.

GIRL STUDENT. We came to University Place. For the first time I saw blood, it was smeared on a wooden cross. It's one thing to hear shooting but another to see blood. There were police in front of the Intercontinental Hotel. But in a crowd you disappear and feel stronger.

TRANSLATOR. Then I saw there were flowers in the guns.

GIRL STUDENT. I saw a tank with a soldier holding a red carnation.

TRANSLATOR. Everyone was hugging and kissing each other, you were kissing a chap you'd never seen before.

GIRL STUDENT. And when I looked again the police had vanished.

STUDENT 2. I saw people climbing on army vehicles, I thought they'd taken them from the soldiers, then I realised the soldiers were driving and I heard people

shouting, 'The army is with us.' Then I started to
cry and I shouted too, 'The army is with us.'

TRANSLATOR. There were no words in Romanian or English
for how happy I was.

SECURITATE. On the 22 the army went over to the side of the
people. I gave my pistol to an army officer and
both magazines were full. That's why I'm here
now. I had no more superiors and I wanted to get
home. I caught the train and stayed in watching
what happened on TV.

HOUSEPAINTER. We leave our six children with my mother
and we follow some tanks with people on them.
They are go to the TV station. We are there with
the first people who make revolution.

BULLDOZER DRIVER. I work till half past ten or eleven, then
I see tanks not with army, with men on them.
I think I will take the bulldozer. But when I get
to the gates my boss says, 'There is no need,
Ceauşescu is no more, Ceauşescu nu mai e.' I see
no Securitate so I go home to my family.

DOCTOR.   Out of the window I saw a silver helicopter and
pieces of paper falling – we thought the people had
won and they were celebration papers.

GIRL STUDENT. There were leaflets thrown down from heli-
copters saying, Go home and spend Christmas
with your family.

DOCTOR.   A boo went up outside when people saw what they
said.

GIRL STUDENT. Suddenly I heard bangbang and I thought my
heart would explode, but it was small children
throwing celebration crackers against the walls.
My father had an attack of cramp and couldn't
move any further.

STUDENT 1. In the Palace Square when the tanks turn round
we are afraid they will fire on us again. But they
turn towards Ceauşescu's balcony.

STUDENT 2. I saw books and papers thrown down from the
balcony and I thought I must do something so
I went to the radio station. I heard people singing
'Wake Up Romanian' and realised it was a victory.

DOCTOR.   About 12.30 I heard on the radio 'Wake Up
Romanian', the anthem which used to be banned,
and announcers who apologise for not telling the
truth, they had been made to lie. Everyone began
to cry and laugh. The doctors and the orderlies
were equal.

GIRL STUDENT. We saw an appeal on TV at a friend's house
for blood so l went to the hospital with our friend's
son-in-law. There were hundreds of people waiting
to give blood but only fifty bottles, luckily I was
able to give blood.

STUDENT 2. I bought some champagne and went home to my
family to celebrate.

DOCTOR.   I went home about 3 and my husband has bought
6 bottles of champagne and we called our neigh-
bours in. For the first time in my life I felt free to
laugh.

GIRL STUDENT. We went to the TV station, it was surrounded
by cars beeping, soldiers wearing armbands to
show they were with the people. We were told the
water was poisoned by Securitate so I ran to buy
some milk so my doggie could have something to
drink.

STUDENT 1. In the afternoon I go to meet my mother when she
comes out of the school. Everyone is shouting 'Ole
ole ole ole' and cars hoot their horns. Then I go to
see my grandmother to show her I am all right.

Pause.

PAINTER.   That night the terror shooting started. There was
no quiet place.

TRANSLATOR. When the terror shooting started, I was at home
and heard it. My legs buckled, I vomited, I couldn't
go out. It took me weeks to get over that.

STUDENT 1. About 7 o'clock we heard on the radio, 'Help, our
building is being attacked.' So I went out again.

HOUSEPAINTER. At the radio station I am scared, my husband
says, 'Why you come then?' Terroristi shoot from
a building and my husband goes with men inside
and catch them. There are many wounded and
I help. I am the only woman.

SOLDIER. They say us it is not Hungarians. It is terroristi. We
          guard the airport. We shoots anything, we shoots
          our friend. I want to stay alive.

PAINTER. They are asking on TV for people to defend the
          TV station. My girlfriend and I go out. We stop
          a truck of young people and ask where they're
          going, they say, 'We are going to die.' They say
          it like that. We can do nothing there, everyone
          knows it.

STUDENT 1. There was a gypsy who had a gun and he says,
          'Come with me, I want people strong with
          courage.' He says we must go to the factory of
          August 23 where they have guns for the guards.
          The Romanian people are cowards and have no
          courage to get in the truck, but at last we go to the
          factory. There are more than one hundred people
          but only 28 get guns, I get one, they say, 'Be
          careful and come back with the gun.' Then we
          go to a police station because we know they are
          on the side of the people and we ask for bullets.
          At first they don't want to give them, they say,
          'We need them to defend our building.' We say,
          'Give us at least one bullet each to be of some use.'

STUDENT 2. People were shouting, 'Come with us,' but I
          thought, 'It's a romantic action, it's useless to go
          and fight and die.' I thought I was a coward to be
          scared. But I thought, 'I will die like a fool
          protecting someone I don't know. How can I stop
          bullets with my bare hands? It's the job of the
          army, I can do nothing, I will just die.' So I went
          home.

BOY STUDENT 1. At the TV station I am behind the wall of a
          house and they shoot across me from both sides. I
          go into a house, the terroristi are gone, I telephone
          my mother to tell her where I am. If I stay ten
          minutes longer I am dead because they shoot that
          house. In the road a boy stands up and is shot. A
          month later is his eighteenth birthday. I ask myself
          if he is shot by our soldiers. I am standing looking
          round, bullets are flying. After a while you don't
          feel scared.

PAINTER.   My girlfriend and I were at the TV station. I didn't know who we were fighting with or how bad it was. I was just acting to save our lives. It is terrible to hate and not to be able to do something real.

GIRL STUDENT. That evening I wanted to put on my army clothes and go out and shoot – I got three out of three in the shooting test when I was in the army. But my father had locked the door again and hidden the key.

HOUSEPAINTER. At ten o'clock we go back to the TV station with some bread.

STUDENT 1. A lot of people bring tea and food though they didn't know if there will be better days and more to eat. They bring things they save for Christmas. Some people say the food is poisoned so that people who bring it must eat and drink first.

PAINTER.   I was with my girlfriend so l felt I should act as a man and be confident. I was curious to know what I would feel in difficult moments.

STUDENT 1. There are children of 12 or 13 moving everywhere, they are harder to see, bringing us bullets, saying, 'What do you need? what shall I bring you?'

PAINTER.   A man was shot in the throat in front of me. Some people couldn't look but I was staring, trying not to forget. I had an insane curiosity. It was like an abattoir. He was like an animal dying with no chance. He had an expression of confusedness. It was incredible he had so much blood. I felt empty.

HOUSEPAINTER. At half past eight we go to buy some bread, then home to sleep. My mother ask where I was and I say I go out to buy some bread, just that.

DOCTOR.   On the 23 I went to work. Two boys came in with a young man on a stretcher, which they put down, then one of them fell to the ground and began to scream – he sees the wounded man is his older brother. His friend takes him down the hall to get a tranquilliser, it is very dark and when they come back the friend trips over something, it is the body

of the older brother, who is dead waiting for
surgery. The younger brother was only 14.
He threw himself on the corpse and won't move,
he said he wants to die with his brother.

STUDENT 1. On the morning of the 23 I went home and I slept
for two hours. I kept the gun with me in bed.

GIRL STUDENT. I was about to go out to defend my school
when my grandmother began to panic and
we thought she would have a heart attack, so
I promised to stay in, and I spent the day passing
messages to people on the phone. Some people
don't like me because of my father.

STUDENT 2. The train didn't go that day so I stayed at home.
I thought, 'This is not my town. I will go to my
own town and act there.'

DOCTOR. I stayed in the hospital without going home till
the 28. We had enough medicine for immediate
cases. Once or twice we had to use out of date
anaesthetic and the patient woke up during the
operation, not often but it happened. We had no
coffee or food. When my husband came to see me,
more than seeing him I was pleased he had 30
packets of cigarettes. We ate what the patients left
and people brought some bread and some jam so
on Christmas day we had jam sandwiches.

SECURITATE. When I heard about the execution on the 25
I came at night with my father to the authorities to
certify what I was doing during the event. I was
detained three days by the army, then told to
remain at home. I will say one thing. Until noon
on the 22 we were law and order. We were brought
up in this idea. I will never agree with unorder.
Everyone looks at me like I did something wrong.
It was the way the law was then and the way they
all accepted it.

STUDENT 1. On the 25 we hear about the trial and their
deaths. It is announced that people must return
their weapons so we go to the factory and give
back our guns. Of the 28 who had guns only
4 are alive.

BULLDOZER DRIVER. I stay home with my family till the 28, then I go to work. They say the time I was home will be off my holidays. There is no more work on the People's Palace, nobody knows if they finish it.

PAINTER. Painting doesn't mean just describing, it's a state of spirit. I didn't want to paint for a long time then.

III FLORINA'S WEDDING

1. Cîinelui e foame. The dog is hungry.

Night, outside. A shrine. A DOG *is lying asleep. A man approaches. He whistles. The* DOG *looks up. The man whistles. The* DOG *gets up and approaches, undecided between eagerness and fear. The man is a* VAMPIRE.

VAMPIRE.   Good dog. Don't be frightened.

              DOG *approaches, then stops. Growls. Retreats, advances. Growls.*

              No no no no no. You can tell of course. Yes, I'm not a human being, what does that matter? It means you can talk to me.

DOG.   Are you dead?

VAMPIRE.   No, no I'm not unfortunately. I'm undead and getting tired of it. I'm a vampire, you may not have met one before, I usually live in the mountains and you look like a dog who's lived on scraps in the city. How old are you?

DOG.   Five, six.

VAMPIRE.   You look older but that's starvation. I'm over five hundred but I look younger, I don't go hungry.

DOG.   Do you eat dogs?

VAMPIRE.   Don't be frightened of me, I'm not hungry now. And if I was all I'd do is sip a little of your blood, I don't eat. I don't care for dogs' blood.

DOG.   People's blood?

VAMPIRE.   I came here for the revolution, I could smell it a long way off.

DOG.   I've tasted man's blood. It was thick on the road, I gobbled it up quick, then somebody kicked me.

VAMPIRE.   Nobody knew who was doing the killing, I could come up behind a man in a crowd.

DOG.   Good times.

VAMPIRE.   There's been a lot of good times over the years.

DOG.   Not for me.

VAMPIRE.   Do you belong to anyone?

DOG.   I used to but he threw me out. I miss him. I hate him.

VAMPIRE.   He probably couldn't feed you.

DOG.   He beat me. But now nobody talks to me.

VAMPIRE.   I'm talking to you.

DOG.   Will you keep me?

VAMPIRE.   No, I'm just passing the time.

DOG.   Please. I'm nice. I'm hungry.

VAMPIRE.   Vampires don't keep pets.

DOG.   You could feed me.

DOG approaches VAMPIRE carefully.

VAMPIRE.   I've no money to buy food for you, I don't buy food, I put my mouth to a neck in the night, it's a solitary – get off.

As the DOG reaches him he makes a violent gesture and the DOG leaps away.

DOG.   Don't throw stones at me, I hate it when they throw stones, I hate being kicked, please please I'd be a good dog, I'd bite your enemies. Don't hurt me.

VAMPIRE.   I'm not hurting you. Don't get hysterical.

DOG approaches again.

DOG.   I'm hungry. You're kind. I'm your dog.

DOG is licking his hands.

VAMPIRE.   Stop it, go away. Go. Go. Go away.

DOG *slinks a little further off then approaches carefully.*

DOG.   I'm your dog. Nice. Yes? Your dog? Yes?

VAMPIRE.   You want me to make you into a vampire?
            A vampire dog?

DOG.   Yes please, yes yes.

VAMPIRE.   It means sleeping all day and going about at night.

DOG.   I'd like that.

VAMPIRE.   Going about looking like anyone else, being
            friendly, nobody knowing you.

DOG.   I'd like that.

VAMPIRE.   Living forever, / you've no idea. All that

DOG.   I'd –

VAMPIRE.   happens is you begin to want blood, you try to put
            it off, you're bored with killing, but you can't sit
            quiet, you can't settle to anything, your limbs ache,
            your head burns, you have to keep moving faster
            and faster, that eases the pain, seeking. And
            finding. Ah.

DOG.   I'd like that.

VAMPIRE.   And then it's over and you wander round looking
            for someone to talk to. That's all. Every night.
            Over and over.

DOG.   You could talk to me. I could talk to you. I'm your
            dog.

VAMPIRE.   Yes, if you like, I don't mind. Come here. Good
            dog.

            VAMPIRE *puts his mouth to the* DOG's *neck.*

**2. Toată lumea speră ca Gabriel să se însănătoşească repede.
Everyone hopes Gabriel will feel better soon.**

i.

GABRIEL *is in bed in hospital.*

FLORINA, *working there as a nurse, passes his bed.*

FLORINA.   I see less of you working here than if I came for
            a visit.

GABRIEL.   Wait.

FLORINA.   I can't.

GABRIEL.   We won. Eh? Ole . . . Yes?

FLORINA.   Yes but don't talk. Wait for your visitors.

GABRIEL.   Rodica?

FLORINA.   Mum and dad.

GABRIEL.   Something wrong with Rodica?

FLORINA.   No.

GABRIEL.   You'd tell me / if she was hurt.

FLORINA.   Don't talk, Gabriel, rest. She's not hurt.

GABRIEL.   Do nurses tell the truth?

FLORINA.   I do to you.

            She goes.

            IRINA *and* BOGDAN *arrive with food.*

IRINA.   Eggs in the shops. We're getting the benefit
            already. I'll ask Florina who I should give it to.
            Keep the apples here. Make sure you get it all, you
            fought for it.

GABRIEL.   Where's Rodica?

IRINA.   She couldn't come.

GABRIEL.   I want her.

IRINA.   Don't, don't, you're not well, I'll never forgive her,
            she's perfectly all right.

GABRIEL.   What?

IRINA.   She's frightened to go out. Now when there's nothing happening. She sends her love.

BOGDAN has a bottle of whisky.

BOGDAN.   This is for the doctor. / Which doctor

GABRIEL.   No need.

BOGDAN.   do I give it to?

GABRIEL.   No.

IRINA.   Yes, a little present for the doctor so he's gentle with you.

GABRIEL.   That was before. Not now.

BOGDAN.   When your mother had her operation, two bottles of whisky and then it was the wrong doctor.

IRINA.   They can't change things so quickly, Gaby.

BOGDAN.   You do something for somebody, he does something for you. Won't change that. Give my father a cigarette, he puts it behind his ear. Because you never know.

GABRIEL.   Different now.

BOGDAN.   Who shall I give it to? I'll ask Florina.

MIHAI, FLAVIA and RADU arrive. RADU takes GABRIEL's hand.

MIHAI.   Radu wanted to visit his friend Gabriel so we thought we'd come with him.

FLAVIA.   We've brought a few little things.

MIHAI.   To pay our respects to a hero.

They stand awkwardly. Then FLAVIA embraces IRINA.

IRINA.   Radu's a hero too.

FLAVIA.   The young show us the way.

BOGDAN.   We're glad you're safe, Radu.

FLAVIA.   And Florina's here?

IRINA.   Yes, she's working.

MIHAI.   You must be proud of her.

BOGDAN.   She worked for five days without stopping.

RADU.   I'll go and find her.

FLAVIA.   Yes, find her, Radu.

            RADU goes.

MIHAI.   We're so glad the young people no longer have a
            misunderstanding. We have to put the past behind
            us and go forward on a new basis.

BOGDAN.   Yes, nobody can be blamed for what happened in
            the past.

IRINA.   Are you warm enough, Gaby? I can bring a
            blanket from home.

ii.

*Evening in the hospital. Patient(s) in dressing-gown(s). Someone
comes looking for a doctor.*

SORE THROAT. I'm looking for the doctor. I have a sore throat.
            I need to get an antibiotic.

            *A patient shuffles slowly about, taking the person
            down corridors and opening doors, looking for a
            doctor. Different sounds come from the rooms – a
            woman crying, a man muttering (it's the patient
            from iii, we barely hear what he's saying, just get
            the sound of constant questions), a priest chanting.
            They go off, still looking.*

iii.

*A couple of weeks after i. Sunlight. GABRIEL is much better,
sitting up. RODICA is sitting beside him holding his hand.
Flowers. A PATIENT in a dressing-gown comes to talk to them.*

PATIENT.   Did we have a revolution or a putsch? Who was
            shooting on the 21st? And who was shooting on

the 22nd? Was the army shooting on the 21st or did some shoot and some not shoot or were the Securitate disguised in army uniforms? If the army were shooting, why haven't they been brought to justice? And were they still shooting on the 22nd? Were they now disguised as Securitate? Most important of all, were the terrorists and the army really fighting or were they only pretending to fight? And for whose benefit? And by whose orders? Where did the flags come from? Who put loudhailers in the square? How could they publish a newspaper so soon? Why did no one turn off the power at the TV? Who got Ceauşescu to call everyone together? And is he really dead? How many people died at Timişoara? And where are the bodies? Who mutilated the bodies? And were they mutilated after they'd been killed specially to provoke a revolution? By whom? For whose benefit? Or was there a drug in the food and water at Timişoara to make people more aggressive? Who poisoned the water in Bucharest?

GABRIEL.   Please stop.

PATIENT.   Why weren't we shown the film of the execution?

GABRIEL.   He is dead.

PATIENT.   And is the water still poisoned?

GABRIEL.   No.

PATIENT.   And who was shooting on the 22nd?

GABRIEL.   The army, which was on the side of the people, was fighting the terrorists, who were supporting Ceauşescu.

PATIENT.   They changed clothes.

GABRIEL.   Who changed clothes?

PATIENT.   It was a fancy dress party. Weren't you there? Didn't you see them singing and dancing?

GABRIEL.   My sister's coming from America.

PATIENT.   Does she know what happened?

GABRIEL.   She'll have read the newspapers.

PATIENT.   Then you must tell her. Do you know?

GABRIEL.   I can't talk about it now.

PATIENT.   Are you a Communist?

GABRIEL.   No but my sister's / coming now.

PATIENT.   Communist. I hope you die.

FLORINA, RADU *and* LUCIA.

LUCIA *embraces* GABRIEL *and* RODICA.

LUCIA.   All the way over on the plane I was terrified of
what I was going to see. But you look beautiful.
In America everyone's thrilled. I told my friends,
'My brother was there, he was wounded, he's a
hero.' I watched TV but they never showed
enough, I kept playing it and stopping when there
was a crowd, I thought I must know somebody,
I was crying all the time, I was so ashamed not to
be here. I've brought you some chocolate, and
oranges.

GABRIEL.   How's America?

LUCIA.   If you mean how's Wayne he's fine, he has an
allergy but let's forget that, he has a lot of
meetings so he can't be here. But America. There
are walls of fruit in America, five different kinds
of apples, and oranges, grapes, pears, bananas,
melons, different kinds of melon, and things
I don't know the name – and the vegetables, the
aubergines are a purple they look as if they've
been varnished, red yellow green peppers, white
onions red onions, bright orange carrots somebody
has shone every carrot, and the greens, cabbage
spinach broad beans courgettes, I still stare every
time I go shopping. And the garbage, everyone
throws away great bags full of food and paper and
tins, every day, huge bags, huge dustbins, people
live out of them. Eat some chocolate.

They eat the chocolate.

PATIENT *comes back again.*

PATIENT.   Have they told you who was shooting on the 22nd?
/ And why was it necessary to kill

GABRIEL.   Please, not now.

PATIENT.   Ceauşescu so quickly?

LUCIA.   Have some chocolate.

             PATIENT *takes some chocolate and puts it in his pocket.*

PATIENT.   Who has taken the supplies we were sent from the west? Nurse?

FLORINA.   I'm not on duty.

PATIENT.   Did we have a revolution? Or what did we have?

RADU.   Come on, let's find your bed.

             RADU *takes him off still talking.*

PATIENT.   Why did they close the schools a week early? Why did they evacuate the foreigners from the geriatric hospital? Who were the men in blue suits who appeared on the streets before the 21st?

             Silence.

LUCIA.   They have mental patients in here with the wounded? That's not very good.

FLORINA.   He was wounded on the head. / He has

LUCIA.   That explains a lot.

FLORINA.   headaches and gets upset. Yes, he's a bit crazy.

             Pause.

LUCIA.   Hungarians were fighting beside us they said on TV. And Ianoş wasn't hurt, that's good. I think Americans like Hungarians.

GABRIEL.   The poor Hungarians have a bad time because they're not treated better than everyone else. How did they treat us when they had the chance? They go abroad and insult Romania to make people despise us.

LUCIA.   This is what we used to say before. Don't we say something different?

GABRIEL.   Ask granny about Hungarians.

LUCIA.   It's true, in America they even like the idea of gypsies, they think how quaint. But I said to them you don't like blacks here, you don't like hispanics, we're talking about lazy greedy crazy people who drink too much and get rich on the black market. That shut them up.

GABRIEL.   But Ianoş doesn't count as Hungarian.

RADU comes back.

LUCIA.   So you got rid of the lunatic all right? Have some more chocolate.

RADU shakes his head.

Go on, there's plenty more.

RADU.   We're not greedy, Lucia. We don't just think about food.

LUCIA.   It's a celebration, it's fun to have chocolate, can't you have fun?

RADU.   No I can't. Celebrate what?

FLORINA.   Radu, not now.

RADU.   Who was shooting on the 22nd? That's not a crazy question.

FLORINA.   Lucia's just arrived. Gabriel's still not well.

RADU.   The only real night was the 21st. After that, what was going on? It was all a show.

LUCIA.   No, it was real, Radu, / I saw it on television.

FLORINA.   I don't want to hear / all this now.

RADU.   Were they fighting or pretending to fight? Who let off firecrackers? Who brought loudhailers?

Pause.

LUCIA looks at FLORINA.

FLORINA.   At the Municipal Hospital the head doctor gave medical supplies from the west to the police to sell on the black market. / And

LUCIA.   That I can believe.

RADU.   he locked the wounded in a room with no one to
               take care of them so he could hand them over / to
               the Securitate and some of them died.

LUCIA.   But that's just him. It's not a plot.

               Pause.

FLORINA.   How many people were killed at Timişoara? Where
               are the bodies? There were bodies found in a
               sandpit for the longjump. / Where are the rest?

LUCIA.   But what does that mean?

RADU.   Why did no one turn off the power at the TV
               station?

               Pause.

LUCIA.   Gabriel? Rodica?

GABRIEL.   I'm too tired.

               RODICA *turns her head away.*

iv.

Some time later. IRINA *helping* GABRIEL *to walk. He reaches
a chair and falls into it laughing.*

IRINA.   Good. Good.

               Silence.

               I used to say more with the radio on.

GABRIEL.   Have you heard people say that by the 22nd / the
               revolution had been stolen?

IRINA.   No no no no no. I've no time for all that nonsense.

GABRIEL.   But –

IRINA.   No. No no no. Now. Walk.

3. Rodica mai are coşmare. Rodica is still having nightmares.

RODICA *is wearing a cloak and a big fur hat with dollars and flowers on it. Two soldiers come in.*

SOLDIER 1. We're the last soldiers, your Majesty. The rest of the army's on the side of the people.

SOLDIER 2. The helicopter's going to rescue you.

> *She takes a telephone from under her cloak and dials endlessly.*

> *The* SOLDIERS *take off their uniforms and get dressed again in each other's identical clothes. Meanwhile* GABRIEL *comes in wearing a huge Romanian flag, his head through the hole. He gives* RODICA *a box of matches and goes.*

SOLDIER 2. Why doesn't anyone love you after all you've done for them?

SOLDIER 1. Have you enough money to pay for the helicopter?

> *She gives them money from her hat. They pocket each thing she gives them and hold out their hands for more till she has nothing left on her hat. She gives them the hat. They hold out their hands for more.*

SOLDIER 1. Give us your hands.

> *Her hands disappear under her cloak.*

SOLDIER 2. Give us your feet.

> *Her feet disappear under her cloak and she sinks down till she is kneeling.*

SOLDIER 1. There's no helicopter. You'll have to run.

> *The* SOLDIERS *go.*

> RODICA *opens the matchbox – 'ole ole ole ole' chanted by huge crowd. She opens and closes it several times and the song continues each time. Sound of gunfire. She looks round in a panic for somewhere to hide the matchbox. She puts it under her cloak, then changes her mind and takes it out. It is now a pill, which she swallows.*

A SOLDIER *comes in and searches, kicking at anything in the way.*

He goes to her and opens her mouth.

'Ole ole ole ole' chanted by huge crowd.

He opens and closes her mouth several times, the chant continues each time.

4. Cînd am fost să ne vizităm bunicii la ţară, era o zi însorită. When we went to visit our grandparents in the country it was a sunny day.

FLORINA, LUCIA, RADU *and* IANOŞ *are visiting* FLORINA *and* LUCIA's GRANDPARENTS *in the country, so they can meet* RADU *before the wedding. The* GRANDPARENTS *are peasants.* IANOŞ *has a child with him, a boy of about 8,* TOMA. *The following things happen in the course of a long sunny afternoon, out of doors, immediately outside the* GRANDPARENTS' *house where there is a bench, and nearby.*

i.

THE GRANDPARENTS *embrace* LUCIA *and* FLORINA, *greet* RADU *warmly,* IANOŞ *more formally.* TOMA *clings shyly to* IANOŞ.

ii.

IANOŞ *has a ball and tries to interest* TOMA *in playing with him and* RADU. *They go off.*

GRANDMOTHER. That young man's a Hungarian.

LUCIA.   He's a friend of Radu and Gabriel's, granny.

GRANDMOTHER. I knew a woman married a Hungarian.
              His brother killed her and ripped the child out
              of her stomach.

FLORINA.   He's just a friend of Gabriel's, granny.

GRANDMOTHER. Radu seems a nice young man. He's
            Romanian. What's wrong with that child?

FLORINA.   He's been in an orphanage.

GRANDMOTHER. Is it a gypsy?

LUCIA.   Of course not.

GRANDMOTHER. They wouldn't let him adopt a Romanian.

iii.

LUCIA *with* IANOŞ *and* TOMA.

LUCIA.   Do we have to have him with us all the time?

IANOŞ.   He likes me.

LUCIA.   I like you but I'm not getting much chance to
            show it.

IANOŞ.   He'll settle down.

LUCIA.   Can he talk?

IANOŞ.   Yes of course.

LUCIA.   I haven't heard him.

IANOŞ.   He doesn't know you.

LUCIA.   I think your parents are remarkable. What if it goes
            wrong? Can you give him back?

IANOŞ.   We don't want to give him back. We're adopting
            him.

LUCIA.   Your parents are adopting him.

IANOŞ.   Yes but me too.

            LUCIA *rolls the ball.*

LUCIA.   Don't you want to play with the ball, Toma?

            She goes and gets it herself.

            Ball. Ball. Can you say ball, Toma?

            TOMA *buries himself in* IANOŞ.

LUCIA.   I think your parents are sentimental.

IANOŞ.   Are you going back to America?

            LUCIA shrugs.

            I still owe your husband money.

LUCIA.   Did you borrow money from him?

IANOŞ.   He paid for the abortion.

LUCIA.   But he didn't know. It was money he gave me, it
            was my money. You can't pay him back, he'd want
            to know what it was for.

IANOŞ.   I haven't got the money anyway.

            Pause.

            Aren't you ashamed?

LUCIA.   What of? No.

IANOŞ.   Not the abortion.

LUCIA.   What?

IANOŞ.   I don't know. The wedding?

LUCIA.   No, why?

IANOŞ.   I'm ashamed.

LUCIA.   Why?

            Pause.

IANOŞ.   I'm ashamed of loving you when I think you're
            probably not very nice.

            Silence.

LUCIA.   Shall I stay here and marry you?

            Silence.

            This is the last of the chocolate.

            As she gets it out, TOMA *pounces on it and runs a
            little way off, stuffing it all into his mouth.*

            You horrible child. I hate you.

IANOŞ   Don't shout at him. How can he help it? You're so
            stupid.

LUCIA. Don't shout at me.

TOMA *whimpers. He starts to shake his head obsessively.*

IANOȘ Toma. Come here.

TOMA *goes on.*

IANOȘ *goes to him.*

Toma.

TOMA *hits* IANOȘ *and starts to bellow with panic.*

IANOȘ *holds him, he subsides into whimpering.*

IANOȘ *sits on the ground holding him.*

LUCIA. Did you tell anyone about us after I left?

IANOȘ. No.

LUCIA. It might be better if we're seen as something new.

Silence.

LUCIA. Is he very naughty?

IANOȘ. Not yet. Most of the time he's so good it's frightening. The babies there don't cry.

LUCIA. He's going to be terrible. I won't be much use.

Silence.

IANOȘ. I'd like to go to America. I've got a passport.

LUCIA. Just for a holiday. I don't like America.

IANOȘ. So is that the only reason you want to stay here? I hoped you loved America.

Pause.

Would your family let you marry a Hungarian?

iv.

RADU *and* FLORINA. RADU *drawing.*

RADU.   Iliescu's going to get in because the workers and
             peasants are stupid.

             Pause.

             Not stupid but they don't think. They don't have
             the information.

             Pause.

             I don't mean your family in particular.

FLORINA.   You're a snob like your father. You'd have joined
             the party.

RADU.   Wouldn't you?

             Silence.

             He touches her face.

FLORINA.   I used to feel free then.

RADU.   You can't have.

FLORINA.   I don't now and I'm in a panic.

RADU.   It's because the Front tricked us. / When we've got
             rid –

FLORINA.   It's because I could keep everything out.

             Pause.

RADU.   But you didn't have me then.

FLORINA.   No but I thought you were perfect.

RADU.   I am perfect.

             Silence.

RADU.   What?

FLORINA.   Sometimes I miss him.

RADU.   What? Why?

FLORINA.   I miss him.

RADU.   You miss hating him.

FLORINA.   Maybe it's that.

RADU.   I hate Iliescu.

FLORINA.   That's not the same.

RADU.   I hate him worse. Human face. And he'll get in
              because they're stupid and do what they're told.
              Ceauşescu Ceauşescu. Iliescu Iliescu.

FLORINA.   I don't have anyone to hate. You sometimes.

RADU.   Me?

FLORINA.   Not really.

RADU.   Me?

v.

The GRANDPARENTS *are sitting side by side on the bench,
the others around them. The* GRANDPARENTS *speak slowly,
the others fast.*

GRANDFATHER. He was killed while he was putting up
              posters.

RADU.   You see? They're murderers. / It's the same

LUCIA.   For which party, grandpa?

RADU.   tactics / of intimidation.

IANOŞ.   Who killed him?

GRANDFATHER. Posters for the Peasants Party.

FLORINA.   Is that / who you support?

RADU.   The Front claim the country supports them but it's
              only / because of intimidation.

IANOŞ.   So did they find out who killed him?

GRANDMOTHER. Yes, it was gypsies killed him.

RADU.   Gypsies? / They were probably paid by the

FLORINA.   How did they know it was them?

RADU.   Front.

IANOŞ.   They'd hardly need paying to murder somebody.

RADU.   Or it could have been Front supporters /

LUCIA.   Or Securitate.

RADU.   and they put the blame on the gypsies.

GRANDFATHER. It was two gypsies, a father and son, who
                used to work in his garden. They had a quarrel
                with him. He used to beat them.

LUCIA.   So was it just a quarrel, / not politics at all?

FLORINA.   Did anyone see them?

GRANDMOTHER. But that quarrel was years ago.

GRANDFATHER. A lot of people didn't like him because he
                used to be a big landowner. The Peasants Party
                would give him back his land.

FLORINA.   So was he killed because / the rest of the

LUCIA.   I thought the Peasants Party was for peasants.

IANOŞ.   No, they're millionaires the leaders of it.

FLORINA.   village didn't want him to get all the land?

L.UCIA.   He should get it / if it's his.

FLORINA.   No after all this time working on it / everyone –

RADU.   Never mind that, he was against the Front, that's
                why they killed him. He was against the
                Communists.

GRANDFATHER. He was a party member. He was very big
                round here. He was a big Securitate man.

LUCIA.   So whose side was he on?

GRANDMOTHER. He wasn't a nice man. Nobody liked him.

vi.

GRANDFATHER is *sitting on the bench, the others lying on the
grass, each separately except that* TOMA *is near* IANOŞ. *Long
silence.*

IANOŞ.   I want to go to Peru.

RADU.   Rome. And Pompeii.

LUCIA.   A holiday by the sea.

Pause.

FLORINA.   Sleep late in the morning.

Pause.

RADU.   Paint what I see in my head.

FLORINA.   Go into work tomorrow and everyone's better.

LUCIA.   Gabriel walking.

IANOŞ.   Rodica talking.

They laugh.

FLORINA.   New shoes.

RADU.   Paintbrushes with fine points.

Pause.

FLORINA.   Drive a fast car.

LUCIA.   Be famous.

IANOŞ.   Toblerone.

Pause.

RADU.   Make money.

Pause.

IANOŞ.   Learn everything in the world by the end of the week.

Pause.

LUCIA.   Not be frightened.

The pauses get longer.

RADU.   Make Florina happy.

Long pause.

IANOŞ.   Make Toma happy.

Silence.

FLORINA.   Live forever.

Longer silence.

LUCIA.   Die young.

Very long silence.

FLORINA.   Go on lying here.

Very long silence.

5 . Mai doreşti puţină brînză?
Would you like some more cheese?

MIHAI *and* FLAVIA *eating cheese and salami.*

FLAVIA.   You know when Radu was born and they said he'd
           be born dead. Three days, no hope. And then
           Radu. The pain stops just like that. And then joy.
           I felt the same the morning of the 22nd. Did you
           ever feel joy before?

MIHAI.   I'm not sure I did.

FLAVIA.   All those years of pain forgotten. You felt that?

MIHAI.   It was certainly a remarkable experience.

FLAVIA.   It can't last of course. Three days after he was
           born I was crying. But I still loved Radu. And what
           have we still got from the 22nd?

MIHAI.   The work on the People's Palace will probably
           continue as soon as its new function has been
           determined.

FLAVIA.   What?

MIHAI.   If not I'm sure they'll find me some other work.
           I'm not in any way compromised, I was on the
           streets, I'm clearly a supporter of the Front. And in
           any case –

FLAVIA.   I wasn't talking about you.

MIHAI.   Good, I had the impression you might be worried.

           Pause.

FLAVIA.   All I was trying to do was teach correctly. Isn't
           history what's in the history book? Let them give
           me a new book, I'll teach that.

MIHAI.   Are you losing your job?

FLAVIA.   I didn't inform on my pupils, I didn't accept
           bribes. Those are the people whose names should
           be on the list.

MIHAI.   Are they not on the list?

FLAVIA.   They are on the list but why am I with them? The
           new head of department doesn't like me. He knows
           I'm a better teacher than he is. I can't stop
           teaching, I'll miss the children.

           Silence during which RADU *comes in.*

           Why are you always out, Radu? Come and eat.

           RADU *is already making sandwiches.*

MIHAI.   I hope you're going to join us for a meal.

           RADU *goes on making sandwiches.*

RADU.   Have you noticed the way Iliescu moves his
           hands? And the words he uses?

MIHAI.   He comes from a period when that was the style.

RADU.   Yes, he does, doesn't he.

MIHAI.   Not tonight, Radu. Your mother's had bad news at
           work about her job.

FLAVIA.   The new head of department –

RADU.   There you are. It's because of me. No one who's
           opposed to the Front / will get anywhere.

MIHAI.   Radu, I don't know what to do with you. Nothing
           is on a realistic basis.

RADU.   Please don't say that.

MIHAI.   What's the matter now?

RADU.   Don't say 'realistic basis'.

FLAVIA.   It's true, Mihai, you do talk in terrible jargon from
           before, it's no longer correct.

MIHAI.   The head of department is in fact a supporter of
           the Liberals.

RADU.   Is he?

FLAVIA.   It may not come to anything.

RADU.   You mean it's because of what you did before?
         What did you do?

MIHAI.   Radu, this is not a constructive approach.

RADU.   It won't come to anything, don't worry. It's five
         weeks since we made our list of bad teachers.
         Nobody cares that the students and staff voted. It
         has to go to the Ministry.

FLAVIA. Do you want me to lose my job?

RADU.   If you deserve to.

         FLAVIA *slaps* RADU.

         Silence.

RADU.   Do you remember once I came home from school
         and asked if you loved Elena Ceauşescu?

FLAVIA. I don't remember, no. When was that?

RADU.   And you said yes. I was seven.

FLAVIA. No, I don't remember.

         Pause.

         But you can see now why somebody would say
         what they had to say to protect you.

RADU.   I've always remembered that.

FLAVIA. I don't remember.

RADU.   No, you wouldn't.

         Pause.

FLAVIA. Why are you saying this, Radu? Are you making it
         up? You're manipulating me to make me feel bad.
         I told you the truth about plenty of things.

RADU.   I don't remember,

FLAVIA. No, you wouldn't.

         Silence.

         Now. We have some dried apples.

RADU.   I expect dad got them from someone with a human
         face.

RADU *is about to leave.*

MIHAI.   Radu, how do you think you got into the Art Institute?

RADU.   The still life with the green vase was the one / they particularly –

MIHAI.   Yes your work was all right. I couldn't have managed if it was below average.

RADU *leaves* MIHAI *with the sandwiches and goes.*

Silence.

MIHAI.   Who do we know who can put in a word for you?

FLAVIA.   We don't know who we know. Someone who put in a word before may be just the person to try and keep clear of.

Pause.

But Radu's painting is exceptional.

MIHAI.   Yes, in fact I didn't do anything.

FLAVIA.   You must tell him.

MIHAI.   He won't believe me.

Pause.

FLAVIA.   Twenty years marching in the wrong direction. I'd as soon stop. Twenty years' experience and I'm a beginner. Yes, stop. There, I feel better. I'm not a teacher.

MIHAI.   They might just transfer you to the provinces.

Pause.

It won't happen. Trust me.

Silence. MIHAI *goes on with his meal.*

FLAVIA.   Granny. Granny?

Her GRANDMOTHER *doesn't come. Silence.* FLAVIA *goes on with her meal.*

6. Gabriel vine acasă diseară. Gabriel is coming home tonight.

Downstairs in the block of flats where GABRIEL *and* RODICA *live.* GABRIEL, *with a crutch, is arriving home from hospital with* RADU, FLORINA, LUCIA, IANOŞ, *and other friends. They have been for a drink on the way and have some bottles with them.*

ALL.   The lift's broken.

               How do we get Gaby up the stairs?

               We'll have the party here.

               Rodica's waiting in the flat.

               We shouldn't have stayed so long at the Berlin.

               We can carry him up.

               We need a drink first.

               Let's do it here.

               Do it, I've never seen it.

               Yes, Radu, to celebrate Gaby coming home.

               Someone announces:

               The trial and execution of Nicolae and Elena Ceauşescu.

               RADU *and* FLORINA *are the Ceauşescus.*

IANOŞ.   Hurry up. Move along.

RADU.   Where are they taking us, Elena?

FLORINA.   I don't know, Nicu. He's a very rude man.

RADU.   Don't worry we'll be rescued in a minute. This is all part of my long-term plan.

               CEAUŞESCU (RADU) *keeps looking at his watch and up at the sky.*

IANOŞ.   Sit down.

FLORINA.   Don't sit down.

RADU.   My legs are tired.

FLORINA.   Stand up.

IANOŞ.   Sit down.

RADU.   The Securitate will get in touch with my watch.

IANOŞ   Answer the questions of the court.

RADU.   What court? I don't see any court. Do you, Elena?

FLORINA.   No court anywhere here.

RADU.   The only judges I recognise are ones I've
              appointed myself.

SOMEONE.   You're on trial for genocide.

FLORINA.   These people are hooligans. They're in the pay of
              foreign powers. That one's just come back from
              America.

ALL.   Who gave the order to shoot at Timişoara?

              What did you have for dinner last night?

              Why have you got gold taps in your bathroom?

              Do you shit in a gold toilet? Shitting yourselves
              now.

              Why did you pull down my uncle's house? *etc.*

FLORINA.   Where's the helicopter?

RADU.   On its way.

FLORINA.   Have these people arrested and mutilated.

RADU.   Maybe just arrested and shot. They are our
              children.

FLORINA.   After all we've done for them. You should kiss
              my hands. You should drink my bathwater.

ALL.   That's enough trial.

              We find you guilty on all counts.

              Execution now.

FLORINA.   You said there'd be a helicopter, Nicu.

IANOŞ.   Stand up.

FLORINA.   Sit down.

              They are roughly pushed to another place.

RADU.   You can't shoot me. I'm the one who gives the orders to shoot.

FLORINA.   We don't recognise being shot.

ALL.   Gypsy.

             Murderer.

             Illiterate.

             We've all fucked your wife.

             We're fucking her now.

             Let her have it.

             They all shoot ELENA (FLORINA), *who falls dead at once.* GABRIEL, *who is particularly vicious throughout this, shoots with his crutch. All make gun noises, then cheer.* CEAUŞESCU (RADU) *runs back and forth. They shout again.*

ALL.   We fucked your wife.

             Your turn now.

             Murderer.

             Bite your throat out.

             Meanwhile CEAUŞESCU (RADU) *is pleading.*

RADU.   Not me, you've shot her that's enough, I've money in Switzerland, I'll give you the number of my bank account, you can go and get my money –

IANOŞ.   In his legs.

             They shoot and he falls over, still talking and crawling about.

RADU.   My helicopter's coming, you'll be sorry, let me go to Iran –

IANOŞ.   In the belly.

             They shoot, he collapses further but keeps talking.

RADU.   I'll give you the People's Palace –

IANOŞ.   In the head.

             They shoot again. He lies still.

They all cheer and jeer.

CEAUŞESCU (RADU) *sits up.*

RADU.   But am I dead?

ALL.   Yes.

He falls dead again.

More cheering, ole ole ole etc.

RADU *and* FLORINA *get up, everyone's laughing.*

IANOŞ *hugs* LUCIA *lightly.*

GABRIEL *suddenly hits out at* IANOŞ *with his crutch.*

GABRIEL.   Get your filthy Hungarian hands off her.

IANOŞ.   What?

GABRIEL.   Just joking.

A MAN looks out of one of the doors of the flats to see what the noise is. They go quiet. He shuts the door.

7. Abia terminase lucrul, cînd a venit Radu.
She had just finished work when Radu came.

Hospital at night. A corridor. FLORINA has just come off duty. RADU is meeting her. They hug.

FLORINA.   Someone died tonight. It was his fifth operation. When they brought him in all the nurses were in love with him. But he looked like an old man by the time he died.

RADU.   Was he one of the ones shot low in the back and out through the shoulder?

FLORINA.   He was shot from above in the shoulder and it came out low down in his back.

RADU.   No, all those wounds are / from being –

FLORINA.   You don't know anything about it. I was nursing him.

RADU.   A doctor told me.

FLORINA.   What does it matter? / He's dead anyway.

RADU.   They were in the crowd with us shooting people in the back.

            Pause.

            And where are they now?

            Pause.

FLORINA.   So what have you done today? Sat in the square and talked?

RADU.   I know you're tired.

FLORINA.   I like being tired, I like working, I don't like listening to you talk.

RADU.   People are talking about a hunger strike.

FLORINA.   Fine, those of you who weren't killed can kill yourselves.

            Pause.

RADU.   Do you want to know what it's for?

FLORINA.   No.

            Pause.

            I hope you're not thinking of it.

RADU.   Someone's been getting at you, haven't they?

FLORINA.   Because if you do / the wedding's off.

RADU.   Someone's threatened you. Or offered you something.

FLORINA.   It's what I think. / Did you really say that?

RADU.   I don't like what you think.

FLORINA.   I don't like what you think. You just want to go on playing hero, / you're weak, you're lazy –

RADU.   You're betraying the dead. Aren't you ashamed? Yes, I'm a hooligan. Let's forget we know each other. / Communist.

FLORINA.   You don't know me.

RADU *goes.*

FLORINA is *alone.*

She is joined by the GHOST *of a young man.*

GHOST.   I'm dead and I never got married. So I've come to
find somebody. I was always looking at you when
I was ill. But you loved Radu then. I won't talk
like he does. I died, that's all I want to know about
it. Please love me. It's lonely when you're dead. I
have to go down a secret road. Come with me. It's
simple.

8. Multă fericire. We wish you happiness.

FLORINA *and* RADU's *wedding party at a hotel. Both families
are there, and old peasant* AUNT *of Bogdan's and a* WAITER.
*Music in background. The following conversations take place,
sometimes overlapping or simultaneously.*

i.

*It's some time into the party so everyone's had a few drinks
without being drunk yet.*

1.

FLAVIA.   What's so wonderful about a wedding is everyone
laughs and cries and it's like the revolution again.
Because everyone's gone back behind their masks.
Don't you think so?

BOGDAN.   I don't know. Perhaps. You could say that.

2.

MIHAI.   I forgot to take my windscreen wipers off last
night so of course they were stolen. Still, my son
doesn't get married every day.

3.

IRINA.   She and her followers talk without speaking, they
             know each other's thoughts. She just looks at you
             and she knows your troubles. I told her all about
             Gaby.

LUCIA.   So you told her your troubles. No wonder she
             knows.

IRINA.   When they send him to Italy for his operation
             maybe we won't need a clairvoyant. She said I
             could take him to see her.

LUCIA.   He'll just laugh.

IRINA.   She says we have no soul. We've suffered for so
             many years and we don't know how to live. Are
             people very different in other countries, Lucia?

LUCIA.   Cheer up, have a drink. It's Florina's wedding day.

IRINA.   I'll miss Florina.

4.

LUCIA is *talking to a smiling* WAITER.

WAITER.   I remember your wedding last year. That was a
             very different time. We had bugs in the vases.
             Mind you. Can I help you change some dollars?

LUCIA.   No thank you.

WAITER.   I used to help your husband. It's easier now. My
             brother's gone to Switzerland to buy a Mercedes.
             You're sure I can't help you? Top rate, high as
             Everest.

LUCIA.   Thank you but I've no dollars left.

             The WAITER*'s smile disappears.*

5.

BOGDAN.   I know someone at work killed his son-in-law. He
             put an axe in his head. Then he put a knife in the
             dead man's hand to make out it was self-defence,
             and said anyway he wasn't there, it was his son.
             And he got away with it. Clever eh?

RADU.   What happened to the son?

BOGDAN.   Luckily he had some money, he only got six years.

RADU.   What's he going to do to his dad when he gets out?

            They laugh.

6.

FLAVIA.   How's your little brother?

IANOȘ.   He wakes up in the night now and cries.

FLAVIA.   How's your mother?

            They laugh.

7.

FLORINA.   I thought I was going to get the giggles.

RADU.   It was good though.

FLORINA.   It was lovely.

8.

IANOȘ.   Lucia and I are going to start a newspaper.

LUCIA.   A friend's sending us magazines from America and
            we'll translate interesting articles.

IANOȘ   (*to* LUCIA). Do people really dress like in Vogue?

9.

IRINA.   I bought these shoes in the street.

FLAVIA   Did they want dollars?

IRINA.   Yes, Lucia's last dollars went on the wedding.

FLAVIA.   Black market prices have shot up.

IRINA.   It's not black market, it's free market.

10.

IANOȘ.   A French doctor told me 4000 babies / have it.

GABRIEL.   I hate the French, they're so superior.

IANOȘ.   Yes, they do like to help.

GABRIEL.   Merci, merci.

IANOȘ   Can you really sterilise infected needles with
            alcohol?

GABRIEL.   I'm sterilising myself with alcohol.

11.

Old peasant AUNT *shouts ritual chants at* FLORINA.

AUNT.   Little bride, little bride,
            You're laughing, we've cried.
            Now a man's come to choose you
            We're sad because we lose you.
            Makes you proud to be a wife
            But it's not an easy life.
            Your husband isn't like a brother
            Your mother-in-law's not like a mother.
            More fun running free and wild
            Than staying home to mind a child.
            Better to be on the shelf
            Only have to please yourself.
            Little bride don't be sad,
            Not to marry would be mad.
            Single girls are all in tears,
            They'll be lonely many years.
            Lovely girl you're like a flower, /
            Only pretty for an hour –

BOGDAN.   Hush, auntie, you're not in the country now.

FLORINA.   No, I like it. Go on.

ii.

*Later. People have had more to drink and are more cheerful,
emotional, aggressive.*

1.

IRINA.   If only he'd stayed in University Square.

LUCIA.   He could have been shot there.

IRINA.   The bullets missed Ianoş.

LUCIA.   Do you wish they'd hit him?

IRINA.   No but of course anyone else.

2.

FLORINA.   Be nice to your mum and dad.

RADU.   I am nice.

3

BOGDAN.   Whinge whinge. Gaby was shot, all right. Every-
           one whinges. Layabout students. Radu and Ianoş
           never stop talking, want to smack them in the
           mouth. 'Was it a revolution?' Of course it was. /
           My son was shot for it and we've got

MIHAI.   Certainly.

BOGDAN.   This country needs a strong man.

MIHAI.   And we've got one.

BOGDAN.   We've got one. Iliescu's a strong man. We can't
           have a traffic jam forever. Are they going to clear
           the square or not?

MIHAI.   The government has to avoid any action that would
           give credibility to the current unsubstantiated
           allegations.

BOGDAN.   They're weak, aren't they.

FLAVIA.   I'm going to write a true history, Florina, so we'll
           know exactly what happened. How far do you
           think Moscow was involved / in planning the coup?

FLORINA.   I don't know. I don't care. I'm sorry.

FLAVIA.   What did you vote? Liberal?

FLORINA.   Yes of course.

FLAVIA.   So did I, so did I.

            She hugs FLORINA.

            Mihai doesn't know. And next time we'll win. Jos
            Iliescu.

5.

RADU.   Look at Gaby, crippled for nothing. They've voted
            the same lot in.

IRINA.   It's thanks to Gaby you can talk like this.

6.

JANOS.   Have another drink.

LUCIA.   I've had another drink.

JANOS.   Have another other drink.

            They laugh.

7.

IRINA.   Ceauşescu shouldn't have been shot.

RADU.   Because he would have exposed people / in the
            Front.

IRINA.   He should have been hung up in a cage and stones
            thrown at him.

            They laugh.

8.

BOGDAN   (*to* MIHAI). If Radu had been hurt instead of
            Gaby, he'd be in hospital in Italy by now.

9.

GABRIEL.   I can't work. Rodica can't work. What's going to
           happen to us? I wish I'd been killed.

FLORINA.   You're going to Italy.

GABRIEL.   When? Can't you do something to hurry things up,
           Florina? Sleep with a doctor? Just joking.

10.

IRINA.   I don't like seeing you with Ianoş.

LUCIA.   He's Gabriel's friend.

IRINA.   I was once in a shop in Transylvania and they
           wouldn't serve me because I couldn't speak
           Hungarian. / In my own country.

LUCIA.   Yes, but –

IRINA.   And what if the doctor only spoke Hungarian / and
           someone wanted a doctor?

BOGDAN.   Stuck-up bastards.

IRINA.   Are you going back to America? You're not going
           back.

LUCIA.   Didn't you miss me?

IRINA.   Aren't you ashamed? Two years of hell to get your
           precious American and you don't even want him.
           Did he beat you?

LUCIA.   I got homesick.

IRINA.   Was Ianoş going on before?

LUCIA.   Of course not. You didn't think that?

IRINA.   I don't know what I thought. I just made the
           wedding dress.

LUCIA.   You like Ianoş.

IRINA.   Go back to America, Lucia, and maybe we can all
           go. You owe us that.

BOGDAN.   You're a slut, Lucia.

11.

FLAVIA   Where are the tapes they made when they listened
           to everyone talking? All that history wasted. I'd
           like to find someone in the Securitate who could
           tell me. Bogdan, do you know anyone?

BOGDAN.   Why me?

FLAVIA.   I used to know someone but she's disappeared.

BOGDAN.   They should be driven into the open and punished.
           Big public trials. The Front aren't doing their job.

FLAVIA.   There wouldn't be enough prisons.

BOGDAN   (*to* MIHAI). There's a use for your People's
           Palace.

12.

MIHAI.   I was in the British Embassy library reading the
           Architect's Journal and there's a building in Japan
           forty stories high with a central atrium up to
           twenty stories. So the problem is how to get light
           into the central volume. The German engineer has
           an ingenious solution where they've installed
           computerised mirrors angled to follow the sun so
           they reflect natural light into the atrium according
           to the season and the time of day, so you have
           sunlight in a completely enclosed space.

13.

FLORINA.   I'm glad about you and Ianoş.

           They kiss.

           Tell me something.

LUCIA.   Don't ask.

FLORINA.   No, tell me.

LUCIA.   Two years is a long time when you hardly know
           somebody. I'd lost my job, I had to go through
           with it, I wanted to get away.

FLORINA.   But you loved Wayne at first? If you didn't I'll kill you.

LUCIA.   Of course I did. But don't tell Ianoş.

14.

PRIEST.   You can't blame anybody. Everyone was trying to survive.

BOGDAN.   Wipe them out. Even if it's the entire population. We're rubbish. The Front are stuck-up bastards. They'd have to wipe themselves out too.

PRIEST.   We have to try to love our enemies.

BOGDAN.   Plenty of enemies. So we must be the most loving people in the world. Did you love him? Give him a kiss would you?

PRIEST.   When I say love. It's enough not to hate.

BOGDAN.   Handy for you having God say be nice to Ceauşescu.

PRIEST.   You're your own worst enemy, Bogdan.

BOGDAN.   So I ought to love myself best.

PRIEST.   Don't hate yourself anyway.

BOGDAN.   Why not? Don't you? You're a smug bugger.

iii

Later. Two simultaneous conversations develop so that there are two distinct groups. Everyone has drunk a lot by now. BOGDAN, who is too drunk to care if anyone listens, puts remarks at random to either group.

1.

BOGDAN.   a. Private schools, private hospitals. I've seen what happens to old people. I want to buy my father a decent death.

b. I support the Peasants Party because my father's a peasant. I'm not ashamed of that. They should have their land because their feet are in the earth and they know things nobody else knows. Birds, frogs, cows, god, the direction of the wind.

c. CIA, KGB, we're all in the hands of foreign agents. That's one point where I'm right behind Ceauşescu.

2.

MIHAI, RADU *and* FLORINA, *joined by* FLAVIA.

MIHAI.   The Front wouldn't fix the vote because they knew they were going to win. Everyone appreciates the sacrifice made by youth. The revolution is in safe hands. This isn't a day for worrying, Florina and Radu, you take too much on yourselves. I wish you could let it all go for a little while. Please believe me, I want your happiness.

FLORINA.   We know you do.

She kisses him.

RADU.   Yes, I know. I appreciate that.

MIHAI.   After all, I'm not a monster. Most of the country supports the Front. It's only in my own home it takes courage to say it. We have a government of reconciliation.

FLAVIA.   Why don't the Front tell the truth and admit they're communists? / * Nothing to be

MIHAI.   Because they're not.

RADU.   * I don't care what they're called, it's the same people.

FLAVIA.   ashamed of in communism, / nothing to be

FLORINA.   They should have been banned / from

MIHAI.   That's your idea of freedom, banning people?

FLORINA.   standing in the election.

RADU.   We've got to have another revolution.

FLAVIA.   ashamed of in planning the revolution if they'd just
            admit it. You never dared speak out against
            Ceauşescu, Mihai, and you don't dare speak out
            now. Say it, I'm a communist and so what. / Say it,
            I'm a communist.

RADU.   Jos comunismul, jos comunismul. / Jos Iliescu. Jos
            tiranul. Jos Iliescu. Jos Iliescu.

FLORINA.   Radu, don't be childish.

            BOGDAN *joins in shouting 'Jos comunismul',
            then turns his attention to the other group.*

3. GABRIEL *at first in group with* MIHAI *then with* LUCIA,
IANOŞ *and* IRINA.

GABRIEL.   The only reason we need an internal security force
            is if Hungary tried to invade us / we'd need to be
            sure –

LUCIA.   Invade? Are you serious?

IANOŞ.   When we get Transylvania back it's going to be
            legally / because it's ours.

IRINA.   You're not going to marry a Hungarian.

LUCIA.   I'm married already.

IANOŞ.   Gaby, the Hungarians started the revolution. With-
            out us you'd still be worshipping Ceauşescu. / And
            now the

            GABRIEL *jeers.*

LUCIA.   We didn't worship him.

IRINA.   Gaby's a hero, Ianoş.

IANOŞ.   Romanians worship Iliescu. Who's the opposition?
            Hungarians.

GABRIEL.   That's just voting for your language.

LUCIA.   Why shouldn't they have their own schools?

IRINA.   And lock Romanian children out in the street. If it
            wasn't bad enough you going to America, now a
            Hungarian, / and Gaby crippled, and Radu's
            irresponsible, I worry for Florina.

GABRIEL.   If they want to live in Romania / they can

LUCIA.   In the riots on TV I saw a Hungarian on the

GABRIEL.   speak Romanian.

IANOȘ.   We can learn two languages, we're not stupid.

LUCIA.   ground and Romanians kicking him.

GABRIEL.   That was a Romanian on the ground, and
             Hungarians – you think we're stupid?

IANOȘ.   You were under the Turks too long, it made you
             like slaves.

LUCIA.   You think I'm a slave? I'm not your slave.

             GABRIEL *pushes* IANOȘ, *who pushes him back.*
             BOGDAN *arrives.*

BOGDAN.   Leave my son alone. Hungarian bastard. And don't
             come near my daughter.

IANOȘ.   I'm already fucking your daughter, you stupid
             peasant.

             BOGDAN *hits* IANOȘ.

             RADU *restrains* BOGDAN.

             LUCIA *attacks* BOGDAN.

             BOGDAN *hits* RADU.

             MIHAI *pushes* BOGDAN.

             BOGDAN *hits* MIHAI.

             FLAVIA *attacks* BOGDAN.

             IANOȘ *pushes* GABRIEL.

             IRINA *protects* GABRIEL.

             GABRIEL *hits* IANOȘ.

             RADU *attacks* BOGDAN.

             MIHAI *restrains* RADU.

             RADU *attacks* MIHAI.

             FLORINA *attacks* RADU.

             GABRIEL *hits out indiscriminately with his crutch
             and accidentally knocks* BOGDAN *to the floor.*

Stunned silence.

FLAVIA.   This is a wedding. We're forgetting our programme. It's time for dancing.

They pick themselves up, see if they are all right.

Music – the lambada. Gradually couples form and begin to dance. BOGDAN and IRINA, MIHAI and FLAVIA, FLORINA and RADU, LUCIA and IANOŞ. GABRIEL tries to dance on his crutch. For some time they dance in silence. The ANGEL and VAMPIRE are there, dancing together. They begin to enjoy themselves.

Then they start to talk while they dance, sometimes to their partner and sometimes to one of the others, at first a sentence or two and finally all talking at once. The sentences are numbered in a suggested order. At 14, every couple talks at once, with each person alternating lines with their partner and overlapping with their partner at the end. So that by the end everyone is talking at once but leaving the vampire's last four or five words to be heard alone. At first they talk quietly then more freely, some angry, some exuberant. They speak Romanian.

BOGDAN.   1. Ţara asta are nevoie de un bărbat puternic. (This country needs a strong man.)

5. Sîntem un gunoi. (We're rubbish.)

13. Dă-le una palma peste gură. (Smack them in the mouth.)

Ei ştiu lucruri pe care nimeni altcineva nu le ştie, păsări, broaşte, vaci, dumnezeu, direcţia vîntului. (They know things nobody else knows, birds, frogs, cows, god, the direction of the wind.)

IRINA.   3. Ea spune că noi nu avem suflet. (She says we have no soul.)

12. El ar trebui spînzurat într-o cuşcă, să dea lumea cu pietre în el. (He should have been hung up in a cage and stones thrown at him.)

14. Tu n-o să te mariţi cu-n ungur. (You're not going to marry a Hungarian.)

Datorită lui Gaby poţi să vorbeşti aşa. (It's thanks to Gaby you can talk like this.)

MIHAI. 8. Nimic nu e pe baze realistice. (Nothing is on a realistic basis.)

Trebuie să lăsăm trecutul în spate. (We have to put the past behind us.)

Frontul doreşte să înlesnească democraţia. (The Front wish to facilitate democracy.)

Ei nu vor aranja votarea, fiindcă ştiu ei că vor învinge. (They wouldn't fix the vote because they knew they were going to win.)

FLAVIA 2. Nu este istoria ce e în cartea de istoria? (Isn't history what's in the history books?)

14. Vreau să predau corect. (I want to teach correctly.)

Unde sînt casetele? (Where are the tapes?)

Voi scrie o istorie adevarată, ca să ştim exact ce s-a întîmplat. (I'm going to write a true history so we'll know exactly what happened.)

Am votat cu liberalii. (I voted Liberal.)

FLORINA. 4. Uneori îmi este dor de el. (Sometimes I miss him.)

14. Doctorul şef a încuiat răniţii într-o cameră. (The head doctor locked the wounded in a room.)

Comuniştii nu trebuie să candideze în alegeri. (The communists shouldn't stand in the election.)

Imi place să fiu obosită, nu-mi place să te aud vorbind. (I like being tired, I don't like listening to you talk.)

RADU. 9. Cine a tras în douazeci şi doi? Nu e o întrebare absurdă. (Who was shooting on the 22nd? That's not a crazy question.)

Cine a aruncat pocnitori? Cine a adus difuzoare? (Who let off firecrackers? Who brought loud-hailers?)

Nu-mi pasă cum se numesc, este acelaşi popor.
(I don't care what they're called it's the same
people.)

Trădezi morţii. (You're betraying the dead.)

LUCIA.   11. Mi-a fost ruşine ca nu am fost acolo. (I was so
ashamed not to be here.)

14. Dar ce inseamna asta? De ce parte a fost el?
(But what does it mean? Whose side was he on?)

De ce n-au şcolile lor? (Why shouldn't they have
their own schools?)

Nu sint sclava ta. (I'm not your slave.)

IANOŞ.   7. Eşti acuzat de genocid. (You're on trial for
genocide.)

Cine este opozitia? Ungurii. (Who's the opposition? Hungarians.)

Voi aţi fost prea mult sub turci, sînţeti ca sclavii.
(You were under the Turks too long, you're like
slaves.)

Vreau sa invăţ tot. (I want to learn everything.)

GABRIEL.   10. Sînt aşa de fericit, ca sînt de cealaltă parte.
(I'm so happy I've put myself on the other side.)

14. Diferit acum. (Different now.)

Ii urasc pe francezi. (I hate the French.)

Ungurii îi fac pe oameni să ne dispreţuiască. (The
Hungarians make people despised us.)

Aş vrea să fi fost omorît. Glumesc. (I wish I'd been
killed. Just joking.)

ANGEL.   6. Nu-ţi fie ruşine. (Don't be ashamed.)

13. Nu libertatea din afară ci libertatea interioară.
(Not outer freedom of course but inner freedom.)

Am încercat sa mă ţin departe de politică. (I try to
keep clear of the political side.)

Zburînd în albastru. (Flying about in the blue.)

VAMPIRE.   11. Nu-ţi fie frică. (Don't be frightened.)

14. Nu sînt o fiinţă umană. (I'm not a human being.)

Incepi sa vrei sînge. Membrele te dor, capul îţi arde. Trebuie să te mişti din ce în ce mai repede. (You begin to want blood. Your limbs ache, your head burns, you have to keep moving faster and faster.)

LIVES OF THE GREAT POISONERS

Introduction *by Caryl Churchill, 1993*

In 1979 I saw *The Seven Deadly Sins* at the Coliseum, with Julie
Covington singing one Anna and Siobhan Davis dancing the other,
and thought of working with three performers, one of whom would
speak, one dance and one sing. But it was ten years before I worked
on that kind of piece.

Meanwhile, I saw Trisha Brown talking while she danced, the Pina
Bausch shows at Sadlers Wells in 1982 and work by Second Stride,
and gradually got nearer to working with dancers. Les Waters and
I asked Ian Spink and Siobhan Davis to work with us on the project
that became *Fen*, but neither of them was free. There was a string
quartet and a choreographed riot in Howard Davies' production of
Softcops at the RSC. *Midday Sun* (1984) was a collaboration
arranged by John Ashford with performance devisers Geraldine
Pilgrim and Pete Brooks; Sally Owen, a Second Stride performer,
was the choreographer. In 1986 Les Waters and I approached Spink
again and he worked with us and writer David Lan on *A Mouthful of
Birds* for Joint Stock. The piece was made during twelve weeks, the
writing mainly done in the middle four. Some of the performers
were mainly dancers and some mainly actors, but everyone took
part in the large movement pieces and everyone had spoken parts,
though there were places where dancers danced and the actors had
more to say. *Fugue* (Channel 4, 1988) was a film with a final dance
piece, using movements that had happened in the story.

The big difference with *Lives of the Great Poisoners* was singing.
Orlando Gough, Spink and I started meeting every few weeks and
decided quite soon to have singers who sang, dancers who danced
and actors who spoke, rather than everyone doing everything. This
would mean scenes between, say, a character who spoke and one
who sang or one who sang and one who danced. Orlando decided
he wanted the singing to be *a capella*, which had two big effects.
One was that he needed four singers; we felt there should be the
same number of dancers (it was after all a Second Stride show) and
since cost meant we could only have nine performers this left only
one place for an actor, so we decided to bend our rule and make one
of the performers both sing and speak. The other effect was that the
words had on the whole to be written first. This, combined with our
decision that – because the rehearsal period would be short – the
words and music should be written before it started, meant they
were more or less fixed before the movement was made. This
doesn't mean that the text constantly dominates what happens.

'Death of Creusa and Creon – dance. They are sung to death by
Medea and Poisons,' left everything to Orlando and Spink.
Sometimes the text is conversational, although Midgley moves
in and out of song and Crippen and Cora speak and sing to each
other. Sometimes it's more like verse ('If I put my hand in fire.')
Sometimes it's bits of documentary ('Brinvillier's confession.')
Sometimes it's just a few words which are used for a far longer
piece of music ('Don't kill yourself.')

I think it was Orlando who started us on poison and we played
around for some time with the idea of a toxic waste ship of fools
unable to put in to any port. That faded but poison stories stayed.
Midgley, an American inventor discovered by Spink, turned out
to be a way of turning three stories into one. So did spotting love
triangles – Cora murdered by Crippen could come back for her
revenge as Medea, and the story fell into place. There would be
Crippen/Jason/Sainte-Croix (actor), Cora/Medea/Brinvilliers
(singer) and Ethel/Creusa/Mme Sainte-Croix (dancer), and their
friend Midgley. After that the details of the story were fairly quick
to work out. There was soon a scenario we all agreed on and I went
off to write the words, sending scenes to Orlando as I went on.
At the beginning of rehearsal some characters had large parts down
on paper while others still had their parts to be made. Similarly this
book gives more weight to the sung and spoken characters because
description can only give a glimpse of what was going on physically
throughout the piece.

Some background information: Crippen's name as a poisoner is well
known, though the details of his story may not be. Lequeux was a
prolific writer of mystery novels; Crippen apparently wrote to him
with ideas for plots involving perfect murders. His reading is made
up of quotations from 'An Eye for an Eye'. Everything Crippen says
to Ethel is taken from his letters to her. Medea's story is too well
known to need telling here. Less well known is that she also used
her knowledge of potions to restore youth, as she did for Jason's
father Aeson. Brinvilliers was a notorious poisoner in seventeenth-
century France. She learned about poison from her lover Sainte-
Croix, who learned from Exili, an international political poisoner.
Many of Mme de Sevigny's lines are taken from her letters.
'Brinvilliers' Confession' is based on her written confession.
Thomas Midgley was an American industrial chemist in the early
part of this century. He put the lead in petrol and CFCs in fridges,
two inventions that seemed a good idea at the time but were
inadvertently poisonous. An idea he never put into practice was that
surplus corn production in America could be restricted by increasing
the ozone in the earth's atmosphere. Our Midgley has no resem-
blance to the real Midgley, apart from these inventions. In the
Brinvilliers section he is based on her children's tutor, Briancourt.

Introduction *by Ian Spink, 1993*

Since its formation in 1982 Second Stride has developed a habit
of attempting a marriage of mixed theatre forms (text, music,
performance and dance) with the result that its productions are often
difficult to define. A critic once wrote 'Is it dance, opera or theatre?
Who cares, it's great.' The work to which he was referring was
Heaven Ablaze in his Breast (1989), a collaboration which involved
composer Judith Weir, designer Antony McDonald and myself.
Based on a story by E.T.A. Hoffmann, the piece was performed
jointly by Vocem Electric Voice Theatre and a group of Second
Stride dancers. All the performers shared singing, dancing and
spoken text and *Heaven Ablaze* probably fitted more into the
category of music theatre.

Lives of the Great Poisoners was already in the planning stages
well before *Heaven Ablaze* hit the stage. It marked the return of
composer Orlando Gough to the company after three years' absence
and included a writer, Caryl Churchill, for the first time. Caryl and
I had worked together before under different circumstances:
A Mouthful of Birds (Joint Stock, 1986) and *Fugue* (Channel 4
Dancelines, 1988). Both of these productions required dancers and
actors to share disciplines. However for *Poisoners* we decided that
the performers would rarely if ever stray from their individual
disciplines. Thus the singers would sing their parts in the manner
of opera, the actors would act their parts and the dancers would
dance their parts, neither speaking nor singing.

Orlando took the brave step of planning an *a cappella* score, that is,
sung and spoken text without instrumental accompaniment. Music
uttered from the stage would energise the narrative along with a
series of 'choreographed' scenes and characterisations. The music
and the text were initially the backbone of this work and a constant
reference point during rehearsals.

The choreography for the four dancers began after the score and
text had been developed. Improvisations with the performers led
to movements which were later developed separately into dances
which were then fitted into the written scenes.

The large mixed-form scenes ('Whist', 'Music Hall Song', 'Death
of Creusa' and 'Hoca') began as separate layers of text, music and
choreography and were woven together so as to allow each element
its own integrity. As one who has moved away from pure dance, my
main concern was that there should never be a flagging in the

narrative line nor indeed in the layers of the texture. For me this meant a subtler kind of dance, one that could appear out of the action as if from nowhere.

During the script development period we spent much time matching the multitude of potential characters from our three stories with the particular skills of our chosen performers. There were aspects of the original characters in our source material which led us to decide what kind of performer should play each part and also provide a central trio of singer/dancer/actor.

The dancer characters were divided thus: Ethel, strong but shy, was reputed to have had 'frog feet' in her childhood. She assisted Crippen in his quack treatments for patients with hearing problems. We decided that she should communicate with an invented sign language. This sign language later informed the radio/semaphore communication used to trap Crippen as he tried to escape to America. Her reincarnation, Creusa, dies as a result of wearing a poisoned dress, suggestive of much anguished physical movement and a counterpoint to the death of Cora in the Crippen section. As the wife of Sainte-Croix, she is unable to say or do anything about his infidelity with Mme de Brinvilliers, except for a final mute confrontation at the end of the piece when she refuses to give up his casket of incriminating love letters and poisons.

Marie Lloyd, a respected music-hall performer, was well known for her innocent yet suggestive stage shows. She was a friend of Cora Crippen and helped in the apprehending of the murderer Crippen. We decided that her theme should be ribbons in her stage show and flags in the 'Ship' section. In the 'Medea' section she becomes one of the poisons who impregnate the dress and kill Creusa. Later, in the 'Brinvilliers' section, she becomes an energetic and not so innocent mistress of the Marquis.

One of Cora's lovers was Bruce Miller. Ex-prize fighter turned music-hall entertainer, he once had a one-man band act. Among other talents, his body and deft, mimed juggling hold a fascination for her. In reality the flashy Bruce eventually left Cora and returned to his wife in America. We have him transforming into Captain Kendall whose delicate investigative work leads to Crippen's capture aboard the SS Montrose. Later Kendall becomes the victim of Medea's poison in the person of Creusa's father, Creon. He returns again as the sad, wavering figure of the Marquis de Brinvilliers, prematurely aged and deformed by years of slow poisoning by his wife.

Aeson, the crippled father of Jason, who is restored to youthful movement by Medea's magic potion in the first section, later returns as Mr Martinetti, a music-hall friend of Cora whose speciality is funny walks and silly faces. He then becomes an energetic sailor on the SS Montrose helping Kendall uncover the escaping couple and communicating with semaphore to the shore. He returns in the 'Medea' section to assist as a poisoner of Creusa. In the final section he becomes the mercurial and devilish La Chaussee, servant to Sainte-Croix and Mme de Brinvilliers.

Three of the dancers (and two of the singers) slip in and out of the roles of a Chorus of Poisons at various points during the piece (see breakdown of performers' roles).

Lives of the Great Poisoners was first performed at the Arnolfini, Bristol, on 13 February 1991. The cast was as follows:

MIDGLEY, *an industrial chemist* — Michael O'Connor (actor/baritone)

DR CRIPPEN
JASON
SAINTE-CROIX, *Mme de Brinvilliers' lover* — Pearce Quigley (actor)

CORA, *Crippen's wife*
MEDEA
MME DE BRINVILLIERS — Angela Tunstall (soprano)

ETHEL, *Crippen's lover*
CREUSA, *Jason's lover*
MME SAINTE-CROIX — Michele Smith (dancer)

LEQUEUX, *novelist*
DEW, *police inspector*
EXILI, *professional poisoner*
DESGREZ, *Chief of Police* — Józic Koc (baritone)

AESON, *Jason's father*
MR MARTINETTI
LA CHAUSSEE, *Sainte-Croix' servant*
DEGREZ'S ASSISTANT
SAILOR — Stephen Goff (dancer)

MRS SMYTHSON
MME DE SEVIGNE — Jackie Horner (mezzo-soprano)

MARIE LLOYD
MME DUFAY, *Marquis de Brinvilliers' mistress* — Sally Owen (dancer)

BRUCE MILLER, *Cora's lover*
KENDALL, *captain*
CREON, *Creusa's father, King of Corinth*
MARQUIS DE BRINVILLIERS — Michael Popper (dancer)

CHORUS OF POISONS
Stephen Goff, Jackie Horner, Józic Koc, Sally Owen

Writer   Caryl Churchill
Composer   Orlando Gough
Musical Directors   Michael Haslam, John Lunn
Director   James Macdonald
Designer   Antony McDonald
Lighting Designer   Peter Mumford
Director/Choreographer   Ian Spink

The original music was included in the first edition published by
Methuen Drama in 1993. A revised and more easily singable
version may be obtained from Orlando Gough, 12 Spencer Rise,
London NW5 1AP, or in case of difficulty from the present
publisher.

Breakdown of Performers' Roles

The piece was made for four dancers, four singers (three singers,
one actor/singer) and one actor.

M/Actor	*M/Actor/Singer* *Baritone*	*F/Singer* *Soprano*	*F/Dancer*
Jason	Medea		
Crippen	Midgley	Cora	Ethel
Jason	Midgley	Medea	Creusa
Sainte-Croix	Midgley	Mme de Brinvilliers	Mme Sainte-Croix

F/Dancer	*F/Singer* *Mezzo-Soprano*	*M/Dancer* *Bass*	*M/Singer*	*M/Dancer*
Poison	Poison	Aeson	Poison	Poison
Marie Lloyd	Mrs Smythson	Mr Martinetti/ Sailor	Lequeux/ Inspector Dew	Bruce Miller/ Capt. Kendall
Poison	Poison	Poison	Poison	Creon
Mme Dufay	Mme de Sevigne	La Chaussee/ Desgrez's Asst	Exili/ Desgrez	Marquis de Brinvilliers

Note on Layout

Speech follows character name, sung passages are indented.

PROLOGUE

Elixir of Life

MEDEA *restores* AESON, JASON*'s father, to youth.*

We hear wordless singing. MEDEA*'s assistants (*CHORUS
OF POISONS*) enter carrying objects which include cup, knife,
metal container (cauldron), henbane, rubber toad. With one
hand the dancers gesture the preparations made for the ritual,
digging a pit, building a fire and collecting herbs.* MEDEA
*enters and takes the henbane and toad and throws them into
the pot. She goes into a spasm.* AESON, *very old and weak, is
carried in by* JASON *and laid on the floor.* MEDEA *takes the
knife (see below), one of the assistants places a cloth under*
AESON*'s head, and* MEDEA *cuts his throat. His body is turned
upside down to drain the blood.* MEDEA, *using the cup, takes
magic potion from the cauldron and pours it into the cut. He
revives in a series of jerks. As the others leave* AESON *does a
small youthful dance and bounds up the wall as it lowers into
the next scene.*

MEDEA.   Hurting you I heal you
                    Killing you I cure you
                    Secrets of death and new life
                    Poisons that heal
                    Fill your blood fill your breath
                    By my skill
                    I kill you and give you new life

DR CRIPPEN

Evening at Hilldrop Crescent

CRIPPEN *and* MIDGLEY. MIDGLEY *is the* CRIPPENS'
lodger.

MIDGLEY.   Red was my first thought, the colour red. You want
to guess how that came to me? You're a country
boy. You ever seen the trailing arbutus that blooms
under snow? That was magic to me. And what
colour are those arbutus leaves? Red. Because the
red absorbs the heat. So –

CRIPPEN.   I don't recall the leaves of the arbutus.

MIDGLEY.   Next time you go home to Michigan you take a
look. So, red, if we could colour the fuel red, do
you follow me?

CRIPPEN.   It would absorb heat –

MIDGLEY.   It would, it would vastly improve its combustion
characteristics and, in a word, prevent knock.

CRIPPEN.   So you found a red dye –

MIDGLEY.   I found iodine. Homely old iodine your ma used to
put on your cut knee. / And would you

CRIPPEN.   No, really? I remember –

MIDGLEY.   believe it? Iodine in the gas stops the knock.

CRIPPEN.   You'll make your fortune. / Mr Midgley, this is
thrilling.

MIDGLEY.   A long way to go. Because it appears it's not after
all the redness. The iodine, by odd chance, but not
the redness. It appears to be a question of
molecular structure. And iodine it turns out is not
commercially viable. So now I'm in search of a
new substance with the correct molecular structure.

CRIPPEN   It's thrilling for me, Mr Midgley, to make the
           acquaintance of a scientist at the frontiers of know-
           ledge. I know in my humble way how hard it is.

MIDGLEY.   Your own career has been devoted to science, /
           I believe.

CRIPPEN.   Humbly devoted to science and medicine. Always
           seeking new methods to lighten men's burdens.
           First with Munyon's Homeopathic Remedies.
           Then Drouet's Institute for the Deaf. Now the Yale
           Tooth Specialists. But of course I can hardly make
           a living. We are reduced to taking lodgers. In the
           case of a guest like yourself of course it's a
           pleasure and an honour.

MIDGLEY.   There's still time yet for both of us, Crippen.

CRIPPEN.   My latest little idea, I call it Sans Peine, the French
           gives it something, I'm about to take out a patent –

MIDGLEY.   There you are.

           LEQUEUX *arrives.* CRIPPEN *introduces him and*
           MIDGLEY.

CRIPPEN.   A great scientist and a great novelist meeting under
           my humble roof at Hilldrop Crescent. Mr Lequeux
           knows secrets thought dead with the Borgias which
           Mr Midgley and I as scientists would be fascinated
           to share. But first he has promised to read to us
           from his latest mystery.

MIDGLEY.   Great admirer. *Wiles of the Wicked, Whoso Findeth
           a Wife, The Veiled Man.*

CRIPPEN.   *The Day of Temptation, The Bond of Black, Secrets
           of Monte Carlo.*

LEQUEUX.   *Eye for an Eye.*

           LEQUEUX *reads from his novel.* MIDGLEY *looks
           over his shoulder and joins in.*

           During this CORA *can be seen putting on jewels
           from a jewel box (the metal container).*

LEQUEUX.   She came into my room

LEQUEUX and MIDGLEY

> a woman whose face, although waxen
> white, was eminently beautiful. Her
> paleness . . . She wore a brooch of rather
> uncommon pattern. It was a playing card,
> a tiny five of diamonds. At that moment
> the truth dawned . . . Quite undue alarm
> I decided. She said, 'Drink that, you'll feel
> better very quickly.' I gulped it down.
> It tasted very bitter but . . . Strange sharp
> pain which struck me across the eyes,
> a paralysis of the limbs and a feeling of
> giddiness . . . most deadly of poisons,
> insidious . . . I saw her in the air, in the
> clouds, everywhere; her voice rang in my
> ears; she was so lovely – yet so vile – a
> poisoner! . . . She knew secrets dead with
> the Borgias . . . She said 'Drink that.'

CRIPPEN.   I get ideas for novels. But I don't have a way with
words, so if you just wrote them up. There's a man
married to a termagant. He's in love with a
beautiful and innocent girl who works as his
secretary. He poisons his wife in the tea but he has
drunk the tea himself without ill effect. How can
this be? He drank an antidote first. The poison is
indetectable. No suspicion falls on him. A perfect
crime. He lives to an old age with his beloved.
Does this idea appeal? I have many others. He kills
his wife with poisoned gloves. / He –

Enter CORA.

CORA.   Is everything ready, Hawley, my love? /

CRIPPEN.   Everything's ready, my love.

CORA.   The guests will be here any minute
and nothing's ready.

CRIPPEN.   Our most respected guests are already here.

CORA.   Enchanté, Mr Lequeux.

LEQUEUX.   Enchanté, Madame.

CORA   (*to* CRIPPEN). My friends, what about my
friends, you've no respect / for them.

CRIPPEN. Respect, my love, I should think not, respect that
tawdry / riff-raff, respect Bruce Miller,

CORA. Tawdry.

CRIPPEN. a one man band, if I were cuckolded by a bank
manager / I might have some respect or if he could
play one single musical instrument to

MIDGLEY. What a charming brooch, Mrs Crippen.

CORA. The rising sun. Do call me Belle.

CRIPPEN. a high professional standard.

CORA. Professional standards? Forgive me
laughing, my husband just made a joke.

CRIPPEN. Have you been to the music hall in London,
Midgley?

MIDGLEY. I'm looking forward to it.

CRIPPEN. Cora will tell you which are the best acts.

CORA. Opera was my first ambition.

MIDGLEY. Bit highbrow for me.

CORA (*to* CRIPPEN). Don't start on me about
Bruce Miller. / What

CRIPPEN. And the German students?

CORA. about your little typewriter? Ethel is a very
dull name. It suits her.

CRIPPEN. Belle is of course my wife's professional name. Her
name is Cora. Or rather her name is Kunigunde,
but that's rather a mouthful we find, Kunigunde
Mackimotzki, Mackimotzki a Polish grocer, not
quite the thing for top of the bill at the Empire
Leicester Square, not that we've made the Empire
Leicester Square yet but hope springs eternal, so
she calls herself Belle Elmore, / you may have
seen her name some way down the bill.

CORA. Dr Crippen is at the top of his profession.
He'll send his diagnosis by mail order.
Rhinitis Chronica Pharyngitis Eustachian
Sulphingitis. The painless wonder. Cures
for diseases that are incurable.

MIDGLEY.   We all have our dreams, Mrs Crippen. You're an
artiste, your husband a physician. What higher
callings?
We all have our dreams, Belle.

Whist

More guests arrive, all music hall friends of CORA*'s.* BRUCE
MILLER, MR MARTINETTI, MRS SMYTHSON, MARIE
LLOYD. *During the following* LEQUEUX *is making a play for*
MARIE LLOYD, CORA *is flirting with* BRUCE MILLER,
CRIPPEN *is standing apart.*

MRS SMYTHSON. Belle.

CORA.   We're eight, that's two tables for whist.

CRIPPEN.   Count me out, my love.

MIDGLEY.   Do play, Crippen.

SMYTHSON.   Oh Dr Crippen, do play.

CORA.   We can do very well without you.

LEQUEUX.   I don't mind not playing.

MRS SMYTHSON. Oh Mr Lequeux, do play.

MIDGLEY.   We'll make one table and take turns. I need
to watch, it's so long since I played.

SMYTHSON.   Oh Mr Midgley, do play.

They settle to playing.

First hand: CORA, MILLER, LLOYD,
MARTINETTI.

The others watch.

MIDGLEY.   What's the stake?

SMYTHSON.   Penny a quarter.

LEQUEUX.   Won't break you.

CORA   (*to* CRIPPEN). Are you going to stand
there all the evening?

LEQUEUX   (*to* CRIPPEN). Cards are a trivial way of
                 passing the time. But I must confess a
                 weakness. Ever since that night in Monte
                 Carlo . . .

CORA.   Oh what a hand.

SMYTHSON.   Don't say a word.

MIDGLEY.   Hearts are trumps.

CORA.   Oh they are, they are.

                 They bid.

LLOYD.   I propose.

MARTINETTI. Pass.

CORA.   I accept. We ladies will show you.

MILLER.   Solo.

CORA.   Solo, you devil.

LLOYD.   Pass.

MARTINETTI. Misere.

SMYTHSON and CORA. Misere!

CORA.   Abondance. There.

MILLER.   Abondance in trumps.

CORA.   Oh Mr Miller, you always have all the
                 hearts.

MIDGLEY.   How many tricks does he have to make?

CORA.   Are you looking at my hand, Mr Midgley?

CRIPPEN.   Just popping out for some air.

MIDGLEY.   Don't go.

                 CRIPPEN *leaves. He goes to visit* ETHEL.

                 Dance of coy tentative passion.

                 *Meanwhile, Evening at Hilldrop Crescent
                 continues.*

                 They play.

SMYTHSON.   He'll never make it.

CORA.   Oh my best card.

SMYTHSON.   Don't say a word.

LEQUEUX.   He's got to win this one.

ALL.   Got you.

> MARTINETTI *and* CORA *win last two tricks.*
> MILLER *fails to make his bid.*

CORA.   Two tricks down.

ALL.   Pay up.

LEQUEUX.   He had the ace.

SMYTHSON.   If you'd led the ten.

MIDGLEY.   Bold play, Belle.

> LEQUEUX *pursues* MARIE LLOYD *round the*
> *table and similarly* CORA *pursues* MILLER.

LEQUEUX   (*to* LLOYD). I sent you roses. I like your
                   style.

MIDGLEY   (*to* CORA). I like your style.

CORA.   Unlucky at cards, lucky in love, Mr Miller.

SMYTHSON.   Oh Mr Midgley, do play.

MIDGLEY.   I will.

SMYTHSON *and* MIDGLEY.

                   Oh Mr Lequeux, do play.

> *Second hand:* MIDGLEY, LEQUEUX,
> SMYTHSON, LLOYD *standing playing and*
> *repeating fragments of movement.*

LEQUEUX. Pass.

SMYTHSON.   I propose.

LLOYD.   Pass.

MIDGLEY.   I accept.

LEQUEUX.   Misere.

SMYTHSON.   Abondance.

LLOYD.   Pass.

MIDGLEY.   Abondance in trumps.

The last round of bidding is repeated while CORA
tells MILLER *she imagines herself singing opera
and he dances seductively in front of her.*

CORA.   I'm at La Scala. I'm gowned by Patou. I'm
                   singing Medea. 'I have my revenge.'

The game continues.

LEQUEUX.   Misere ouverte.

SMYTHSON.   Pass.

LLOYD.   Pass.

MIDGLEY.   Abondance declaree.

MIDGLEY lays his cards on the table.

ALL.   Ooo!

LEQUEUX *again pursues* MARIE LLOYD, *while*
CORA *and* SMYTHSON *turn their attention to*
MIDGLEY.

LEQUEUX   (*to* MARIE LLOYD). I had nothing. I sent
                   you roses.

CORA   (*to* MIDGLEY). You're a genius.

SMYTHSON and MIDGLEY.
                   Beginner's luck.

CORA.   Lucky at cards, lucky in love, Mr Midgley.

LEQUEUX.   Won't you sing for us, Mrs Lloyd?

SMYTHSON.   Oh Mrs Lloyd, do sing.

MIDGLEY.   Won't you sing for us, Mrs Crippen? Oh
                   Belle, do sing.

Music Hall Song

CORA *sings a music hall song. During the song* MARIE
LLOYD *is doing a saucy dance with ribbons on sticks,*
MARTINETTI *is doing funny faces and silly walks,* BRUCE
MILLER *is doing a juggler-magician routine without props,*

CORA *is doing a crass dance routine among them while she sings. She does it badly but is pleased with herself.*

CORA.
> There was a young lady in Paris,
>> as history writers tell
>
> Who poisoned her poor old father
>> and both her brothers as well.
>
> She was pouring a bottle of poison
>> adown of her husband's throat
>
> When her lover says 'No don't bother'
>> and gave him an antidote.
>
> She poisoned him, he poisoned her.
> They both took an antidote.
>
> He poisoned her, she poisoned him.
> Oh! What a to-do.

ALL.
> You can't trust 'em further than you can throw 'em.

LLOYD, MARTINETTI *and* MILLER *do a cod ballet routine with* CORA *performing badly in the centre.*

SMYTHSON.
> Oh Belle, you've got no talent. I can't help admiring you.

MIDGLEY.
> Oh Belle, you've got real talent. I can't help admiring you.

LEQUEUX.
> I'll never forget your magnificent performance. I can't help admiring you though you spurned my roses.

CORA *goes back to music hall song and others go back to previous material.*

CORA.
> She poisoned him, he poisoned her,
> She gave him an antidote.
> Oh what a to-do.
> *Etc.*

During this singing CRIPPEN *finishes his dance with* ETHEL, *who remains on the floor, and enters Hilldrop Crescent. General embarrassment as the guests leave.*

Cora's Death

CRIPPEN *makes cocoa using a cup and spoon.* CORA *takes off her shoes, and her jewels, which she puts in the box.*

CORA.   I won't sell my jewels so don't ask.
                            I like a lot of company and the house full
                                to suffocation, why not?
                            I won three-and-six, you can have that.
                            I should have gone misere.

CRIPPEN.   Drink your cocoa, my love, and we'll go to bed.

CORA.   I want to be famous, I want the gentlemen
                                standing up to cheer and throwing flowers.
                            How's the little typewriter tonight?

                            ETHEL *moves towards* CRIPPEN *and nudges him
                            with her head.*

CRIPPEN.   Drink your cocoa, my love.

CORA.   You're a nasty little quack with no soul.
                            I'm hoping to be on the bill with Marie
                                Lloyd.
                            The Music Hall Ladies Guild Ball – will
                                you try to enjoy it?
                            Mr Midgley's taken a fancy to me.

                            CORA *is getting sleepier.*

                            The CHORUS OF POISONS *singers appear above
                            and start singing her to death and* ETHEL *starts
                            a dance which refers to the fact that she may have
                            suffered a nervous breakdown and that on the
                            evening of the murder she kept putting curlers
                            in hair again and again and the landlady said
                            'You must relieve your mind or you will go
                            absolutely mad.' It's mostly gestural with
                            references to her hair and her ears and spell
                            casting. At the beginning her movements are
                            frantic and repetitive.*

CORA.   Remember the night I thought I was going
                                to die?
                            I said 'Wake up and get a priest, I'm going
                                to die.'

CRIPPEN *embraces* CORA.

CORA.   And you took care of me.

CRIPPEN.   Drink up your cocoa, my love, and we'll go to bed.

CORA.   Poor Belle's unlucky at cards and unlucky
                    in love.
                    They're all cheering me and throwing
                    flowers.

*CORA is getting weaker. She seems to pass out in
CRIPPEN's arms. Suddenly she screams and
becomes frantic.*

*CRIPPEN moves away from her as she jerks up
and crawls around the floor.*

ETHEL's movements become calm.

CORA.   I'm going to die.

CRIPPEN.   What's the matter, my love? Are you ill?

CORA is trying to grab hold of CRIPPEN.

CORA.   Help me. Take care of me. Make me better.
                    Stop the pain.

CRIPPEN.   Go to sleep, Cora, go to sleep.

*CORA and the POISONS go on shrieking while
ETHEL does a rapid triumph dance and
CRIPPEN tries to restrain CORA.*

CRIPPEN.   You're meant to go to sleep. It's not supposed to
                  hurt. It's painless. Be quiet, someone will hear
                  you. What are you doing? Hyoscine's meant to
                  make you go to sleep. You're meant to die quietly,
                  Cora, in your sleep.

Shrieking gets worse. CRIPPEN *gets gun and
shoots* CORA, *thus ending music.* ETHEL *exits.*
CRIPPEN *disposes of the body by putting it out of
sight behind the floor.*

CRIPPEN *alone with his crime.*

CRIPPEN.   When I was a child in Coldwater, Michigan, some
                  nights I couldn't sleep and I crept downstairs.
                  It seemed I was all alone in the house. How could
                  I get away? How could I not be damned? I'd sit for

hours by the stove trying to keep warm. The devil was always in the kitchen.

He remains sitting during the following scene.

Suspicion

SMYTHSON *and* MARIE LLOYD *try to get* INSPECTOR DEW *to take action.* DEW *has a book of missing persons.* MIDGLEY *is with him. Meanwhile* ETHEL *joins* CRIPPEN *and is given* CORA'*s brooch.*

SMYTHSON.	Inspector Dew, my friend has disappeared.
DEW.	Hundreds of people vanish every day.
SMYTHSON.	At first her husband said she'd gone away. And now he says she's dead just as I feared. That woman was seen trying on Belle's dresses. She came to the ball with Dr Crippen wearing Belle's rising sun brooch on her bosom. Belle never in a thousand years would have allowed another woman to wear her jewels.
DEW	(*meanwhile*). Wives often run away. Happens every day.
SMYTHSON.	My suspicions are becoming stronger in the direction of foul play.

ETHEL *enters to* CRIPPEN, *who reaches down to the body as if undressing it and gives* ETHEL CORA'*s dress and then her brooch, which he pins on* ETHEL.

SMYTHSON.	My friend has disappeared. She's dead just as I feared.
MIDGLEY.	I wonder where she's gone. I wonder why.

MARIE LLOYD *moves in to observe* CRIPPEN *and* ETHEL.

SMYTHSON.   There's no trace of her on the passenger
                        lists.
                    He doesn't even know what town she died
                        in, he hasn't got a death certificate.
                    He said she died at his son's house and his
                        son wrote to say he knows nothing
                        about it.

                    My suspicions are becoming stronger in
                        the direction of foul play.

DEW.   Happens every day.

DEW calls on CRIPPEN. ETHEL *leaves.*

DEW.   I'd like to have a word with you about the
                        death of your wife.

CRIPPEN.   Inspector Dew, I want to confess. I have lied. I lied
            when I said my wife was called away suddenly on
            family business. I lied when I said she got
            pneumonia on the ship and the reason I was so
            uncertain about the place of her death is because
            the whole thing was a pack of lies. The truth is my
            wife has left me. She's run off with her lover, a
            prizefighter called Bruce Miller, who has played
            here in music halls as a one man band. I could not
            bear to be laughed at. She was dead to me so I
            pretended she was dead. I have to confess I also
            lied to Miss LeNeve, who now lives with me as
            my wife, believing me a widower. I am sorry to
            have wasted police time by causing unnecessary
            suspicion. I tried to avoid social embarrassment
            and have been punished by being even more
            severely embarrassed.

DEW moves away, satisfied.

*CRIPPEN runs back to the body, which is still out
of sight. His action indicates that he chops the
head off and puts it in a hatbox (the metal
container).*

DEW.   Hundreds of people vanish every day.
                    Wives often run away. Happens every day.

SMYTHSON.   My suspicions are becoming stronger in
                        the direction of foul play.

MIDGLEY.   Belle Elmore is a very charming woman.
                        We're dull dogs. She wanted the bright
                        lights.

DEW and MIDGLEY. Bright lights.

SMYTHSON.   Foul play.

> *They all go off.*

> ETHEL *runs in disguised as a boy. She is wearing
> a suit and carrying a hat. She dances with*
> CRIPPEN. *Her movements are stronger and more
> exuberant. It's like a conversation between her
> movement and* CRIPPEN's *lines.*

CRIPPEN.   It is so precious a thought to me to tell you you are
            always and ever my wifie and that not even death
            can come between us.

            We have been so long one in heart, soul, thought
            and deed that, wifie darling, nothing can separate
            our inward consciousness and spirit.

            No more sacred relations to each other such as
            ours could ever exist.

> CRIPPEN *puts on a false moustache.* ETHEL *puts
> on the hat, tucking up her hair. She makes a move
> towards the hatbox,* CRIPPEN *playfully forestalls
> her and takes the box with him as they run away.*

On the Ship

As they go off, CAPTAIN KENDALL *and the* SAILOR *appear
on the deck of the ship.* ETHEL *and* CRIPPEN *arrive with the
hatbox.*

CRIPPEN.   Allow me to introduce myself. John Philo
            Robinson. My son. We are travelling abroad for his
            health. Owing to his delicate condition we require
            the exclusive use of a cabin for ourselves alone.

> MIDGLEY, DEW, SMYTHSON *appear above
> and start to sing (see below). They are holding up
> plastic evidence bags containing hair, brooch,
> photograph.* ETHEL *and* CRIPPEN *are shown*

> *to their cabin.* KENDALL *is reading a newspaper.*
> ETHEL *and* CRIPPEN *reappear on deck, look at
> the sea and fall asleep.* KENDALL *and* SAILOR
> *retire but still watch the couple.*

ALL.   Evidence.

DEW.   There was one place in the house which
                held a peculiar fascination.
                I couldn't keep my mind from wandering
                back.
                A thrill of excitement.
                Evidence nauseatingly unmistakable.
                The putrified atmosphere.

                Wanted for Murder and Mutilation.

SMYTHSON.   What did I say? Foul play. Murder and
                Mutilation.

MIDGLEY.   I think there's been a mistake.

DEW.   Traces of hyoscine hydrobromide.

MIDGLEY.   Hyoscine is a poison found in henbane or
                deadly nightshade, which commonly grows
                on waste ground. Sticky hairy leaves.
                Yellow and purple blossom. It is poisonous
                in all its parts. Hyoscine has a medical
                application for inducing twilight sleep.

> *During the above,* KENDALL *approaches the
> couple and takes* ETHEL's *hat off so that her hair
> falls down. He signals to the* SAILOR.

DEW.   The message in the air

SMYTHSON.   Racing over the sea.

MIDGLEY.   Ship pursuing ship pursuing ship . . .

> *During the above the* SAILOR *signals to* MARIE
> LLOYD *with flags and she in turn signals to the
> audience.* CRIPPEN *wakes briefly.*

CRIPPEN   (*to* KENDALL). My son enjoyed the ship's concert
                last night. Forgive his not speaking, he is a little
                deaf and rather shy.

> CRIPPEN *goes back to sleep. Signalling
> continues.* KENDALL *replaces* ETHEL's *hair*

under her hat and indicates to the SAILOR *to come and get the hatbox, which* CRIPPEN *is still holding. The* SAILOR *struggles with the sleeping* CRIPPEN, *who finally wakes and snatches the box back.*

SMYTHSON. If you'd listened to me they wouldn't have got away.

MIDGLEY. I think there's been a mistake. If they have run away it's to protect the reputation of Miss LeNeve and to start a new life.

CRIPPEN *watched by* KENDALL *and the* SAILOR *furtively drops the hatbox in the sea.*

DEW. Large pieces of human remains
No arms or legs and no head
Removed the bones and the head.

KENDALL *and* SAILOR *entertain* CRIPPEN *and* ETHEL *with a curious dolphin dance, like formation swimming, in which we can only see their legs upside down.*

DEW. I can't keep my mind from the horror of
what I've seen
The putrified atmosphere
After this I'll never sleep the sleep of the
innocent.

SMYTHSON. If you'd listened to me they wouldn't have
got away
The putrified atmosphere
Hyoscine hydrobromide
Everything points to his guilt.

MIDGLEY. It's to protect the reputation of
Miss LeNeve
I think there's been a mistake
Hyoscine hydrobromide
I'm sure he's innocent.

CORA'*s head appears over the edge of the ship.*

CRIPPEN *recoils.*

LLOYD *does a triumphant flag dance.*

KENDALL *and* SAILOR *continue dolphin dance.*

CORA.   You thought you'd thrown my head into
                         the sea
                     You thought I'd fallen asleep
                     I'm awake, I'm here, I'll never leave
                         you now
                     I can't keep my mind from the horror

                     I want them throwing flowers
                     Murder and mutilation

SMYTHSON.   Murder and mutilation
                     The putrefied atmosphere

MIDGLEY.   He's one of the most agreeable men
                         that I know
                     The putrefied atmosphere
                     Murder and mutilation
                     Please say you're innocent

ALL.   Murder and mutilation
                     The death of your wife.

CRIPPEN.   We were like two children in the great unkind
           world who clung to one another and gave each
           other courage.

           KENDALL *and the* SAILOR *welcome* DEW,
           LLOYD, SMYTHSON *and* MIDGLEY *aboard
           the ship.* DEW *handcuffs* CRIPPEN.

           LLOYD, KENDALL *and* SAILOR *do a
           triumphant dance.*

DEW.   I arrest you for murder
                     And then I'll grow flowers
                     I can't keep my mind

SMYTHSON.   Murder and mutilation
                     To mutilate your own wife

MIDGLEY.   You want to start a new life
                     With the innocent you love.
                     Your wife is magnificent
                     I think there's been a mistake.

CORA.   I'll never leave you now and you'll never
                         escape me
                     You thought I'd gone forever but I'll have
                         my revenge

They all go off leaving CRIPPEN *and* ETHEL *alone.*

CRIPPEN.   One Sunday how early I came for you and we had a whole day together which meant so much to us then. A rainy day but how happy we were with all sunshine in our hearts.

They embrace and walk slowly off watched by CORA *who has transformed into* MEDEA.

MEDEA

Corinth

MEDEA.

If I put my hand in fire
Would the pain rush out of my mind into
   my hand?
I could stand that.

Why my hand?
I want his hand on fire.
Her hand, I wouldn't feel a thing, I might
   still feel his hand.
I want her dead.
Set their house on fire.

CHORUS OF POISONS (*two singers and male
dancer*) *assemble at the side with the metal box of
poisons. Dancer does gestural dance illustrating*
MEDEA's *words.*

MEDEA.

What and get caught?
Poison.
Poison that kills far away like the bite
   of a thought.
Wrap her body in fire.
Wrap fire round her head.

I could stop, I could leave, I could
   stop now.
She could live, he needn't grieve, I could
   go away.

But I have the power.
Poison that eases into her body out of
   my mind.
The pain will burn her body and leave my
   mind cold.
The horror will rush out of my mind.

MIDGLEY *and* JASON *enter as* MEDEA *and*
POISONS *go off.*

MIDGLEY.   Today we've something to celebrate.

JASON.   What? / You've heard – ah, sorry.

MIDGLEY.   You know the knock problem – what?

JASON.   Nothing, go on, yes, the knock in car engines.

MIDGLEY.   I tried everything from ethyl acetate and aluminium fluoride to camphor and melted butter. Thirty thousand chemical compounds.

JASON.   Like those endless days at sea.

MIDGLEY.   I thought this could take my entire life.

JASON.   You think you're going to fall off the world.

MIDGLEY.   You get one that works and it stinks of garlic.

JASON.   Wave after bloody wave, you want to give up.

MIDGLEY.   But then I took a look at the periodic table and, wait for it, everything that was nearly ok was clustered down the bottom. That was like you killing the serpent.

JASON.   And you struck gold.

MIDGLEY.   What I've struck is lead. Lead in the gas stops the knock.

JASON.   You'll make your fortune.

MIDGLEY.   A golden fleece. And leaded gas. So we both have something to celebrate, I guess.

JASON.   I do have something to celebrate. I'm getting married.

MIDGLEY.   I always thought you and Medea were already – congratulations. We'll have a party.

JASON.   Not to Medea. / We did go through a form of

MIDGLEY.   Not to Medea?

JASON.   marriage but it's not legal here.

MIDGLEY.   What?

JASON.   To Creusa. The princess?

MIDGLEY.   My god, has Medea left you? Don't do anything rash. She'll come back. This is terrible. Shall I speak to her for you?

JASON.   No. No, thank you, no. She hasn't left me.

MIDGLEY.   What? For Creusa? You're out of your mind. Medea's – there's no comparison.

JASON.   Maybe you can comfort her.

MIDGLEY.   She wouldn't look at me – what are you saying?

JASON.   No, I mean cheer her up, stop her being angry with me.

MIDGLEY.   She shouldn't be angry?

JASON.   Look, Midgley, you don't live with her. She was wonderful in her own country, dealing with monsters, I owe her a lot. But when you get back to civilisation. Not everyone's as tolerant as you.

MIDGLEY.   And Creusa's father is King of Corinth.

JASON.   She's beautiful, Midgley. And her father's King of Corinth.

MIDGLEY.   It's a career move.

JASON.   It's a brilliant career move. I'm a hero, I can have what I like. But it won't last. Poor old Jason, always going on about his golden fleece, crazy wife.

MIDGLEY.   I thought you loved her.

JASON.   Get a grip, Midgley. When the King dies I'll run Corinth. Would you give up your leaded petrol? Help me talk her round. She likes you.

MIDGLEY.   Does she? Has she said so?

Enter MEDEA.

MEDEA.   I deceived my father for you. I murdered my brother. I betrayed my country and helped you steal its treasure. / I'm sorry

JASON.   Medea, I do appreciate . . .

MEDEA.   that's not enough. I'm sorry I didn't have a sister / so I could drink her blood.

JASON.   I never suggested . . .

MIDGLEY.   Medea, listen.
                  Jason, when you think of all she's done.

MEDEA.   If I could go home to a time before I knew
                  you.

JASON.   When I say I'm going to marry the princess . . .
           Marriage doesn't mean much here. Wives are a
           matter of career. Passion is for a mistress. We've
           turned up in Corinth with nothing except that I'm
           a hero. We've a chance to get in with the royal
           family. I'm doing it for you. I'll buy you a house.

MIDGLEY   (*to* MEDEA). Wives are a matter of career.
           Passion. A house.

           (*To* JASON.) This is terrible.

MEDEA.   Without you I'd be a princess.
           Without me you'd be dead.
           Jason's a hero.
           Who saved you? Who poisoned the
           serpent? Who got the golden fleece?

MIDGLEY.   Is this true?

MEDEA.   Medea's the hero.

           She repeats this through JASON*'s next speech, and*
           MIDGLEY *joins in.*

JASON.   You were nobody. You were desperate to get out of
           that godforsaken country. If you'd stayed there no
           one would ever have heard of you, you're only
           famous for helping me.

MEDEA.   The King should give me his daughter and
           let me rule over Corinth.

MIDGLEY.   I can't stand this. Two people who are so
           magnificent.

JASON.   Marriage doesn't mean much here.

MIDGLEY.   She gave up everything.

MEDEA.   I murdered my brother.

JASON.   This is our chance to be rich and powerful.

MIDGLEY.   She's already made you rich and powerful.

MEDEA.   I'll have my revenge.

JASON.   I'll buy you a house.

MIDGLEY.   But she's magnificent.

MEDEA.   Tell me about the house. Tell me murder's
                  good. Make me hate you more.

MIDGLEY.   I can't defend him. I'm sorry. You're the most
            extraordinary woman. Try not to hate him. Things
            may turn out for the best, you have to keep on and
            sometimes things suddenly . . . I wish I could put
            things right.

            The singer POISONS *enter and begin preparing
            the poison dress, taking poisons from the box.*

MEDEA.   (*to* MIDGLEY). If only I'd loved a man
                  like you. I'd be famous for sweetness.
                  I hate this rage. I'm the same Medea who
                  cures the sick and brings the dead to life.
                  I'll believe he's marrying her to make me
                  happy. I'll live in his house.

                  Take this dress and crown to the princess.

            As MEDEA *gives dress to* MIDGLEY, CREON
            and CREUSA *appear above.* CREUSA *starts to
            descend.*

MEDEA.   Tell her it comes from a great enchantress.
                  Tell her it's woven with spells for her
                      happiness.

MIDGLEY.   Things have turned out for the best. You
                  have to keep on and sometimes things
                  suddenly . . . Today we have something
                  to celebrate.

            JASON *and* MEDEA *go off together.*

            CREUSA *has arrived at the top of a steep slope.*

            MIDGLEY *takes the dress to* CREUSA.

            *Everyone watches in silence as she puts the dress
            on.*

            MEDEA *returns to watch.*

Death of Creusa and Creon

All the POISONS *go to* CREUSA.

Singing POISONS, MEDEA *and* MIDGLEY *begin to sing her to death.*

CREUSA *begins to feel the effects.*

One of the singing POISONS *does an incantation over her.*

The SINGERS *move away with* MEDEA, *leaving* CREUSA *with the dancing* POISONS.

CREON *watches from above.*

MIDGLEY *is watching from the side.*

SINGERS *prod* CREUSA.

DANCERS *move around her as she suffers, jumping over her, dancing with her and pushing her from one to the other.*

CREUSA *is crawling on the floor in agony. She rolls off the floor, runs and falls dead.*

CREON *descends to* CREUSA, *he clasps her in his arms and becomes glued to her body and dies.*

POISONS *and* MEDEA *do a triumphant dance.* MIDGLEY *is watching with horror.*

Lament for Creusa

DANCERS *lay out large white sheet and lay* CREUSA *in it.*

JASON *enters and grieves over her body. She is put in his arms wrapped in the sheet and* CREON *is placed at her feet.*

CHORUS.   O nuit désastreuse, o nuit effroyable, où
               retente tout à coup comme un éclat de
               tonnerre cette étonnante nouvelle: Madame
               se meurt, Madame est morte. Madame est
               passé du matin au soir ainsi que l'herbe du
               champ. Le matin elle fleurissait, avec
               quelle grâce, vous le savez; le soir nous la
               vîmes séchée. Quelle diligence! En neuf
               heures, l'ouvrage est accompli.

MIDGLEY.   I didn't know. I thought I was putting
                   things right. If I could go back to this
                   morning.

Medea's Triumph

MEDEA *sings triumphantly at* JASON, *who circles aimlessly
with the wrapped body of* CREUSA *in his arms.*

MEDEA.   Yes I can bring the dead to life. But not
                       for you.
                   It's no thrill healing, I'd rather kill.

                   A man thinks he's drunk. He's dead.

JASON *collapses, still holding* CREUSA.

MEDEA.   His skin shrivels, his eyes are hollow,
                       his hair goes white, his teeth break like
                       glass.
                   Secret de crapaud. Venin de crapaud.
                   Breath, bite, urine and excrement
                   Crushed in a mortar and left to putrefy.
                   Poison from moles, pigeons, fish
                       and snakes,
                   Poison from hanged men and suicides.

                   I love this rage.
                   How her body melted from its bones.
                   You thought I'd gone forever but I have
                       my revenge.

CREUSA *and* CREON *dissolve out of the scene.
The two dancing* POISONS *briefly become
dragons around* MEDEA.

MEDEA.   My enemies melted in fire
                   Your palace on fire
                   Now I'm flying in fire where you can't
                       come, in the fiery air on the wings of
                       dragons.

MEDEA *goes off with the dragons.*

JASON *and* MIDGLEY *shattered.*

JASON.   I should have known. / Why did I ever get

MIDGLEY.   You couldn't have known.

JASON.   involved with her? She's a maniac. Someone who killed her own brother, I should have known, / I

MIDGLEY.   I should have known. I shouldn't have taken the dress.

JASON.   should never have brought her back with me, I was obsessed – you couldn't have known.

MIDGLEY.   Things don't always turn out the way you think. Impossibly horrible things sometimes happen and that's what's happened here. We have to keep going. You've got to run Corinth. I've got work to do.

JASON.   I can't keep my mind from the horror.

POISONS (two singers, female dancer) assemble with box of poisons, putting labels on bottles.

MIDGLEY comforts JASON.

MIDGLEY.   I've had a new idea, try and listen. It's to keep things cool. Fish and meat and milk so they won't putrefy in hot weather and make people sick. The common refrigerant is ammonia, which is harmful.

Dancing POISON begins sinuous suggestive dance.

MIDGLEY.   By using the periodic table I hit on this in just three days. Dichlorodifluoromethane, we've called it freon, a type of CFC. I took some in my mouth to show it wasn't poison, blew on a flame and it went out.

MIDGLEY and JASON go off as BRINVILLIERS (MEDEA) enters and the POISONS hold out the box of poisons to her.

MME DE BRINVILLIERS

Hospital

MEDEA *is now* MME DE BRINVILLIERS. *She is in the
hospital. 'Many of the ladies of Paris faithfully visited the
sick . . . Brinvilliers was allowed to wander at will. She brought
and administered sweets, wine and biscuits . . . patients who
received gifts from her hands invariably died in greatest agony
. . . Beds built to contain two patients were crowded with six.'*
(Mme de Brinvilliers and Her Times *by H Stokes, Lane, London,
September 1912.*)

The sick are the four dancers, including CREUSA. *They enter
and get under a large sheet.* BRINVILLIERS *gives medicine to
the sick, assisted by the singing* POISONS, *and one by one they
die, using movements reminiscent of the music hall characters.
They are lowered behind the floor, as* CORA's *body was.*

BRINVILLIERS. Healing you I hurt you
              Curing you I kill you
              Secrets of life and new death.
              Poisons that kill
              Fill your blood fill your breath.
              By my skill
              I heal you and bring a new death.

              BRINVILLIERS *goes.*

Laboratory

SAINTE-CROIX, EXILI *and* LA CHAUSSEE *appear in the
laboratory.* EXILI *and* LA CHAUSSEE *are bottling poisons.*
SAINTE-CROIX *is checking orders.* CREUSA *takes her dress
off, becoming* MME SAINTE-CROIX, *and exits.*

EXILI.   Our new product will be so delicate
                 One breath will be fatal
                 The greatest art is indetectable
                 We'll corner the market.

SAINTE-CROIX. We've orders from Hamburg, Venice and
        Madrid.

EXILI.   The death seems natural
                        A little blood coagulates in the heart.
                        Our fame is to be unknown
                        The poison is imperceptible

SAINTE-CROIX. This is the one that's going to make our
        fortune.

EXILI.   To simulate a slow decline
                        An emanation in the air
                        We'll corner the market.

        MIDGLEY *joins them.*

SAINTE-CROIX. This is Signor Exili, the cleverest man in
        the world. Mr Midgley, whom I'm lucky enough
        to have as my children's tutor. A great chemist,
        a great alchemist. You find us as usual in search
        of the philosopher's stone and the elixir of life.

EXILI.   Philosopher's stone. Elixir of life. Great
                        ambitions.

MIDGLEY.   Lead into gold. Eternal youth. Great
                        ambitions.

EXILI.   Do you know the elixirs of Paracelsus?

MIDGLEY.   Not very well.

EXILI.   Primum Ens Melissae.
                        Dissolve a phial of potassium carbonate
                        Macerate leaves of the melissa plant
                        Pour on absolute alcohol.
                        Collect, distil, evaporate to the thickness
                            of a syrup.

                        Primum Ens Sanguinis.
                        Blood from the vein of a healthy young
                          person.
                        Digest with twice the amount of alcahest
                        Caustic lime and absolute alcohol
                        Distilled ten times and set on fire.
                        Separate filter preserve the red liquid.

        MIDGLEY *echoes what he's told, jumps ahead*
        with a bit he remembers, gets something wrong,
        joins in enthusiastically.

MIDGLEY. People must say to you what they say to me, Wild goose chase. But we don't listen.

SAINTE-CROIX. Mr Midgley stops things putrifying by keeping them cold.

MIDGLEY. And the CFCs also have an application in air conditioning.

EXILI. An emanation in the air?

MIDGLEY. I tested them on rats, and they're completely non-toxic.

EXILI. And now if you'll excuse us.

MIDGLEY. May I watch?

SAINTE-CROIX and EXILI are moving up to the laboratory.

SAINTE-CROIX. Unfortunately we're working with dangerous chemicals and we have to wear masks.

MIDGLEY. Do you have a spare mask?

SAINTE-CROIX and EXILI put on their masks and start work.

MIDGLEY. Best of luck then.

MIDGLEY goes.

SAINTE-CROIX. Does he know?

EXILI. He doesn't know.

SAINTE-CROIX. He knows.

They turn back to their work.

Meanwhile MMES DE BRINVILLIERS, DE SEVIGNE, SAINTE-CROIX and DUFAY are doing their toilette. M DE BRINVILLIERS is lying ill at BRINVILLIERS' feet, being fed poisoned wine, MME SAINTE-CROIX is massaging DE SEVIGNE, DUFAY is powdering herself and clouds of powder rise into the air.

MIDGLEY reappears above at the side.

EXILI. To simulate a slow decline
An emanation in the air
We'll corner the market.

MIDGLEY   (*to himself*). Something strange is going
                          on here.
                          There's something in the air.

SEVIGNE.   What rubbish do we rub on our faces?
                          Fat boiled up from the feet of a sheep.
                          Why do we make our heads look like
                             cabbages?
                          The most ridiculous thing we can devise.
                          Why do we stick black patches on
                             our faces
                          And call them flies?
                          Why do we spend half the day asleep?

SEVIGNE and BRINVILLIERS.
                          You do nothing. The days pass. You grow
                             old. You die.

                          MMES SAINTE-CROIX *and* DUFAY *have gone
                          into a face massage dance.*

Hoca

Evening at the DE BRINVILLIERS'. LA CHAUSSEE, *with
wine goblets, leaps onto the gaming table.* EXILI *is the dealer
for the game of Hoca. He has cards and a croupier's rake.
Everyone from the previous scene is there. They all have money.*

*Hoca is played by having a table divided into numbered com-
partments. Player puts stake, banker draws a numbered card
and pays 28 x stake.*

*Behaviour throughout this scene is sexy, bitchy and increas-
ingly savage.* DUFAY *is the mistress of the* MARQUIS DE
BRINVILLIERS. SAINTE-CROIX *is the lover of* MME DE
BRINVILLIERS. *She keeps an eye on the Marquis, who plays
heavily and loses.* MME SAINTE-CROIX *watches* SAINTE-
CROIX *jealously.* MIDGLEY *is new to the game. He is
increasingly infatuated with* MME DE BRINVILLIERS. LA
CHAUSSEE *serves wine, helps* SAINTE-CROIX *and* EXILI
cheat and, as the evening gets wilder, makes rough passes at
DUFAY. DE SEVIGNE *is flirtatious and observant, explaining
things to* MIDGLEY. *The dancers often break into phrases
of movement. Because the* MARQUIS DE BRINVILLIERS

has been poisoned, his movements are deliberate, jerky and unsteady.

| BRINVILLIERS. | Shall we play |
| | Hoca, lansequenet, portique, basset, ombre? |

| OTHERS. | Ombre, basset, portique, lansequenet, hoca? |
| | Hoca, hoca. |

They place bets. The first game.

> The most dangerous game
> Banned in Italy
> Two popes have forbidden the faithful to play
> Parliament wants to ban it
> Magistrates want to ban it
> Six trade guilds want to ban it
> Hoca.

| SEVIGNE. | The mere rumour it's going to be fashionable has given rise to an infinity of tables. |

| ALL. | Hoca. |

MIDGLEY.   What's so dangerous about hoca?

SAINTE-CROIX. There's so many ways of cheating.

MIDGLEY.   Aren't you playing?

SAINTE-CROIX. I've given up. I taught Exili all I knew about gambling and he taught me all he knew.

MIDGLEY.   About?

SAINTE-CROIX. All he knew.

> DUFAY *has won the first game.*

| EXILI. | Thirty-two paying thirty-two, a stake of twenty écus pays five hundred and sixty. |
| | Faites vos jeux. |

Placing bets for second game.

| SEVIGNE. | Dangerous game. |
| MIDGLEY. | Do I dare play? |

SAINTE-CROIX. Madame de Montespan lost half a million and won it back on three cards.

BRINVILLIERS   (*to* MIDGLEY). You could learn a lot from Sainte-Croix.

(*To* MARQUIS.) No good at cards are you, my love?

(*To* MIDGLEY.) He's lost two fortunes, his and mine.

EXILI.   Rien ne va plus.

OTHERS.   Hoca.

MIDGLEY *wins the second game.*

EXILI.   Nine paying nine. Ten écus is two hundred and eighty.

MIDGLEY.   I won, I won. I won all that? This is amazing.

BRINVILLIERS.   Lost again, my love?

MME DE BRINVILLIERS *and the* MARQUIS *quarrel – she sings, he dances.*

BRINVILLIERS.   You've lost two fortunes, can't you stop?

You'll give whatever you win to Madame Dufay.

At least Sainte-Croix knows how to play cards.

Meanwhile, bets for third game.

EXILI.   Faites vos jeux.

MIDGLEY.   Do I dare play?

SEVIGNE.   He can't stop.
Expensive mistress.

SAINTE-CROIX *corrects the cards.*

EXILI.   Rien ne va plus.

OTHERS.   Hoca.

MIDGLEY *wins the third game.*

MIDGLEY.   I won. I won again. This is amazing.

SEVIGNE and EXILI. The Marquis de Brinvilliers has lost five
               thousand.

SAINTE-CROIX (*to* MME SAINTE-CROIX). No of course I'm
               not still in love with Madame de Brinvilliers. The
               woman's a monster.

She goes to place a bet. Fourth game.

EXILI.   Faites vos jeux.

             SAINTE-CROIX *joins* MME DE
             BRINVILLIERS.

BRINVILLIERS.   Beloved, why haven't I killed that man?
             I don't know how I've lived with him
               so long.
             I wish you hadn't married that plain girl.

SAINTE-CROIX. You know marriage doesn't mean anything.
               Wives are a career. Her dowry paid for the
               laboratory.

BRINVILLIERS.   I don't like her.

SEVIGNE.   That poor girl.
             Her dowry paid.

ALL.   Hoca.

             MIDGLEY *wins fourth game.*

MIDGLEY.   I've won again, this is amazing.

SEVIGNE and EXILI. The Marquis de Brinvilliers has lost ten
               thousand.

             BRINVILLIERS *goes to* MIDGLEY.

             MME SAINTE-CROIX *goes to* SAINTE-CROIX
             and slaps his face.

BRINVILLIERS.   Lucky at cards, lucky in love, Monsieur
             Midgley.

MIDGLEY.   Lucky? After what you made me do?

BRINVILLIERS.   I know you will always look after my
               interests.
             That stupid man is quite incapable.
             I don't know how I've lived with him
               so long.
             If only I'd married a man like you.

SEVIGNE.   That poor man.
                        Quite incapable.

                        SAINTE-CROIX beckons LA CHAUSSEE *and
                        secretly gives him a card, which he takes to* EXILI.

SAINTE-CROIX (*to* MME SAINTE-CROIX). I've taught Exili
                        how to play hoca. Put your stake on eighteen.

                        She places her stake. Fifth game.

                        BRINVILLIERS *and* MARQUIS *quarrel.*

BRINVILLIERS.   Can't you stop?
                        This is my money.
                        Correct the cards.

MIDGLEY and SEVIGNE.
                        Extraordinary woman.

                        BRINVILLIERS *joins* SAINTE-CROIX.

                        MIDGLEY *is counting his winnings.*

SAINTE-CROIX. Have you been to the hospital?

BRINVILLIERS.   Twelve doses of weakest solution
                        Can't see or speak
                        The boy has a strong constitution
                        His skin shrivels, his eyes are hollow, his
                            teeth break like glass
                        But he won't die.
                        Venin de crapaud
                        Ruptoire that pierces
                        Hyoscine.

EXILI.   Rien ne va plus.

OTHERS.   Hoca.

EXILI.   Paying number eighteen.

                        MME SAINTE-CROIX *has won the fifth game.*

SEVIGNE and EXILI. The Marquis de Brinvilliers has lost
                        fifteen thousand.

                        SEVIGNE *joins* MIDGLEY *again while others
                        place bets for sixth game.*

SEVIGNE.   Sainte-Croix taught Exili to play hoca.

MIDGLEY.   How do you mean?

SEVIGNE.   And Exili taught Sainte-Croix . . .

MIDGLEY.   What? What?

SEVIGNE.   Signor Exili had to leave Italy.
                  He was employed by the great.

MIDGLEY.   To do what?

She whispers to him. (We hear BRINVILLIERS
who is still singing about poisons with SAINTE-
CROIX.)

SEVIGNE.   Didn't you know?

MIDGLEY.   I don't want to know.

SEVIGNE.   Didn't you know?

MIDGLEY.   Does she know?

SEVIGNE.   I warn you not to give way to her caresses.
                  They're full of danger.

MIDGLEY.   Yes I know. But I don't want to know. I'm
                  enchanted.

Meanwhile.

BRINVILLIERS.   Venin de crapaud
                  Ruptoire that pierces
                  Hyoscine.

EXILI.   Rien ne va plus.

OTHERS.   Hoca.

MME DE SAINTE-CROIX *wins the sixth game.*

SEVIGNE and EXILI. The Marquis de Brinvilliers has lost
                  twenty thousand.

BRINVILLIERS *attacks* MARQUIS *again, they
quarrel furiously. He is unsteady from being
poisoned.*

BRINVILLIERS.   This is my money . . . I was only seventeen
                  . . . your dissipation . . . any woman of
                  spirit . . . my own fortune . . . go on, lose
                  some more, faites vos jeux . . . rien ne va
                  plus.

Meanwhile SEVIGNE *is still warning* MIDGLEY.

SEVIGNE.   I warn you
                  Her caresses are full of danger.

MIDGLEY.   I don't want to know. I'm enchanted.

                  SAINTE-CROIX *seeing the* MARQUIS *has been
                  poisoned goes to* BRINVILLIERS.

SAINTE-CROIX. What have you given him?

BRINVILLIERS.   Venin de crapaud. A slow decline.
                  Beloved. Get rid of that plain girl and
                  marry me.

SAINTE-CROIX. Beloved.

BRINVILLIERS.   Beloved.

                  EXILI *has handed over the bank to* LA
                  CHAUSSEE *and come forward.* SAINTE-CROIX
                  goes to him.

SAINTE-CROIX. She's giving her husband poison. I don't want
                  to marry her. We've already had a long and terrible
                  life. Give me some antidote.

EXILI.   Theriac? Orvietu?

                  They give antidote to the MARQUIS.

                  The seventh game. MIDGLEY *goes to*
                  BRINVILLIERS.

MIDGLEY.   I'm staking all my winnings.

                  They both place bets. So do EXILI *and the*
                  MARQUIS. DUFAY *and* MME SAINTE-CROIX
                  dance wildly.

MIDGLEY.   Let me save you.
                  Let me take you away.

                  SAINTE-CROIX *and* EXILI *are fixing the game.*

SEVIGNE.   I warn you
                  Her caresses are full of danger.

BRINVILLIERS.   Save me?
                  It's I who have the power.
                  I poisoned my father,
                  A slow decline.
                  I poisoned my brothers.

MIDGLEY   (*meanwhile*). Please don't tell me.
                 Let me take you away.

BRINVILLIERS.   Save me?
                 Who's going to hurt me?
                 I killed my father
                 I killed my brothers
                 It's I who have the power

MIDGLEY   (*meanwhile*). Please don't tell me.
                 I'm enchanted.

ALL.   Hoca.

          LA CHAUSSEE *holds up the winning number.*

          Everyone moves onto the table.

          Disappointment, as all go 'Ahhh'.

          EXILI *has won all the money with the seventh
          game.*

SEVIGNE.   Exili won a fortune on one card.

          LA CHAUSSEE, SAINTE-CROIX *and* EXILI *are
          sharing out the money.* MMES SAINTE-CROIX,
          DUFAY *and* DE SEVIGNE *are preparing to go.*
          SEVIGNE *flirts with* EXILI *now that he has won.*

MIDGLEY.   I staked all my winnings and I lost.

EXILI.   Rien ne va plus.

          As they leave, BRINVILLIERS *takes* SAINTE-
          CROIX *aside.*

BRINVILLIERS.   I told him.

SAINTE-CROIX. Why?

BRINVILLIERS.   He adores me.

SAINTE-CROIX. Not enough. We'll have to get rid of him. Ask
          him to come to your room.

          SAINTE-CROIX *leaves.* BRINVILLIERS *and*
          MIDGLEY *are alone.*

BRINVILLIERS.   Come to my room at midnight.

BRINVILLIERS and MIDGLEY.
                 I'm in your power.

MIDGLEY *goes.*

BRINVILLIERS *stays as the scene changes to her bedroom.*

Assignation

SAINTE-CROIX *joins* BRINVILLIERS. *He brings her the box of poisons and then starts to spread a sheet.* MIDGLEY *watches them from above through a window.* SAINTE-CROIX *leads* BRINVILLIERS *to the bed, and taking a knife hides in the room.*

MIDGLEY.   Why? Why? Is he there to watch us
                         make love?
                     I know that should stop me but do I care?
                     Is he there to kill me?
                     Let me just see her and see if I stay
                         with her
                     Let me just breathe the same air.
                     Maybe I don't care if I die.

MIDGLEY *goes into* BRINVILLIERS' *room. She woos him but he is unresponsive.*

BRINVILLIERS.   Come in my sweet. Your hands are cold.
                     Why won't you look at me? You seem so
                     sad. You're the most extraordinary man. If
                     only I'd married a man like you.

They kiss. MIDGLEY *breaks away.*

MIDGLEY.   Why do you want to kill me?

BRINVILLIERS *catches him by the throat.*
SAINTE-CROIX *jumps out, scuffle,* SAINTE-CROIX *runs away.* BRINVILLIERS *rushes to the box and tries to take poison.* MIDGLEY *stops her. She wraps herself in the sheet.*

BRINVILLIERS.   I want to die.

They sit exhausted all night.

MIDGLEY.   Don't kill yourself.

BRINVILLIERS.   Don't leave me.

MIDGLEY.   Don't kill me.

BRINVILLIERS.   Don't betray me.

> *By the end* MIDGLEY *has moved to her and lies down beside her. She sleeps. He covers her with his coat. It is morning.*

Morning After

SAINTE-CROIX *comes in with a cup of coffee. He offers it to* MIDGLEY, *who shakes his head,* SAINTE-CROIX *takes a sip himself and offers it again to* MIDGLEY, *who drinks. They share the coffee while they talk.*

MIDGLEY.   How am I supposed to feel?

> SAINTE-CROIX *shrugs.*

You tried to kill me.

SAINTE-CROIX. That was last night.

MIDGLEY.   And what? This morning, what?

SAINTE-CROIX. You want me to stab you? You want me to cry and kiss you?

> *They drink some coffee.*

There's a middle-aged couple called Brunet, quite rich, musical, they get a famous flautist to play at their parties and Madame becomes his mistress. But, meanwhile, Monsieur is arranging for the musician to marry the daughter. Invitations go out, Madame's wild with jealousy, and she poisons her husband. So what should the young man do? Everyone advises him to switch brides and marry the widow, he gets rich quicker, and the king was at the wedding.

You know Madame de Dreux? Wife of the politician? She's not 30 and she's poisoned three lovers. She did get caught but she just got a little fine and society finds her divinely amusing. Women won't sit next to her latest lover at dinner in case he smiles at them.

MIDGLEY.   Don't people get punished?

SAINTE-CROIX.   Only if you've no connections. And I'll tell
                you another funny thing, the executioner is reliably
                reported to have poisoned his own wife. Come on,
                Midgley. And it's not just love affairs. The whole
                political life of the country depends on poison.
                Richelieu kept cats to smell his food. Colbert is
                constantly ill. Everyone in public life drinks
                antidote every morning. So of course it's a
                constant challenge. Exili and I are working on
                something imperceptible, one breath is fatal.
                People want this, Midgley, we've buyers all over
                Europe. We'll make a fortune.

MIDGLEY.   No.

SAINTE-CROIX.   I don't want to kill you, Midgley. If you can't
                be friends you'd better go away.

MIDGLEY.   I keep thinking I should go home. I could be on a
            ship. But I can't leave her.

SAINTE-CROIX.   Then you're in it with us, aren't you? Don't
                worry. Everything's pointless anyway. People are
                vile. Death doesn't matter.

MIDGLEY.   I'm in love.

            They sit in silence.

            I can't keep awake. Did you give me something?

SAINTE-CROIX. No, you're tired.

MIDGLEY.   It's delicious.

            MIDGLEY *sleeps.*

Breakfast

SAINTE-CROIX *carefully wakes* BRINVILLIERS *and gives
her coffee.*

BRINVILLIERS.   I thought you'd run away.

SAINTE-CROIX. You wish I'd killed him?

BRINVILLIERS.   If someone looks at you, you run away.

SAINTE-CROIX. You want me to kill him?

BRINVILLIERS.   I wish I was waking up into a day that
                 wasn't already spoiled.

SAINTE-CROIX. You started this.

BRINVILLIERS.   You taught me poison.

SAINTE-CROIX. You told me who to kill.

BRINVILLIERS.   We killed them for you.

SAINTE-CROIX. So you could get money.

BRINVILLIERS.   So you could get my money.

SAINTE-CROIX. And for revenge.

        Pause.

BRINVILLIERS.   Do you love me?

SAINTE-CROIX. Why ask?

        Pause.

SAINTE-CROIX. On the one hand you're sick of what we do.
             On the other hand you're trying to kill your
             husband.

BRINVILLIERS.   You gave him antidote to save him.

SAINTE-CROIX. I won't marry you.

        Pause.

BRINVILLIERS.   I've been giving you poison too.

SAINTE-CROIX. I told you you hated me.

BRINVILLIERS.   It may be to kill you. It may just be to
                 reach inside your body.

        Pause.

SAINTE-CROIX. Do you think I didn't know? I'm hard to
             poison, I know the antidotes. And why do you
             think you feel so ill and sad? Remorse? A little
             drop of remorse in your coffee.

BRINVILLIERS.   I know what you give me. I can save
                 myself. I know everything you know.

SAINTE-CROIX. Do we go on like this till we die of old age?

BRINVILLIERS.   I wish I could wake up.

> *They sit in silence.*

> SAINTE-CROIX *gets up.*

BRINVILLIERS.   Where are you going?

SAINTE-CROIX. To work.

BRINVILLIERS.   I feel worse when I'm alone.

> SAINTE-CROIX *goes.*

Death of Sainte-Croix

SAINTE-CROIX *goes off and appears above in laboratory. MME SAINTE-CROIX comes to him and they embrace; BRINVILLIERS sees them and leaves. SAINTE-CROIX puts on glass mask and starts to work. The two dancing POISONS appear. One of them takes off his mask and the other breathes into his mouth, poisoning him. He staggers out of the laboratory breathing painfully and noisily, while they watch. While grabbing the box to find an antidote he collapses on the floor. MME SAINTE-CROIX runs in and he dies at her feet.*

The Casket

MME DE BRINVILLIERS *arrives to confront MME SAINTE-CROIX. MME SAINTE-CROIX won't give up the casket (box of poisons). DESGREZ arrives, discovers the body and the casket and examines the blood on the wall, the knife and the sheet.*

BRINVILLIERS.   I've come to offer my condolences on your husband's unfortunate accident. I've come to collect a casket which is my property and concerns me alone.

DESGREZ.   Mysterious circumstances
Impound all documents
Everything is in the custody of the law.

MIDGLEY *wakes up and sees* SAINTE-CROIX'
stiff body being taken away by LA CHAUSSEE.
SEVIGNE *and* DUFAY *arrive.*

MIDGLEY.   My poor friend.

SEVIGNE.   Another scandal.

MME SAINTE-CROIX *gives the casket to*
DESGREZ. *He opens the casket and takes out
what he finds.*

DESGREZ.   Letters.
                   A number of powders, liquid clear
                       as water.
                   Letters from Madame de Brinvilliers.

DUFAY *and* SEVIGNE *are reading the letters
while* LA CHAUSSEE *returns to hide
incriminating evidence from the casket. The
Marquis appears above and walks across the top
wall, then sits and watches.* MIDGLEY *is trying to
intervene with* DESGREZ.

BRINVILLIERS.   Whose powders? Not mine.

SEVIGNE.   Another scandal.

MIDGLEY.   There's been a mistake.

DESGREZ.   Corrosive sublimate, vitriol, antimony.
                   A casket of poisons.
                   Your property. The casket concerns you
                       alone.

DESGREZ *arrests* BRINVILLIERS. *She says
nothing.*

DESGREZ and SEVIGNE.
                   Everything points to her guilt.

MIDGLEY   (*to* DESGREZ). I'm sure she's innocent.
                   (*To* BRINVILLIERS.) Let me save you. Let
                   me take you away. We could be on a ship.

DESGREZ'S ASSISTANT *administers water
torture to* BRINVILLIERS. *He forces her to drink
water out of a jug. The movement is reminiscent of*
MEDEA *pouring potion into* AESON's *throat.*
MIDGLEY *tries unsuccessfully to prevent it.*

DESGREZ.   What do you know?

MIDGLEY.   I'll tell you what I know.
                  I don't know what I know.
                  There's been a mistake.

SEVIGNE.   Madame Dreux killed three lovers.
                  The king's mistress is a poisoner.
                  Divinely amusing.
                  Why with so many guilty is she the only
                      one to suffer?

The Confession

BRINVILLIERS.   I accuse myself of giving poison.
                  I accuse myself of having given poison to a
                  woman who wanted to poison her husband.
                  I accuse myself that I did not honour my
                  father and did not show him respect.

                  MME SAINTE-CROIX *does a slow dance of
                  triumph.* MARQUIS DE BRINVILLIERS *comes
                  in during this.*

BRINVILLIERS.   I accuse myself of having caused general
                  scandal.
                  I accuse myself of having ruined myself
                  with a man already married and of having
                  given him much money.
                  I accuse myself that this man was the
                  father of two of my children.
                  I accuse myself of having poisoned my
                  father. A servant gave him the poison.
                  I had my two brothers poisoned and the
                  servant was broken on the wheel.
                  I accuse myself of having taken poison and
                  also of giving some to one of my children.
                  I accuse myself of setting fire to a house.

                  I have forgotten.
                  I know nothing about it.
                  I know nothing at all.
                  I know nothing.
                  I do not remember.
                  I do not know.

*MME SAINTE-CROIX has placed the casket to
be the chopping block. DESGREZ, DE SEVIGNE,
DUFAY and MARQUIS DE BRINVILLIERS take
the sheet and drape it over the chopping block.*

Brinvillier's Death

*In silence, BRINVILLIERS lays her head on the block.
DESGREZ'S ASSISTANT takes the knife and places it on
BRINVILLIERS' neck. As he raises it, she falls off the back of
the floor.*

*As SEVIGNE starts to sing, the cloth and casket are removed.
SAINTE-CROIX comes in carrying a tray of coffee and
amaretti, which he serves to everybody. People unwrap their
amaretti and roll up the papers and SAINTE-CROIX sets fire
to them so that the burning paper floats up into the air and the
ash floats down.*

SEVIGNE.   O nuit désastreuse, o nuit effroyable, où
              retentit tout à coup comme un éclat de
              tonnerre cette étonnante nouvelle: Madame
              se meurt, madame est morte.
              After the execution her body was thrown
              into the fire.
              Her head cut off, her body burnt, her ashes
              scattered to the winds.

MIDGLEY.   I can't keep my mind from the horror.

DESGREZ.   She can't be in paradise.
              Her dreadful soul must be kept apart.

SEVIGNE.   The mob are searching for her bones.
              They think she's a saint.

              She is in the air. Her body burnt, her ashes
              scattered to the winds. Now we all breathe
              her in so we'll all catch a mania for
              poisoning which will astonish us.

SEVIGNE and MIDGLEY.
              She's in the air.

DESGREZ.   Her dreadful soul.

*BRINVILLIERS appears above at the side as
SAINT-CROIX goes off. He appears above at the
back and lights his own amaretti paper.*

BRINVILLIERS. I set fire to a house. I poisoned my father,
I poisoned my brothers, I myself took
poison. I do not remember. I do not know.

*As MIDGLEY sings, the four dancers do a happy
inventive dance watched by SAINTE-CROIX,
drinking coffee, and BRINVILLIERS who repeats
her song.*

MIDGLEY. Grief makes it hard to think. But I do have
the glimmering of an idea. To control the
growth of crops by increasing the ozone in
the earth's atmosphere.

DESGREZ. Her dreadful soul

SEVIGNE. She's in the air.

MIDGLEY. Increase the ozone.

BRINVILLIERS. I do not know.

*As the dance and song end, the dancers turn
upstage and join hands with MIDGLEY,
DE SEVIGNE and DESGREZ.*

THE SKRIKER

The Skriker was first performed in the Cottesloe auditorium of the Royal National Theatre, London, on 20 January 1994 with the following cast.

THE SKRIKER	Kathryn Hunter
JOSIE	Sandy McDade
LILY	Jacqueline Defferary
PASSERBY	Desiree Cherrington
YALLERY BROWN	Don Campbell
BLACK DOG	Brian Lipson
KELPIE / FAIR FAIRY	Philippe Giraudeau
GREEN LADY / JENNIE GREENTEETH	Lucy Bethune
GIRL WITH TELESCOPE / LOST GIRL	Melanie Pappenheim
HAG / WOMAN WITH KELPIE	Mary King
BOGLE / RAWHEADANDBLOODYBONES / DARK FAIRY	Stephen Goff
BROWNIE / RADIANT BOY	Richard Katz
MAN WITH BUCKET / NELLIE LONGARMS	Stephen Ley
SPRIGGAN	Robbie Barnett
GRANDDAUGHTER / BLACK ANNIS	Diana Payne Myers
GREAT-GREAT-GRANDDAUGHTER / DEAD CHILD	Sarah Shanson

Director   Les Waters
Designer   Annie Smart
Music   Judith Weir
Movement   Ian Spink
Lighting   Christopher Toulmin

Judith Weir's music is available from Chester Music, Music Sales Ltd, 8-9 Frith Street, London W1V 5TZ.

242

Characters

THE SKRIKER
JOSIE
LILY

JOSIE *and* LILY *are in their late teens*

JOHNNY SQUAREFOOT
THE KELPIE
MAN WITH CLOTH AND BUCKET
YALLERYBROWN
PASSERBY
GIRL WITH TELESCOPE
GREEN LADY
BOGLE
SPRIGGAN
WOMAN WITH KELPIE
BROWNIE
DEAD CHILD
FAIR FAIRY
DARK FAIRY
RAWHEADANDBLOODYBONES
BLACK DOG
NELLIE LONGARMS
JENNIE GREENTEETH
BLACK ANNIS
HAG
LOST GIRL
BUSINESSMEN
THRUMPINS
BLUE MEN
PICNIC FAMILY

GRANDDAUGHTER
GREAT-GREAT-GRANDDAUGHTER

Underworld.

JOHNNY SQUAREFOOT, *a giant riding on a piglike man,*
throwing stones. He goes off.

The SKRIKER, *a shapeshifter and death portent, ancient and*
damaged.

SKRIKER.   Heard her boast beast a roast beef eater, daughter
could spin span spick and spun the lowest form of
wheat straw into gold, raw into roar, golden lion
and lyonesse under the sea, dungeonesse under the
castle for bad mad sad adders and takers away.
Never marry a king size well beloved. Chop chip
pan chap finger chirrup chirrup cheer up off with
you're making no headway. Weeps seeps deeps her
pretty puffy cream cake hole in the heart operation.
Sees a little blackjack thingalingo with a long long
tale awinding. May day, she cries, may pole axed
me to help her. So I spin the sheaves shoves
shivers into golden guild and geld and if she can't
guessing game and safety match my name then I'll
take her no mistake no mister no missed her no
mist no miss no me no. Is it William Gwylliam
Guillaume? Is it John Jack the ladder in your
stocking is it Joke? Is it Alexander Sandro Andrew
Drewsteignton? Mephistopheles Toffeenose
Tiffany's Timpany Timothy Mossycoat? No
't ain't, says I, no tainted meat me after the show
me what you've got. Then pointing her finger says
Tom tit tot! Tomtom tiny tot blue tit tit! Out of her
pinkle lippety loppety, out of her mouthtrap, out
came my secreted garden flower of my youth and
beauty and the beast is six six six o'clock in the
morning becomes electric stormy petrel bomb.
Shriek! shrink! shuck off to a shack, sick, soak,
seek a sleep slope slap of the dark to shelter skelter
away, a wail a whirl a world away.

Slit slat slut. That bitch a botch an itch in my
shoulder blood. Bitch botch itch. Slat itch slit
botch. Itch slut bitch slit.

Put my hand to the baby and scissors seizures seize you sizzle. Metal cross cross me out cross my heartburn sunburn sunbeam in my eyelash your back. Or garlic lickety split me in two with the stink bombastic. Or pin prick cockadoodle do you feel it? But if the baby has no name better nick a name, better Old Nick than no name, because then we can have the snap crackle poppet to bake and brew and broody more babies and leave them an impossible, a gobbling, a no.

I've been a hairy here he is changeling changing chainsaw massacre massive a sieve to carry water from the well well what's to be done? Brother brewed beer in an eggshell. I said I'm old old every so olden dazed but I never see saw marjory before three two one blast off!

Put me on a red hot shovel pushel bushel and a peck peck peck. Gave me red hot metal in a piping hot metal in a pie ping pong what a stink. Call the vicar to exorcise exercise regular sex a size larger six or seventh heaven and hellcat.

Chopped up the hag whole hog higgledy pig in the middle. Kelpie gallops them into the loch stock and barrel of fun fair enough and eats them, falls out of the water into love with a ladylike, his head in her lap lap lap, her hand in his hairy, there is sand in it there is and there is sand and shells shock. Bloody Bones hides in the dark dark dark we all go into the dark cupboard love all. See through the slit where he sits on piles of bloody boney was a warrior and chews whom he likes. Dollop gollop fullup.

But they're so fair fairy fair enough's as good as a feast day. Take them by the handle and dance in the fairy ring a ring ding sweet for a year and a day date data dated her and never finished the first reel first real dance in the fairy ring on your finger and bluebell would wouldn't it. Their friends drag 'em out dragon laying the country waste of time gentlemen. Listless and pale beyond the pale moonlight of heart sore her with spirits with spirit dancing the night away in a mangy no no no come back again.

Eating a plum in the enchanted orchard, cherry orchid, chanted orchestra was my undoing my doing my dying my undying love for you. Never eat a fruit or puck luck pluck a flower if you want to get back get your own back get back to your own back to the wall flower.

When did they do what they're told tolled a bell a knell, well ding dong pussy's in. Tell them one thing not to do, thing to rue won't they do it, boo hoo's afraid of the pig bag. Open bluebeard's one bloody chamber maid, eat the one forbidden fruit of the tree top down comes cradle and baby. Don't put your hand in the fountain pen and ink blot your copy catching fishes eyes and gluesniffer. So he puts his hand in and wail whale moby dictated the outcome into the garden maudlin. Everything gone with the window cleaner.

Don't get this ointment disappointment in your eyes I say to the mortal middlewife but of course she does and the splendoured thing palace picture palace winter policeman's ball suddenly blurred visionary missionary mishmash potato, and there was a mud hit mad hut and the mother a murder in rags tags and bob's your uncle and the baby a wrinkly crinkly crackerjack of all trading places, because of course it was all a glamour amour amorphous fuss about nothing. But she never lets on so she gets home safe and sound the trumpet. But one day I'm in the market with b and put it in the oven helping myself and she sees me and says how's your wife waif and stray how's the baby? And I say what eye do you seize me with? This eye high diddley, she says. So I point my finger a thing at her and strike her blind alley cat o' nine tails.

Serve her right as raining cats and dogshit. Whatever you do don't open the do don't open the door.

I got a sweet sucker sweet till it melts in your mouth. Watched the bride a cock horse in her white lace curtain up trip through the grieve grove graveyard rosy and honeysuckle on her daddy's armour, lurked and looked till the groom for one

moribund strode up the pathtime. Hold this candle
the scandal I said, and he stood till it gutterbed and
went out. Then. What? No wedding party frock! no
broad no breed! no family life jacket potato, no
friends in need you ask! A hungered yours hundred
years later. And a bit a bite a bitter bread and he
was crumbs crumbling to dust panic.

Better forget them, not always be talking stalking
walking working them over and understand still.
Yes better forgotten rotten leaves them alone. We
don't need the knock kneed knead the dough re mi
fa away so there la di da. Never think shrink so
small about them at all a tall dark stranger than
friction. Then stop cockadoodle if you cancan.

They used to leave cream in a sorcerer's
apprentice. Gave the brownie a pair of trousers to
wear have you gone? Now they hate us and hurt
hurtle faster and master. They poison me in my
rivers of blood poisoning makes my arm swelter.
Can't get them out of our head strong.

Then get in their head body and tailor maiden has
a perfect fit a frit a fright a frying tonight jar.

We'll be under the bedrock a bye and by. We'll
follow you on the dark road at nightingale
blowing. No but they're danger thin ice pick in
your head long ago away. Blood run cold comfort
me with apple pie. Roast cats alive alive oh dear
what can the matterhorn piping down the valley
wild horses wouldn't drag me.

Revengeance is gold mine, sweet. Fe fi fo
fumbledown cottage pie crust my heart and hope
to die. My mother she killed me and put me in pies
for sale away and home and awayday. Peck out her
eyes have it. I'll give you three wishy washy. An
open grave must be fed up you go like dust in the
sunlight of heart. Gobble gobble says the turkey
turnkey key to my heart, gobbledegook de gook is
after you. Ready or not here we come quick or
dead of night night sleep tightarse.

LILY *is visiting* JOSIE *in mental hospital.* LILY *is pregnant.*
Also there is the KELPIE, *part young man, part horse.*

JOSIE.   I've a pain in my shoulder. I never used to have
          that did I. It's one of the things they give me here.

LILY.   I don't remember.

          Pause.

          Shall / I rub it?

JOSIE.   The food's not healthy. They put two things the
          same colour like white fish and mash potato.

LILY.   I could bring something in.

JOSIE.   I'm here to be punished.

LILY.   No, you were ill.

JOSIE.   Yes and I'm better now so can I come home with
          you?

LILY.   I don't think they'd let you.

JOSIE.   They will / if you ask.

LILY.   I don't think so.

          Pause.

JOSIE.   They will if you say you'll be responsible but you
          don't want to / be, do you.

LILY.   They wouldn't anyway.

JOSIE.   I don't blame you.

          Pause.

LILY.   All right, I will. I'll ask when I see the nurse. I'd
          love to take you out of here, Josie. I'd love it if I
          had a place of my own to take you and look after
          you, I'd love it.

JOSIE.   Why?

LILY.   Wouldn't you?

JOSIE.   I wouldn't love it, no. I'd do it.

          Pause.

LILY.   Have you made any friends here?

JOSIE.   I don't think so.

LILY.   What are the nurses like?

JOSIE.   I haven't noticed.

LILY.   Do they do things to you? I won't ask if you don't
          want. Like electrocute you. Or put you in a padded
          / cell or –

JOSIE.   They give me pills.

LILY.   What sort? what you got?

JOSIE.   That what you come for?

LILY.   No but if you / got some –

JOSIE.   I haven't got them, they've / got them.

LILY.   Take more when they're not looking, bring a whole
          lot out, be a laugh.

JOSIE.   You've no idea.

LILY.   What? what have I no idea?

          Pause.

          Nurse.

JOSIE.   No.

LILY.   What? Nurse.

JOSIE.   No.

LILY.   Don't you want to?

          Pause.

          Was she being naughty?

JOSIE.   You can't be naughty, a ten day old baby, can you.
          You really don't know anything / about

LILY.   I just meant she might have annoyed you.

JOSIE.   it. What can a ten day old baby do that's naughty?

LILY.   Like crying or – I don't know.

JOSIE.   You wouldn't kill a baby because it annoyed you,
          would you.

LILY.   I don't know.

JOSIE.	Would *you*?
LILY.	I don't know. You tell me.
JOSIE.	Of course you wouldn't.

Pause.

LILY.	Was it difficult?

Pause.

JOSIE.	Licence to kill, seems to me.
LILY.	You're in here.
JOSIE.	They don't hang you.
LILY.	They don't hang anyone.
JOSIE.	It should have been me that died.
LILY.	No, why?

Pause.

It's nicer here than I expected. The garden.

JOSIE.	You're thinking of going home.
LILY.	Not right away, no, but –
JOSIE.	Don't.
LILY.	I'm not.
JOSIE.	Take me with you.
LILY.	Josie, listen. I'm going to run away. But I'll write and tell you where I am, all right? I'm going to London.
JOSIE.	I won't hurt your baby.
LILY.	Of course not, I don't think that.
JOSIE.	If you'd got any sense you would. But you'd be wrong.

Pause.

Are you going then?

LILY.	No.

Pause.

JOSIE.   Wait till I tell you something.

Pause.

I thought it was a patient because if you saw them you'd know what I mean, there's some of them I'm nothing compared. You'd think I was worse because I've done something but some of them think they're someone else and I do know . . . What was I saying?

LILY.   You thought someone was / a patient.

JOSIE.   Yes but she's hundreds of years old. And then I was impressed by the magic but now I think there's something wrong with her.

LILY.   When you say hundreds of years old, you mean like eighty?

JOSIE.   She looks about fifty but she's I don't know maybe five hundred a million, I don't know how old these things are.

LILY.   When you say magic?

JOSIE.   I thought maybe she could go home with you.

LILY.   Josie, you'll be coming out soon. It's better to wait till they say.

JOSIE.   She'd like me to wish the baby back but I won't because she'd make it horrible.

LILY.   How do you know she's not a patient who just thinks she's . . .

Pause.

JOSIE.   Rub my shoulder.

LILY *rubs* JOSIE's *shoulder.*

LILY.   When I get to the front gate is it left or right to the bus?

She goes on rubbing her shoulder. She stops.

All right?

JOSIE *doesn't reply.*

LILY.   Josie?

LILY goes. WOMAN about 50 approaches.
Dowdy, cardigan, could be a patient. It is the
SKRIKER.

SKRIKER.   I heard that.

JOSIE.   What?

SKRIKER.   You don't like me.

JOSIE.   I'm thinking what you'd enjoy and you'd like her
            better than me. She's stronger, she's more fun. I'm
            ill and I think you're ill and I / don't think –

SKRIKER.   You don't want me.

JOSIE.   She'll have a baby and you'll like that.

SKRIKER.   Please, please keep me.

            Pause.

            I'll give you a wish.

JOSIE.   I don't want a wish.

SKRIKER.   I'll be nice.

JOSIE.   It's cold all round you.

SKRIKER.   I can get you out of here. Just say.

JOSIE.   No. Where to? No.

SKRIKER.   Josie.

JOSIE.   All right, I'll have a wish.

SKRIKER.   Yes? Wish.

JOSIE.   I wish you'd have her instead of me.

            Pause. SKRIKER *turns away.*

            Wait. I don't mind you any more.

SKRIKER.   No, I'm not after you.

JOSIE.   You won't hurt her? What do you want from her?

            SKRIKER *starts to go. A* MAN *comes in carrying*
            a white cloth and a bucket of water.

            Oh but I'll miss you now.

            SKRIKER *goes.*

The MAN *spreads the cloth on the floor and
stands the bucket of water on it. He waits.
He isn't satisfied. He picks up the cloth and
bucket and walks about looking for a better spot.*

Meanwhile the KELPIE *goes.*

YALLERY BROWN *is playing music.*

The MAN *puts the cloth and bucket down in
another place. A derelict woman is shouting in the
street. It is the* SKRIKER.

A PASSERBY *comes along the street, throws
down a coin, and then starts to dance to the music.*

LILY *comes along the street.*

SKRIKER.   What's the wires coming out of your head for?

Collecting his brain in a box, mind you don't lose
it. You've got a dead pig on your back.

She falls down in front of LILY. LILY *helps her up.*

Can you help a poor old lady, lost my bus pass,
price of a cup of tea, you've got a kind face
darling, give you the white heather another time.

LILY *gives her money and starts to go away but*
SKRIKER *holds her.*

The MAN *puts the cloth and bucket down in a new
place.*

Do I smell? It's my coat and my cunt. Give us a
hug. Nobody gives us a hug. Give us a kiss. Won't
you give us a hug and a kiss.

LILY *suddenly hugs and kisses her.*

There's a love. Off you go, Lily.

SKRIKER *goes.*

The MAN *is satisfied with the position of cloth and
bucket and goes off without them.*

LILY.   How do you know my name? – What? what's
happening? my teeth. I'm sick. Help me. What is
it? It's money. Is it? Out of my mouth?

*Pound coins come out of her mouth when she
speaks. She stops talking and examines the money.*

A YOUNG GIRL *is looking through a telescope.*

LILY *speaks carefully, testing.*

When I speak, does money come out of my mouth? Yes.

Through the telescope THE GIRL *sees a* GREEN LADY *dancing with a* BOGLE.

The PASSERBY *goes on dancing.*

LILY *goes.*

A YOUNG MAN, *who is a* BROWNIE, *comes in and starts sweeping and cleaning.*

The GREEN LADY *and* BOGLE *disappear when the girl looks away from the telescope. The* GIRL *looks again but they don't reappear. The* GIRL *goes.*

The PASSERBY *never stops dancing.*

SKRIKER *tells* LILY*'s story.*

SKRIKER.   So lily in the pink with a finnyanny border was talking good as gold speaking pound coins round coins pouring roaring more and more, singing thinging counting saying the alphabetter than nothing telling stories more stories boring sore throat saw no end to it fuckit buckets and buckets of bloodmoney is the root of evil eye nose the smell hell the taste waste of money got honey to swallow to please ease the sore throat so could keep on talking taking aching waking all night to reach retch wrench more and more and more on the floor on the bed of a hotel tell me another not another wish it would stop stop talking now and sleep at last fast asleep and woke to find she can eek peak speak can I speak without can I without and about now changing the cash dash flash in the panic of time. And now in the hotel bar none but the brave deserve a drink I think for lily the

LILY *at a bar talking to an American woman of about 40 who is slightly drunk. It is the* SKRIKER. *There is a TV.*

There is a SPRIGGAN, *grotesquely ugly and ten foot tall, who is invisible to* LILY, *having a drink.*

Later the **KELPIE** *arrives. Then a* **WOMAN** *who drinks with the* **KELPIE.**

The **BROWNIE** *goes on cleaning. Later he finishes work and goes down on his hands and knees to lap a saucer of milk, then goes.*

SKRIKER.   So how does this work?

LILY.   How?

SKRIKER.   How does it –

LILY.   You want to turn it off?

SKRIKER.   No, how does that picture get here. From wherever.

LILY.   How does it *work?*

SKRIKER.   Yes.

LILY.   Oh you know, I don't know, you know, it's – isn't it the same in America?

SKRIKER.   Take your time. In your own words.

LILY.   It has to be plugged in so it's got power, right, electricity, so it's on so you can turn it on when you press the button, so the light's on and that shows it's on, ok?

SKRIKER.   But what's / the electricity – ?

LILY.   It's got all these tubes / and anyway –

SKRIKER.   No how do you see / all over the world?

LILY.   And meanwhile, let's say this is something live we're seeing, there's a camera there pointing at the picture at the thing that is the picture, camera, you want me to explain – the light gets in and there's the film, tape, the tape, it picks up the light somehow and it gets the picture *on* it, don't ask me, and there you are if it was a tape like you hire a tape down the video shop / that's it, they

SKRIKER.   No, tell me.

LILY.   make a whole lot of copies.

SKRIKER.   It's happening *there* and it's / *here.*

LILY.   I'm telling you, hang about, how it gets sent, I can't quite, through the air, if it's live, or even if

it's not of course, if it happened before and they
recorded – say it's live, it's coming – not the whole
picture in the air obviously, it's in bits like waves
like specks and you need an aerial / to

SKRIKER. This is crap.

LILY. catch it and this changes it back into the picture /
and it's not a solid thing, it's all dots

SKRIKER. But how for fuck's sake?

LILY. and lines if you look, I can't help it. If it's on the
other side of the world they bounce it off a satellite
yes I'm explaining satellite which is a thing a
thing they put up in space ok, they put it up I'm
explaining that too and it's going round like a star,
stars don't go round, like a moon but it looks like
a star but moving about you sometimes see it at
night, and it bounces off the satellite / all right –

SKRIKER. What bounces off?

LILY. The picture.

SKRIKER. The picture bounces off?

LILY. The waves, the – what is this?

SKRIKER. You're holding out on me.

LILY. I don't have all the technical if you want the jargon
if you want the detail you'll have to ask someone
else.

SKRIKER. Don't fuck with me.

LILY. Look, / that's all I –

SKRIKER. And flying. I suppose / you don't know

LILY. What?

SKRIKER. how you fly? / And the massive explosions that –

LILY. I don't fly.

SKRIKER. No idea, huh? Never fly, never flown / across the
sea –

LILY. Fly you mean go in a plane no but even if I had / I
wouldn't –

SKRIKER.   Or how you make poisons?

LILY.   What?

SKRIKER.   You people are killing me, do you know that? I am
sick, I am a sick woman. Keep your secrets, I'll
find out some other way, I don't need to know
these things, there are plenty of other things
to know. Just so long as you know I'm dying,
I hope that satisfies you to know I'm in pain.

LILY.   Are you ill? Can I help? / Can I get something?

SKRIKER.   No no no, forget it. Really.

LILY.   You're in pain?

SKRIKER.   Not at all, no, I'm just fine, forget it. I don't have
much aptitude for science. I guess you don't either.
No big deal. We can just watch what comes over.

Pause.

LILY.   You feel all right?

SKRIKER.   You are a sweet girl. You are just such a sweet girl.

Pause.

Running away from home is a great start. I did it
myself. It can get to be a habit. You keeping the
baby?

LILY.   Yes of course.

SKRIKER.   Because I'm looking for one, no I'm kidding.
Look at it floating in the dark with its pretty empty
head upside down, not knowing what's waiting for
it. It's been so busy doubling doubling and now it's
just hovering nicely decorating itself with hair and
toenails. But once it's born it starts again, double
double, but this time the mind, think of the energy
in that. Maybe I could be the godmother.

LILY.   You're staying in London?

SKRIKER.   Do you have friends in London?

LILY.   No but –

SKRIKER.   You now have one friend in London. And I have
one friend in London. ok? Not ok?

LILY. Yes yes I do want to be friends. I just –

Pause.

SKRIKER. Anyone would think you were frightened of me. I'm frightened of you.

LILY. You're the one Josie said.

SKRIKER. But I want to be friends.

LILY. Why am I frightening?

SKRIKER. Lily, I'll level with you, ok? You ready for this? I am an ancient fairy, I am hundreds of years old as you people would work it out, I have been around through all the stuff you would call history, that's cavaliers and roundheads, Henry the eighth, 1066 and before that, back when the Saxons feasted, the Danes invaded, the Celts hunted, you know about any of this stuff? Alfred and the cakes, Arthur and the table, long before that, long before England was an idea, a country of snow and wolves where trees sang and birds talked and people knew we mattered, I don't to be honest remember such a time but I like to think it was so, it should have been, I need to think it, don't contradict me please. That's what I am, one of many, not a major spirit but a spirit.

LILY. And why are you here?

SKRIKER. I am here to do good. I am good. You look as if you doubt that.

LILY. No, of course not.

SKRIKER. I am a good fairy.

LILY. You do good magic?

SKRIKER. That's exactly what I do.

LILY. And you'll do it for me?

SKRIKER. Where do you think your money comes from?

LILY. I'm not ungrateful.

SKRIKER. You're the one I've chosen out of everyone in the world.

LILY.   Why?

SKRIKER.   Because you're beautiful and good. Don't you
            think you are? Yes everyone sometimes thinks
            they're beautiful and good and deserve better than
            this and so they do. Are you telling me I made a
            mistake? I'd be sorry to think I'd made a mistake.

LILY.   No. No I'm glad.

SKRIKER.   And you accept?

LILY.   What?

SKRIKER.   Accept my offer. Accept my help.

LILY.   Yes. I think – what offer?

SKRIKER.   My help.

LILY.   Do I have to do something?

SKRIKER.   Just accept my help, sweetheart.

            Pause.

LILY.   No, I . . . It's very kind of you but . . . I don't like
            to say no but . . .

SKRIKER.   You might as well say yes. You can't get rid of me.

LILY.   No.

SKRIKER.   Who the fuck do you think you are?

            Pause.

            Whatever you say.

LILY.   You should have stayed with Josie. She's braver
            than me.

SKRIKER.   She wished I'd go with you.

LILY.   Did she? I wish she'd come and help me then.

SKRIKER.   That's the way. You'll begin to get a taste for it.

LILY.   For what?

SKRIKER.   Wishes.

LILY.   I didn't –

SKRIKER.   Yes.

Pause.

Tell me how the TV works and I'll trade.

LILY.　　　I don't know how the TV works.

SKRIKER.　Would you like a ring that when you look at the stone you can tell if your loved one is faithful?

LILY.　　　I don't have a loved one.

SKRIKER.　I can fix that, no problem. Just tell me how / the TV –

LILY.　　　I don't know how the TV works.

LILY goes.

The WOMAN *gets on the* KELPIE's *back and rides off.*

SPRIGGAN *goes.* SKRIKER *goes.*

The MAN *comes back to his bucket and cloth. He skims a gold film off the top of the water in the bucket which he makes into a cake. He puts the cake on the cloth, draws a circle around it and sits down to wait. The* PASSERBY *is still dancing.*

A DEAD CHILD sings.

DEAD CHILD.

　　　My mother she killed me and put me in pies
　　　My father he ate me and said I was nice
　　　My brothers and sisters they picked my bones
　　　And they buried me under the marley stones.

Derelict WOMAN *muttering and shouting in the street. It is the* SKRIKER. JOSIE *comes by.*

SKRIKER.　I know my son is writing me letters all the time and the army is stopping them because the officers are devils and do what you tell them because they are DEVILS and the letters are in sacks in the Bank of England waiting for the Day of Judgment when you will go to HELL and lose sight of me and stop moving me about but you can't move me now because my fingers are just so because I'm in charge of the devils and if I keep it up the devils will let my son go LET MY SON GO. What are you staring at?

JOSIE. You.

SKRIKER. Can you spare the price of a cup of / tea darling

JOSIE. No.

SKRIKER. because I haven't eaten all day, bless you for a sweet kind face. / I haven't eaten today but never

JOSIE. I said no.

SKRIKER. mind if you've no money my darling, that happens to all of us, just give me a kiss instead. Won't you give me / a kiss sweetheart?

JOSIE. Get off, you stinking crazy –

SKRIKER. You're a nasty girl, Josie, always were.

SKRIKER goes.

JOSIE. Is it you, come back, you – What? uh uh I'm sick, what, it's alive, it's – it's toads is it, where from, me is it, what?

As she speaks toads come out of her mouth. She speaks carefully, testing.

When I speak, do toads – ?

They do.

She opens her mouth to cry out in rage after SKRIKER, and shuts it, forcing herself to be silent to prevent more toads. She goes.

A FAIR FAIRY comes and tries to pick up the cake, the MAN won't let her have it, she goes. He sits waiting. The PASSERBY is still dancing.

JOSIE and LILY are sitting on a sofa. LILY is wrapped in a blanket. The SKRIKER is part of the sofa, invisible to them.

During this, a DARK FAIRY tries unsuccessfully to get the cake.

JOSIE. So you think it was just her got me out?

LILY. Because I wished it.

JOSIE. No I'm better, that's why.

LILY. And they bought you a train ticket?

JOSIE.	They do that when they discharge you from hospital.
LILY.	And how did you bump into me in the street?
JOSIE.	Because I'm lucky.
	Pause.
JOSIE.	Aren't you glad to see me?
LILY.	I don't feel very well. Is it cold in here?
JOSIE.	No, it's fine.
LILY.	I'm freezing.
JOSIE.	You must be ill then.
LILY.	Yes, I think I am.
JOSIE.	Or that could be her.
	Pause.
LILY.	What could?
JOSIE.	She's cold.
LILY.	I'm cold because I'm ill, all right?
JOSIE.	All right.
	Pause.
JOSIE.	Toads. She thinks she's funny. She's got it coming.
	Pause.
LILY.	Don't you think it's sad . . .
JOSIE.	What?
	Pause.
LILY.	I think I'm fainting.
	Pause. LILY *touches* SKRIKER.
	Josie, there's something icy.
JOSIE.	You better go to bed.
LILY.	There's a thing. It's got a face.
JOSIE.	Stop it.
LILY.	Feel.

JOSIE.   No.

LILY.   I can see her. Josie, see her, you must.

JOSIE.   She's for you now. You took her money.

LILY.   No, I can't bear it, I wish / you'd –

JOSIE.   Don't.

LILY.   I wish you'd see her too.

Pause.

JOSIE.   So I see her, so what?

SKRIKER.   Josie's not frightened.

JOSIE.   Toads, what you do that for, I'm not toads inside,
            it's you that's toads.

            SKRIKER *leaps up out of the sofa. She's wearing
            a short pink dress and gauzy wings.*

SKRIKER.   Here I am as you can see
            A fairy from a Christmas tree.
            I can give you heart's desire
            Help you set the world on fire.

LILY.   This is a dream, it's a nightmare and I'll wake up.
            I know I think other things happened like the
            money but that's because I'm remembering it in
            the dream.

JOSIE.   It's not a dream. She made me / speak toads.

LILY.   You would say that because you're just somebody
            in my dream.

JOSIE.   I'm not, it's me, I'm awake.

SKRIKER.   Don't you want a wish, Lily?

LILY.   I'll tell you about it in the morning.

SKRIKER.   What would you like, Lily?

JOSIE.   Lily, / be careful.

LILY.   I can't wake up yet but I can make it stop being a
            nightmare.

JOSIE.   Lily –

LILY.   I wish for flowers.

Flowers fall from above. SKRIKER *takes* LILY's *hand and puts it against her face.*

SKRIKER.   I'm warmer now, feel.

LILY.   And if it's not a dream it's even better.

The GREEN LADY *comes for the cake. The* MAN *gives it to her and she eats it. They go off together. The* PASSERBY *goes on dancing.*

There is a row of small houses. The SPRIGGAN *and* RAWHEADANDBLOODYBONES *tower over them.*

A BLACK DOG.

LILY *is in a park. A* SMALL CHILD *approaches her. It is the* SKRIKER.

THE GIRL WITH THE TELESCOPE *is looking through it but not seeing the* GREEN LADY. *She is tired and sad.*

LILY.   Can you play cat's cradle?

SKRIKER shakes her head.

Shall I show you?

SKRIKER nods. LILY *shows her cat's cradle.*

Put your fingers in here and take it. Good. Now I take it back. Now put your fingers, see, in there. Careful, that's it. Now I take it. Now you – that's right. This one's called fish in a dish. You use your little fingers and cross over – Oh it's all in a tangle.

SKRIKER.   Do it again.

LILY.   I'll show you one you can do by yourself.

LILY does it, SKRIKER *watches.* JOSIE *comes and watches too.*

LILY.   There, do you like that?

SKRIKER.   Show me again.

LILY.   Watch what I'm doing. Get it like this to start. What's your name?

SKRIKER.   I can do it. / Let me do it.

LILY.   Wait. Where do you live?

SKRIKER.   In the flats.

LILY.   Have you got any brothers and sisters?

SKRIKER.   Are you going to have a baby?

LILY.   Yes.

SKRIKER.   When?

LILY.   Soon. There, do you like that?

           LILY *shows* SKRIKER *the cat's cradle.*

SKRIKER.   Can I be its sister?

LILY.   You can't really be its sister.

SKRIKER.   I can, I can be, please let me. I want a baby, I want
           a baby brother or a baby sister.

LILY.   You'll have to ask your mum to have a baby.

SKRIKER.   I haven't got a mum. Please let me be a sister. Say
           yes. Say yes. Please say yes.

LILY.   Yes all right.

SKRIKER.   I'll be its sister and you can be my mum.

LILY.   Who do you live with?

SKRIKER.   Please say yes. Pretend.

LILY.   I'll be your pretend mum.

SKRIKER.   Will you give me real dinner or pretend dinner?

LILY.   Pretend dinner.

SKRIKER.   Real sweets or pretend sweets?

LILY.   I might find / some real sweets.

JOSIE.   Do you like this child?

SKRIKER.   Where? / Get some now. What kind?

LILY.   Yes, I do.

JOSIE.   She's horrible. There's something wrong with her.

           JOSIE *takes hold of* SKRIKER *to look at her.*

LILY.   Leave her alone.

SKRIKER.   Leave me alone, I'll tell my mum.

JOSIE.   She's not your mum. You haven't got a mum.

SKRIKER.   Mum! mum!

LILY.   Josie, stop it. It's all right, pet, she's just / teasing.

JOSIE.   Get out you little scrounger. / Leave Lily alone.

SKRIKER.   Mum, don't let her / hit me.

LILY.   Josie.

JOSIE.   I know you, you bastard. How you like toads?
You like dirt in your mouth? Get away from us.
You come in the house I'll put you in the fire,
then we'll see what you look like.

*JOSIE picks up dirt from the ground and stuffs it in
the SKRIKER's mouth. LILY rescues SKRIKER.*

LILY.   Get away, you're crazy. / (*To* SKRIKER.) It's all

JOSIE.   It's her.

SKRIKER.   Mum, make her go away.

LILY.   right. (*To* JOSIE.) I never want / to see you.

JOSIE.   It's her.

LILY.   Of course it's not her, it's a child, you're mad, you
should have stayed in hospital, I can't look after
you, you go round attacking people they'll take
you away again and I won't care, I won't help you
get out next time, / now go away and leave us
alone.

JOSIE.   She can have you then, I don't care, I'm not
helping you.

JOSIE goes further away and watches.

LILY.   Let's wipe your mouth. Poor baby. Did she hurt
you? Nasty Josie.

SKRIKER.   Nasty Josie. Nasty Josie. Nasty Josie.

LILY.   Now where's our piece of string?

SKRIKER.   Give me a cuddle. Let me sit on your lap.

LILY.   Careful, mind my tummy.

SKRIKER.   You're fat.

LILY.   It's the baby.

SKRIKER.   I'm the baby.

LILY.   No, you're the baby's big sister.

SKRIKER.   Fat fat fat.

LILY.   Careful.

SKRIKER.   Nasty baby.

She hits LILY*'s stomach.*

LILY.   Don't. Get off.

SKRIKER.   Mum. Mum.

LILY.   Come on then but be careful. Don't hurt the baby.

SKRIKER.   Cuddle.

LILY.   Cuddle cuddle.

SKRIKER.   Kiss.

LILY *kisses her.*

LILY.   Better now?

SKRIKER.   Let's go home.

LILY.   Home where?

SKRIKER.   Where we live.

LILY.   This is our house here.

SKRIKER.   No I mean go home. To your house.

LILY.   I better not take you back there. Someone's going to wonder where you are.

SKRIKER.   No one's going to wonder. I want to go home. Take me home.

LILY.   Let go, you're / pulling my hair.

SKRIKER.   No no, hold me. Hold me.

LILY.   Get down, / let go. Mind the baby.

SKRIKER.   Hold me tight.

LILY.   Let go. I'm telling you. / Now let go.

SKRIKER.   Never never never / never.

LILY.   You'll get a smack. Now get off. You're hurting.
            Get off.

            She hits SKRIKER *and pushes her away.*
            SKRIKER *lies on ground crying.* JOSIE *comes
            back.*

            Have I hurt her?

JOSIE.   Not enough.

            SKRIKER *sits up.*

SKRIKER.   You touch me I'll tell my dad you'll be sorry, get
            my brother on you he's bigger than you, I got lots
            of friends / everywhere set them on you watch out
            get in your head get in your eyes turn you into
            dogshit on my shoe.

JOSIE.   What you hurt me for, toads, what you do that for,
            I was looking for you, I'm not frightened, you're
            frightened, only did toads when I wasn't ready
            I'm ready now you just try you're no good there's
            something wrong with you you're a spastic fairy
            you need us more than we need you should have
            thought of that / before you done that to me too
            late.

LILY.   Josie, it's not.

SKRIKER.   You're stupid, aren't you, Lily. Josie knows.

JOSIE.   Leave her alone, she can't – . You can come back
            to me.

SKRIKER.   I don't want to. I like Lily.

JOSIE.   But I wish it.

SKRIKER.   I don't have to do what you wish. Lily doesn't
            wish it, do you?

LILY.   I don't know.

SKRIKER.   No because I might give you nice things. And
            Josie wants nice things. That's why she wants me.
            Not to help Lily. So you both want me. / That's
            nice.

LILY.   I don't, no I don't.

SKRIKER.   Josie's not frightened.

JOSIE.   What do you want?

SKRIKER.   I want a lot but so do you. We could both have it.

JOSIE.   Have what?

SKRIKER.   Whatever you like.

LILY.   Josie, don't do it. When you feel her after you it's . . . Josie, remember what it felt like / before, don't do it.

JOSIE.   But when you've lost her you want her back. Because you see what she can do and you've lost your chance and it could be the only chance ever / in my life to –

LILY.   Josie, don't.

SKRIKER.   I knew you were desperate, that's how I found you. Are you ready now?

LILY.   Josie, I wish / you wouldn't.

SKRIKER.   You don't count any more.

Pause.

JOSIE.   Yes.

Blackout. A horrible shriek like a siren that goes up to a very high sound and holds it. Gradually it relents little by little breaking up into notes and coming down till it is pleasant and even melodious.

Underworld. As SKRIKER and JOSIE arrive it springs into existence. Light, music, long table with feast, lavishly dressed people and creatures, such as YALLERY BROWN, NELLIE LONGARMS, JENNY GREENTEETH, THE KELPIE, BLACK DOG, RAWHEADAND-BLOODYBONES, THE RADIANT BOY, JIMMY SQUAREFOOT, BLACK ANNIS (with a blue face and one eye). It looks wonderful except that it is all glamour and here and there it's not working – some of the food is twigs, leaves, beetles, some of the clothes are rags, some of the beautiful people have a claw hand or hideous face. But the first impression is of a palace. SKRIKER *is a fairy queen, dressed grandiosely, with lapses.*

As they arrive the rest burst into song. Everyone except JOSIE *and the* SKRIKER *sings instead of speaking. They press food and drink on* JOSIE, *greet her, touch her.*

SPIRITS.   Welcome homesick
drink drank drunk
avocado and prawn cockfight cockup cocksuck
red wine or white wash
champagne the pain is a sham pain the pain is a sham
fillet steak fill it up stakes in your heart
meringue utang
black coffee fi fo fum.

A HAG *rushes in shrieking. She seizes food, scattering it, searching. She sings.*

HAG.   Where's my head? where's my heart? where's my arm? where's my leg? is that my finger? that's my eye.

The SPIRITS *laugh and jeer at her and repeat what she says, singing.*

SPIRITS.   Headlong . . . heartbreak . . . harmful . . . legless . . . finicky . . . eyesore.

HAG.   Give me my bones.

JOSIE *and* SKRIKER *speak, everyone else sings.*

JOSIE.   What is it? what's the matter?

HAG.   They cut me up. They boiled me for dinner.
Where's my head? is that my shoulder? that's
my toe.

SKRIKER.   They chopped her to pieces, they chipped her to
pasties. She's a hag higgledepig hog. She's a my
my miser myselfish and chips.

SPIRITS.   A miser a miserable

HAG.   Give me my bones.

The SPIRITS *jeer and pelt the* HAG *with bits of food and drive her away.*

*They repeat previous singing about the feast. A lost
girl takes* JOSIE *aside and sings to her under
cover of the other singing.*

GIRL. Don't eat. It's glamour. It's twigs and beetles and a
dead body. Don't eat or you'll never get back.

The SPIRITS *urge food on* JOSIE *and the* GIRL
has to move away. But she manages to get back.

Don't drink. It's glamour. It's blood and dirty
water. I was looking for my love and I got lost in
an orchard. Never take an apple, never pick a
flower. I took one bite and now I'm here forever.
Everyone I love must be dead by now. Don't eat,
don't drink, or you'll never get back.

SPIRITS *push her aside and sing on, louder and
more chaotically.* SKRIKER *offers* JOSIE *a glass
of red wine.*

SKRIKER. Your wealth, Josie, happy and gory.

JOSIE. I'm not thirsty.

SKRIKER. Thirst and worst, mouth drouth dry as dustbowl.

JOSIE. Yes, but I don't –

SKRIKER. Dizzy dozy chilly shally.

JOSIE. Yes but I don't want –

SKRIKER. Don't you want to feel global warm and happy
ever after? Warm the cackles of your heartless.
Make you brave and rave. Look at the colourful,
smell the tasty. Won't you drink a toasty with me,
Josie, after all we've done for?

JOSIE *drinks. Everyone is silent and attentive for
a moment. Then they all burst out singing again
triumphantly, among them* THE GIRL *sings.*

GIRL. Twigs and beetles and dead body. Water and blood.
You'll never get back.

But JOSIE *doesn't notice her. She is happy now
and eats the food they pile in front of her, not
noticing the difference between cake and twigs.
The* SPIRITS *celebrate, congratulating the*
SKRIKER.

SPIRITS.   We won wonderful
            full up at last
            last man's dead.

            One by one the spirits get up and dance, and
            JOSIE *and the* SKRIKER *too, increasing frenzy.*
            Some of them fly into the air.

            In the confusion the feast disintegrates. Finally
            everything and everyone has gone except the
            PASSERBY *still dancing.*

            Silence and gloom. JOSIE *appears on her hands*
            and knees scrubbing the floor. A MONSTER
            comes to watch her. It is the SKRIKER. *There is*
            a fountain.

SKRIKER.   Better butter bit of better bitter but you're better
            off down here you arse over tit for tattle, arsy
            versy, verse or prose or amateur status the nation
            wide open wide world hurled hurtling hurting hurt
            very badly. Wars whores hips hip hoorays it to the
            ground glass. Drought rout out and about turn off.
            Sunburn sunbeam in your eye socket to him. All
            good many come to the aids party. When I go
            uppety, follow a fellow on a dark road dank ride
            and jump thrump out and eat him how does he
            taste? toxic waste paper basket case, salmonele-
            phantiasis, blue blood bad blood blue blood blad
            blood blah blah blah. I remember dismember the
            sweet flesh in the panic, tearing limb from lamb
            chop you up and suck the tomorrow bones. Lovely
            lively lads and maiden England, succulent suck
            your living daylights, sweet blood like seawater
            everywhere, every bite did you good enough as
            good as a feast.

JOSIE.   And now no one tastes any good?

SKRIKER.   Dry as dustpans, foul as shitpandemonium. Poison
            in the food chain saw massacre.

JOSIE.   If I could just go and see. I'd come back.

SKRIKER.   Shall I take you in my pocket pick it up and tuck
            it in?

JOSIE.   Yes please.

SKRIKER.   Up in the smokey hokey pokey? up in the world
            wind? up in the war zone ozone zany grey?

JOSIE.   Because it's years. I think I've lived longer than
            they do up there. If I don't go now I won't know
            anyone.

SKRIKER.   What will you pay me say the bells the bells?

JOSIE.   Sip my blood?

SKRIKER.   Haven't I sipped lipped lapped your pretty twist
            wrist for years and fears? What's happy new,
            what's special brew hoo?

JOSIE.   I had a dream last night.

SKRIKER.   Haven't I wrapped myself up rapt rapture ruptured
            myself in your dreams, scoffed your chocolate
            screams, your Jung men and Freud eggs, your
            flying and fleeing? It was golden olden robes you
            could rip tide me up in but now it's a tatty bitty
            scarf scoff scuffle round my nickneck. Give a
            dog a bone.

JOSIE.   Tell you something I remember.

SKRIKER.   Haven't I drained rained sprained ankles and
            uncles, aunts and answers, father and nearer?
            What do you know about your selfish you haven't
            worn down out?

JOSIE.   Got a new one.

SKRIKER.   Bran tub new? lucky dipstick?

JOSIE.   Never even thought it myself. Something I saw
            when I was three.

SKRIKER.   What?

JOSIE.   Will you take me up?

SKRIKER.   What?

JOSIE.   A little bit of stony ground.

SKRIKER.   And?

JOSIE.   It had little stones on it.

SKRIKER.   Were you alonely?

JOSIE.   I don't remember. Probably alone. No, probably
            someone nearby. I remember the stones.

SKRIKER.   What can I do with a scrap crap wrap myself up
            in it? Ground to a halt. Stone death.

JOSIE.   But you'll take me with you?

SKRIKER.   That doesn't bye bye a trip up. You're dry as dead
            leaves you behind.

JOSIE.   Please.

SKRIKER.   You'll never go home on the range rover's return
            again witless.

JOSIE.   Why not, if I'm useless?

SKRIKER.   When I'm weak at the need, you'll be a last tiny
            totter of whisky whistle to keep my spirits to keep
            me stronger linger longer gaga. And while I'm
            await a minute, don't touch the water baby.

JOSIE.   Don't touch the water in the fountain because
            I'll die.

            SKRIKER *goes.*

            JOSIE *goes to the fountain and almost puts her
            hand in the water.*

            *She shrieks and plunges her hands in. A shrieking
            sound gets louder and louder.*

            Darkness.

            JOHNNY SQUAREFOOT *throwing stones at*
            BLACK DOG.

            JOSIE, LILY *and the* SKRIKER *as child are
            exactly as they were in the park.* SKRIKER *runs
            off.*

            The BLACK DOG *is in the park. The* GIRL WITH
            THE TELESCOPE *sits depressed. The* KELPIE
            and the WOMAN *who rode off on his back stroll
            as lovers.*

LILY.   (*shouting after* SKRIKER). We're not scared of
            you. (*To* JOSIE.) It's just a child anyway.

JOSIE. Too bright. No it's bright there. My eyes don't
        work. Hold me.

LILY.   Now what?

JOSIE. You smell like people. Your hair's like hair. It was
        like putting a gun to my head because they always
        said I'd die if I did that. Liars, you hear me? I got
        away. Yah. Can't get me.

LILY.   Stop it. You can stop it.

JOSIE. I was ready to die. I thought I'd never get back.

LILY.   Don't. It makes me lonely.

JOSIE. That's right I'm not dead? We're not both dead?
        Lily, you didn't die while I was away?

LILY.   Josie.

JOSIE. No, tell me are we dead?

LILY.   No we're not. Stop it.

JOSIE. How long's it been?

LILY.   How long's what?

JOSIE. I went for.

LILY.   Come on, let's go home.

JOSIE. I had a whole life. How long? I'm very old.

LILY.   You went? what?

JOSIE. Years and years, longer than I lived here, I wasn't
        much than a child here hardly. I've got
        children there, Lily, and they're grown up but I
        didn't mean to leave them, I thought I'd just die,
        won't I ever see them? I don't want to go back.
        How can I live now?

LILY.   You can't be old. Look at you. Look at me.

JOSIE. Yes, how do you do that? You've travelled into the
        future. You're not real. You're something she's
        made up.

LILY.   Josie.

        LILY *hugs her.*

JOSIE.   Are you glad to see me?

LILY.   I never stopped seeing you.

JOSIE.   But you're glad?

LILY.   Yes.

JOSIE.   When is this? I don't know when it is.

LILY.   It's just today like it's been all day. We went to the shops. We met a child in the park.

JOSIE.   That's horrible.

LILY.   Please, I'm tired. My stomach hurts.

JOSIE.   No time at all?

As they go the BUCKET AND CLOTH MAN *and the* GREEN LADY *go by. He is weak and stumbling. The* BLACK DOG *follows them off. The* DEPRESSED GIRL *goes on sitting.*

A BUSINESSMAN *with a* THRUMPIN *riding on his back. He doesn't know it's there. The* GIRL *leaves. He is joined by colleagues, all with* THRUMPINS, *for a meeting. They are talking but we can't hear what they say. All we can hear is a shrill twittering wordless conversation among the* THRUMPINS. *Still* PASSERBY *dancing.*

A smart WOMAN *in mid thrties. It is the* SKRIKER.

SKRIKER.   So the Skriker sought fame and fortune telling, celebrity knockout drops, TV stardomination, chat showdown and market farces, see if I carefree, and completely forgetmenot Lily and Josie. Lovely and Juicy, silly and cosy, lived in peaces and quite, Jerky still mad as a hitter and Lively soon gave happy birth to a baby a booby a babbly byebye booboo boohoo hoooooo. What a blossom bless 'em. Dear little mighty.

LILY *and* JOSIE *and the baby are on the sofa.* RAWHEADANDBLOODYBONES *sits on a shelf watching, invisible to them.* SKRIKER *and* MEN *with* THRUMPINS *leave.*

LILY.   Everyone says you'll be tired or they . . . bunnies
           or fluffy . . . everything too sweet and you think
           that's really boring, makes you want to dress her in
           black but she's not sweet like pink and blue. Or
           you get them moaning about never get enough
           sleep or oh my stitches or like that, no one lets on.

JOSIE.   Are you listening to me?

LILY.   Day and night.

JOSIE.   But in fact never.

LILY.   I'm tired.

JOSIE.   You just said tired wasn't it.

LILY.   It's not all about it but I'm still tired.

JOSIE.   So what's the big secret?

LILY.   Not a secret.

JOSIE.   What's so wonderful wonderful only you're
           brilliant enough to feel it?

LILY.   Nothing.

JOSIE.   Everyone gets born you know. It's not something
           you invented. Walk down the street you'll see
           several people that were born.

           Silence.

LILY.   So tell me again.

           Silence.

           Josie, it's over.

JOSIE.   How can it be over if it didn't happen?

LILY.   What you thought what you dreamed whatever is
           over.

JOSIE.   But I did go.

LILY.   Josie, I was with you all the time.

JOSIE.   But I did go.

LILY.   All right.

JOSIE.   Smash your face in. I did go. They need us you
           know, they think we're magic. They drink your
           blood. I miss the dancing.

Silence.

JOSIE. So what is it about her?

LILY. I know everyone's born. I can't help it. Every
thing's shifted round so she's in the middle. I never
minded things. But everything dangerous seems
it might get her. I know she's just . . . But if she
wasn't all right it'd be a waste, wouldn't it.

JOSIE. What happened to me is like that. As big as that is
to you. I promise.

LILY. But it happened in no time at all.

JOSIE. Yes. But where I was it was years.

LILY. Yes.

JOSIE. All right then.

LILY. And it's over now.

JOSIE. Everything's flat here like a video. There's
something watching us.

LILY. Yes but there's not.

JOSIE. I can't go back because they hate me for getting
away.

LILY. You want to go back?

JOSIE. I'm never going to be all right.

LILY. You know how they say 'oh their little fingers' and
of course they've got little fingers, they couldn't
have fingers like us. But that's not what they mean.
I mean look at her fingers.

JOSIE. She's a changeling.

LILY. She what?

JOSIE. That's not your baby. They've put one of theirs and
taken yours off.

LILY. Don't say that, don't.

JOSIE. Changeling. / Changeling.

LILY. I warn you, I'll kill you / don't say it,

JOSIE. You believe me don't you?

LILY.   I don't want, I don't believe you no / but I

JOSIE.   Lucky for them.

LILY.   don't want to hear it.

JOSIE.   They'll keep yours down there. It makes them
           stronger. They'll breed from it. And you'll always
           have this one watching you. Look at its little slitty
           eye.

LILY.   Don't even think it. / I'm not listening.

JOSIE.   Shall I tell you what? If you want your own one
           back? You put the changeling on a shovel and put
           it in the fire, that's what they used to do. So we'd
           use the cooker and put it over the gas. And
           sometimes they turn into a cat and go up the
           chimney. How'd it get out of here? Round and
           round the walls. I'll open the window. Then you
           get your own one back in the cot.

LILY.   I can't live with you if you're like this.

JOSIE.   You've got to fight them. You say you love her and
           you won't even do something to get her back. This
           isn't human. I can tell.

LILY.   Whatever you are, if you're really there, if you can
           hear me, I want a wish.

JOSIE.   She'll come back, look out.

LILY.   I wish Josie wasn't mad.

JOSIE.   Don't wish me.

           Silence.

LILY.   Did anything happen?

JOSIE.   What have you done?

LILY.   What have I done?

JOSIE.   Hurts.

LILY.   Where? what?

JOSIE.   Inside.

LILY.   What have they done to you?

JOSIE.   Here.

LILY.	I wish –
JOSIE.	Don't don't don't.
LILY.	What have they done?
JOSIE.	I don't think anything's broken. They haven't really put bits of metal. I killed her. Did I? Yes. I hadn't forgotten but. She was just as precious. Yours isn't the only. If I hadn't she'd still. I keep knowing it again, what can I do? Why did I? It should have been me. Because under that pain oh shit there's under that under that there's this other / under that there's –
LILY.	Wait, stop, I'm sorry, I'll / fix it
JOSIE.	Don't let me feel it. It's coming for me. Hide me. This is what. When I killed her. What I was frightened. Trying to stop when I. It's here.
LILY.	No please I'll –
JOSIE.	Save me. Can you? There's no one to save.
LILY.	I wish –
JOSIE.	No.
LILY.	If I wish you happy, no, you could kill people and still, don't feel pain no, just all right what does that mean, I wish I hadn't, no I'd do it again, I wish you were like before I wished, does that, I wish –
JOSIE.	You mustn't keep wishing or she'll get you.
LILY.	Are you all right now?
JOSIE.	There's something.
LILY.	What?
JOSIE.	Gone.
LILY.	It doesn't hurt?
JOSIE.	What?
	Silence.
LILY.	I should have asked you.
JOSIE.	Well ask me.

LILY.   If you really thought . . .

JOSIE.   Are you starting again? I was there for years.

LILY.   No, if you thought she was a changeling.

JOSIE.   Shall we do some tests? Yeah? Be a laugh.

LILY.   No we won't. We'll take care of her.

JOSIE.   Have you been wishing? Stupid. She'll get you
            now.

            Many couples dancing. They include KELPIE *and*
            WOMAN, GREEN LADY *and* BUCKET MAN,
            who is weak, BROWNIE, SKRIKER *as man,*
            RAWHEADANDBLOODYBONES, BLACK
            DOG, JOHNNY SQUAREFOOT, NELLIE
            LONGARMS. *There is a large shoe and when
            they've finished dancing they climb on it. It is
            identical to* LILY's *shoe which she has kicked off
            She is sitting on the sofa with a* MAN *about 30. It
            is the* SKRIKER. JOSIE *is chopping vegetables.
            The* BABY *is in a carrycot.*

SKRIKER.   I'd wait down the end of the road and see you
            come out with the pram. I'd watch you in the park.

LILY.   When did you?

SKRIKER.   You knew I was there though.

LILY.   No, when?

SKRIKER.   You meant me to follow you or I wouldn't have
            done it.

LILY.   I never saw you.

SKRIKER.   Unconsciously meant. Or in your stars. Some
            deep . . .

LILY.   Oh like that.

SKRIKER.   Yes some fateful . . . So that when we met it
            wasn't for the first time. You felt that. Some people
            are meant to be together. I'd walk out of meetings
            because of this overpowering . . . I'd accelerate to
            fifty on a short block up to a red light. Anything
            that wasn't you my eyes veered off. I couldn't
            sleep, of course, not that sleep's my best – do you
            sleep?

LILY.   If she lets me.

SKRIKER. How do you do that? No what do you do, tell me.
          You go to bed.

LILY.   I go to bed.

SKRIKER. You take anything?

LILY.   Not to sleep, no, be a waste.

SKRIKER. So you just lie down.

LILY.   I might look at a magazine for about ten minutes
          but then I'm too sleepy.

SKRIKER. So what's that like when you get sleepy?

LILY.   You know what it's like.

SKRIKER. No, what's it like.

          JOSIE *goes out.*

LILY.   My eyes keep shutting by themselves. I'm reading
          something and then I see my eyes are shut so
          I open them and think I'll just finish that story
          and the words are going double so I don't bother.
          So I put out the light.

SKRIKER. And then what?

LILY.   I go to sleep.

SKRIKER. No, how? What happens.

LILY.   I'm lying there. And . . .

SKRIKER. And thoughts.

LILY.   Maybe thoughts a bit about the day or –

SKRIKER. Rush through your head.

LILY.   Not rush but . . . and I might see things.

SKRIKER. See . . . ?

LILY.   Like a tree with its leaves or somebody . . .

SKRIKER. Frightening things?

LILY.   No but nothing to do with anything, not dreams
          exactly but bright – and I know something I've just
          thought isn't right, like maybe there's two things

that seem to be something to do with each other
but they're not but I can't remember what it was –

SKRIKER.   Your mind's going out of control like when there's
going to be an accident. / When any

LILY.   No.

SKRIKER.   minute people are going to be mangled in some
machinery and it's going very slowly but you
can't / stop it.

LILY.   No, not like that.

SKRIKER.   Like what?

LILY.   Nothing, I'm asleep after that.

SKRIKER.   So maybe that's something I'd pick up. I'd slide
off into sleep beside you.

LILY.   Why don't you sleep?

SKRIKER.   I have slept. It's partly my legs, they can't get
right. And things in my head. Well I'll tell you
there was this . . . He was quite highpowered, he
thought he was. He was going to help me, he was
going to manage me because I was a conjuror at
this point, I could do these amazing – I was
entitled to recognition. He didn't deliver. So I'd lie
awake. Well he subsequently died in fact. So that
was good. But I've got a lot on my mind. You'll
help me with that.

LILY.   I don't know.

SKRIKER.   Yes because you have faith in me.

JOSIE *comes back.*

Have you noticed the large number of
meteorological phenomena lately? Earthquakes.
Volcanoes. Drought. Apocalyptic meteorological
phenomena. The increase of sickness. It was
always possible to think whatever your personal
problem, there's always nature. Spring will return
even if it's without me. Nobody loves me but at
least it's a sunny day. This has been a comfort to
people as long as they've existed. But it's not
available any more. Sorry. Nobody loves me

and the sun's going to kill me. Spring will return
and nothing will grow. Some people might feel
concerned about that. But it makes me feel
important. I'm going to be around when the
world as we know it ends. I'm going to witness
unprecedented catastrophe. I like a pileup on the
motorway. I like the kind of war we're having
lately. I like snuff movies. But this is going to be
the big one.

JOSIE *goes out.*

Your friend doesn't like me.

LILY.   I'm sorry.

SKRIKER.   I'm getting uncomfortable.

LILY.   She doesn't like anyone.

SKRIKER.   I can't tolerate being disliked. So never mind.
             We'll go away together. You'd like a holiday. We'll
             bring the baby, no problem, I love kids, babies are
             cupid. What are you doing tomorrow?

LILY.   No, I –

SKRIKER.   You think this is sudden. I think it's sudden. No
             I don't. I've been looking for you. It's going to
             happen.

LILY.   What's going to happen?

SKRIKER.   Us being together forever. We both know that. So
             there's no point taking a long time getting to the
             point which we got to the first time no even before
             we met no even before I ever set eyes on you
             because this kind of thing is meant. Don't you
             agree?

LILY.   Yes I do. I think I do.

SKRIKER.   What's this 'I think'?

LILY.   I just . . .

SKRIKER.   Are you backing out?

LILY.   No. What? I –

SKRIKER.   Don't do this to me. I warn you. Quite straight-
             forwardly as one human being to another.

LILY.   I didn't mean –

SKRIKER.   Don't don't don't don't don't look startled. You're
              the only good person I've ever met. Everyone else
              has tried to destroy me. But you wish me well. You
              wouldn't deny that.

LILY.   No, I –

SKRIKER.   No.

LILY.   No I –

SKRIKER.   What? what? don't dare. This is a high voltage
              cable. Are you going to grab it? I'm going to take
              care of you and the baby. You're coming with me.
              You don't have to worry about anything any more.

              JOSIE *comes in again.*

LILY.   I do like you. I can't look away from you. But a bit
              slower. It's no use getting angry because I can't –

SKRIKER.   I hate it when I'm so unkind. This sometimes
              happens. I won't go into my childhood just now. I
              can't forgive myself. I feel terrible.

LILY.   I didn't mean –

SKRIKER.   I'm useless, I get something beautiful and I ruin it.
              Everything I touch falls apart. There are some
              people who deserve to be killed and I believe it's
              important to be completely without remorse. I
              admire that if someone has no compassion because
              that's what it takes. But other people such as
              yourself. You won't want to see me again. How
              could I do that? I worship you. I'm so ashamed.
              I feel sick. Help me. Forgive me. Could you ever
              love me?

              JOSIE *attacks him with a knife, slashing his arm
              and chest. Blood on his shirt.*

              Do you love me? Do you love me?

LILY.   Yes, yes I do.

              *He takes off the bloodstained shirt and tie.
              Underneath, identical clean ones.*

SKRIKER   (*to* JOSIE). You're getting into a lot of trouble. She
              loves me.

LILY.   No I don't. What are you?

SKRIKER.   But you do you know. See you later.

            He goes.

LILY.   These things only come because of you. Go and
            live somewhere else.

            GREEN LADY *pushing* BUCKET MAN *in a
            wheelchair.*

            KELPIE *with the body of* WOMAN *who went
            away with him.*

            TELESCOPE GIRL *distraught and searching.*

            JOSIE *leaves with* BLACK DOG.

            PASSERBY *still dancing.*

            MARIE, *a young woman about* LILY's *age, is
            visiting* LILY. *It is the* SKRIKER. *The* KELPIE
            cuts up the woman's body.

SKRIKER.   Can I pick up the baby?

LILY.   No.

SKRIKER.   Sorry.

LILY.   I don't remember you.

SKRIKER.   I've grown up.

            Silence.

            Someone's going to kill me. Marie never hung out
            with the right people. I need somewhere to stay.

LILY.   I can't help you.

SKRIKER.   You're not the only person I know. I'm almost a
            celebrity. My face has been on the covers – not
            this face exactly but a face. But I'm the same old
            Marie. Those are silver, these are gold. There's a
            lot of people out there who pretend to be your
            friend. They say they are. But you and me and
            Josie swore in blood.

LILY.   I don't remember.

SKRIKER.   You remember the waste ground? you remember
            the corner with the nettles? you remember Josie?

LILY.   Of course I remember Josie.

SKRIKER.   You've forgotten Marie.

LILY.   I'm sorry . . . I can't . . . I'm not sure.

SKRIKER.   When we left messages in the wall?

LILY.   Yes I do remember the wall.

SKRIKER.   The tree.

LILY.   Corner shop after school.

SKRIKER.   Sherbet lemons.

LILY.   But were you . . . ?

SKRIKER.   It's funny how much of our life we forget. You
            can't help it. You never liked me best. Let me stay
            with you. There's room now Josie's gone. I'd be
            safe here.

LILY.   No.

SKRIKER.   My dad did things to me. I never told you that.
            My mum shut me in the cupboard.

LILY.   Go somewhere else.

SKRIKER.   My boyfriend's going to kill me.

LILY.   You're not Marie.

SKRIKER.   No, but I'm still in danger. That's why I came.
            Look, I'm not pretending anything. That's good
            isn't it? You've got to love me.

LILY.   How would that help?

SKRIKER.   Yes, help me Lily. I don't work properly.
            You've got to come with me. You can save me.
            You want to.

LILY.   I don't love you at all. I don't like you. I don't care
            if you die. I'm never going to see you again.

            SKRIKER *goes.* LILY *sits exhausted. Later she
            goes.*

            A FAMILY *having a picnic on a beach. The beach
            is covered with* BLUE MEN. PASSERBY *still
            dancing.*

JOSIE *and the* BLACK DOG *are in a small room, visited by a shabby respectable* MAN *about 40. It is the* SKRIKER.

JOSIE.   She didn't know anyone. She didn't have anywhere to stay the night. I slipped a wire loop over her head.

SKRIKER *laughs.*

So that'll do for a bit, yeh? You'll feel ok. There's an earthquake on the telly last night. There's a motorway pileup in the fog.

SKRIKER.   You're a good girl, Josie.

JOSIE.   There's dead children.

SKRIKER.   Tell me more about her.

JOSIE.   She had red hair. She had big feet. She liked biscuits. She woke up while I was doing it. But you didn't do the carcrash. You'd tell me. You're not strong enough to do an earthquake.

SKRIKER *coughs.*

I'll do terrible things, I promise. Just leave it to me. You don't have to do anything. Don't do anything. Promise.

SKRIKER *coughs.*

You won't do anything to Lily?

SKRIKER.   Who's Lily?

JOSIE.   Nobody. Someone you used to know. You've forgotten her.

SKRIKER *laughs.*

Have you forgotten her?

SKRIKER *coughs.*

I think you'd like me to do something tomorrow.

SKRIKER *coughs.*

The BUCKET MAN *comes slowly in his wheel-chair, moving it himself now. He stops and dozes. The* TELESCOPE GIRL *comes in, she has*

bandaged wrists. RAWHEADANDBLOODY
BONES, KELPIE *and* JOHNNY SQUAREFOOT
rush across wildly, tangling with the PASSERBY,
who keeps dancing.

SKRIKER.   Josie went further and murther in the dark, trying
to keep the Skriker sated seated besotted with
gobbets, tossing it giblets, to stop it from wolfing,
stop it engulfing. But still there was gobbling
and gabbling, giggling and gaggling, biting and
beating, eating and hating, hooting and looting
and lightning and thunder in the southeast
northwest northeast southwest northsouth crisis.
Lily doolalley was living in peacetime, no more
friend, no more fiend, safe as dollshouses. But
she worried and sorried and lay far awake into
the nightmare. Poor furry, she thought, pure feary,
where are you now and then? And something
drove her over and over and out of her mind how
you go.

BLACK ANNIS *has small houses in a glass
aquarium. She slowly fills it with water.*

LILY, *with the* BABY, *arrives at the hospital,
where there is a very ill old woman. It is the*
SKRIKER.

LILY.   What you doing in hospital? If you're really asleep
I'll say it again after. I thought you'd be in the
government or the movies by now. I went to
stations when people were coming off trains or
closing time coming out of pubs. I'd put her in the
pram, she'd go back to sleep. There are things out
in the night. I think you should be glad I've come,
and open your eyes. When I made you go I didn't
know you'd really gone, anyone spoke to me I was
frightened. Then one day there was someone going
to jump from a building and when it wasn't you
I started looking.

SKRIKER.   Don't kill me.

LILY.   It's Lily.

SKRIKER.   They've taken my friends away. Not me.

LILY.   I'll take care of you.

SKRIKER.   You're a liar, Lily.

LILY.   I came to find you.

SKRIKER.   I had a friend fed her cat on tins and it was frightened of real food. Put a bit of raw meat down and it leapt back. It smelt blood. Thought it was going to eat it. The dinner the cat. I've enemies in here. Shh.

LILY.   I came to say I'd go with you.

SKRIKER.   Where are you going, dear?

LILY.   You said you wanted me to. Like Josie.

SKRIKER.   I've no idea who these people are.

LILY.   Yes because I miss . . . You'll leave everyone else alone if I do that, I'm not bringing the baby so don't ask, you're to leave her alone always. And Josie alone. Because if I go it'll help, won't it?

SKRIKER.   Have you tried dialling 999?

LILY.   I know I said I didn't love you.

SKRIKER.   Aren't you afraid a fade away?

LILY.   No because if it's what Josie did I'll be back in no time. It could feel like hundreds of years and I wouldn't leave the baby for five minutes but when I get back she won't know I've gone.

SKRIKER.   Gone with the wind hover crafty.

LILY.   Even if it's a nightmare. I'll be back the same second. I'll make you safe. Take me with you.

SKRIKER leaps up. It is no longer the old woman. It is the SKRIKER from the beginning of the piece, but full of energy.

SKRIKER.   Lily, my heartthrobber baron, my solo flighty, now I've some blood in my all in veins, now I've some light in my lifeline nightline nightlight a candle to light you to bedlam, here comes a –

SKRIKER lights a candle and gives it to LILY.

Watch the lightyear. Here you stand in an enchanted wood you or wouldn't you. Just hold this candle the scandal I said and she stood till stood still stood till what?

LILY *stands holding the candle. Everything else is dark. A blackbird sings.*

An OLD WOMAN *and a* DEFORMED GIRL *sitting together. They see* LILY *appear. The* GIRL *cries out. The candle goes out and* LILY *sees them.*

The SKRIKER *is the ancient creature it was at the beginning of the piece. The* PASSERBY *is still dancing.*

Lily appeared like a ghastly, made their hair stand on endless night, their blood run fast. 'Am I in fairylanded?' she wandered. 'No,' said the old crony, 'this is the real world' whirl whir wh wh what is this? Lily was solid flash. If she was back on earth where on earth where was the rockabye baby gone the treetop? Lost and gone for everybody was dead years and tears ago, it was another cemetery, a black whole hundred yearns. Grief struck by lightning. And this old dear me was Lily's granddaughter what a horror storybook ending. 'Oh I was tricked tracked wracked,' cried our heroine distress, 'I hoped to save the worldly, I hoped I'd make the fury better than she should be.' And what would be comfy of her now? She didn't know if she ate a mortal morsel she'd crumble to dust panic. Are you my grand great grand great are you my child's child's child's? But when the daughters grand and great greater greatest knew she was from the distant past master class, then rage raging bullfight bullroar.

The GIRL *bellows wordless rage at* LILY.

'Oh they couldn't helpless,' said the granddaughter, 'they were stupid stupefied stewpotbellied not evil weevil devil take the hindmost of them anyway.' But the child hated the monstrous.

GIRL *bellows.*

'Leave her alone poor little soul-o', said the grin dafter, 'cold in the headache, shaking and

shocking. Have a what drink, wrap her in a blanket
out, have a sandwhich one would you like?' So
Lily bit off more than she could choose. And she
was dustbin.

The OLD WOMAN *holds out some food and* LILY
puts out her hand to take it.

The PASSERBY *stops dancing.*

End.

THYESTES
by Seneca

Introduction

'Now could I drink hot blood,' says Hamlet,'and do such bitter business as the day would quake to look on.' He wants to be a hero in a Seneca play. I didn't know that till I read *Thyestes*.

In the summer of 1992 I went to see Ariane Mnouchkine's production of the *House of Atreus* plays, and wondered why there were no Greek plays about the beginning of the story. But there had been, James Macdonald told me, though none of them survived. What did survive was a Latin *Thyestes* by Seneca. I got the Loeb edition with Latin on one page and English opposite. At first I was attracted by the Ghost of Tantalus and a Fury, then by the revenge story, the drought (it was a hot dry summer), the fears of the world ending, which all felt oddly topical. Then I started getting interested in the language, in trying to get through the opaque screen that a translation can't help being to see what Seneca had actually said. I'd studied Latin at school, and with the Loeb and a dictionary began to pick my way through a few bits that interested me.

Loeb's translation was printed in 1912 and though very helpful is written in a style archaic then: 'Who from the accursed regions of the dead haleth me forth. . . ' What struck me was how simple and direct the Latin was. Because it's a language without 'the' or 'a', because it's a language where person and tense are tucked into the verb (we say 'I will kill', they say 'kill' with endings that means 'I' and 'in the future'), it uses fewer words than we do and they're more full of action. In Latin you can say 'black dog kills white cat, white cat kills black dog, black dog cat white kills, cat kills white black dog' and it will still be clear that the black dog killed the white cat because tucked into each word is who's doing it, who's having it done to them, which colour goes with which animal, and this means they can achieve subtleties of emphasis just with word order where we might need a few extra words.

English is full of Latin words, but for us they're not our most basic ones, not the ones that mean the thing itself. It's spade *v* horticultural implement, and it's loving *v* amorous, death *v* mortality, brotherly *v* fraternal. We're lucky to have both and

we've gained shades of meaning by having more words to play
with. But reading Latin I realised the obvious, that to the
Romans Latin words were the only words, the ones that most
directly meant the things they wanted to say, not words that were
elevated or remote.

So though my vague idea of Seneca, rather confirmed by dipping
into translations, had been of a grandiloquent, rhetorical, florid
writer, I began to feel he was far blunter, faster and subtler than
I'd thought, and I began for my own pleasure to puzzle out what
was there. Sometimes I stayed so close to the Latin that I could
feel the knobbly foreign constructions just under the English
skin, and liked that, though often I made something less literal
of it. I put it into verse, counting syllables rather than stresses;
often five and six alternating, fives to move faster, or sevens. It
forced me to be concise, since something had to be happening in
every five syllable line. The choruses have verse patterns done
by syllables. I've condensed the choruses a little, but otherwise I
feel I've kept close to what Seneca wrote, though my choices of
words must be as typical of me and my time as Jasper
Heywood's are of him and his time.

Heywood's was the first English translation of *Thyestes*, in 1560.
He wrote:

> Thus when my days at length are overpass'd
> And time without all troublous tumult spent,
> An aged man I shall depart at last
> In mean estate to die full well content.
> But grievous is to him the death that, when
> So far abroad the bruit of him is known
> That known he is too much to other men,
> Departeth yet unto himself unknown.

I wrote:

> When my days have passed
> without clatter,
> may I die
> old and ordinary.
>
> Death lies heavily
> on someone who
> known to all
> dies unknown to himself.

Loeb wrote:

So when my days have passed noiselessly away, lowly may
I die and full of years. On him does death lie heavily who,
but too well known to all, dies to himself unknown.

Seneca wrote:

sic cum transierint mei
nullo cum strepitu dies
plebeius moriar senex.
illi mors gravis incubat
qui notus nimis omnibus
ignotus moritur sibi.

Which could be more literally translated as

so when willhavepassed my
no with wildconfusednoise days
oneofthecommonpeople mayIdie old.
thatone death heavy lieson
who known toomuch toall
unknown dies tohimself.

Most of Heywood's translation is written in the rollicking
rhyming alliterative fourteeners that were often used before
blank verse took over:

What fury fell enforceth me to flee th'unhappy seat,
That gape and grasp with greedy jaw the fleeing food to eat?

He manages it very skilfully, without getting too trapped by
alliteration. The Penguin collection of Seneca's tragedies gives
excerpts from other Elizabethan translations of Seneca in the
appendix, some far harder to take seriously than Heywood.
I particularly like this, from John Studley's *Medea:*

O flittring Flockes of grisly ghostes that sit in silent seat
O ougsome Bugges, O Goblins grym of Hell I you intreat.

Where, I thought, had I heard something like this before? Then I
remembered:

Thy mantle good,
What! stain'd with blood?
Approach ye Furies fell!
O fates! come, come;
Cut thread and thrum;
Quail, crush, conclude and quell.

It is of course 'Pyramus and Thisbe', the play Bottom and his friends are putting on in *A Midsummer Night's Dream*. I hadn't realised before what it was that was being parodied.

Nor had I realised till I read *Thyestes* quite what was meant by Seneca being an influence on Elizabethan theatre, though I'd known it was through Seneca that classical tragedy burst into the sixteenth century – they didn't know the Greek originals. Shakespeare must have had his own reasons from his own time and his own life for writing about horrors, but Seneca showed a way of doing it: ghosts, banished kings, vengeful brothers; drinking blood, asking mountains to fall on you, calling up spirits; night, eclipses, thunderbolts. There are essays or whole books in this, and I'm sure they've been written. And of course it's not all there is to Shakespeare. But the similarities suddenly leapt out at me, and not just the obvious one of *Titus Andronicus*, where the children are served up for dinner.

One of the most specific, following Atreus' thought:

> LEAR. I will have such revenges on you both
> That all the world shall – I will do such things –
> What they are yet I know not – but they shall be
> The terrors of the earth.

And others less close but belonging in the same world that Atreus and Thyestes live in:

> LADY MACBETH.   Come you spirits
> That tend on mortal thoughts, unsex me here,
> And fill me from the crown to the toe top full
> Of direst cruelty. . .
>   . . . Come, thick night,
> And pall thee in the dunnest smoke of hell,
> That my keen knife see not the wound it makes,
> Nor heaven peep through the blanket of the dark
> To cry Hold, hold.

This way of writing and thinking could be used seriously or mocked. When Laertes has jumped into Ophelia's grave –

> Now pile your dust upon the quick and dead
> Till of this flat a mountain you have made
> To o'er top old Pelion. . .

Hamlet sends the whole convention up:

> And if thou prate of mountains, let them throw
> Millions of acres on us till our ground,
> Singeing his pate against the burning zone

> Make Ossa like a wart. Nay an thou'lt mouth
> I'll rant as well as thou.

I wonder what Shakespeare's attitude is to Lear in the storm.

> You sulphurous and thought-executing fires
> Vaunt-couriers to oak-cleaving thunderbolts
> Singe my white head.

I used to think it was Shakespeare's rhetoric, not Lear's, Shakespeare's way of writing about Lear's real suffering. But it seems to me now that the style is deliberately chosen for the grandiose Lear who demanded speeches of love, and is part of the self importance he's on the way to losing but hasn't lost yet.

But it's not just words, it's a type of tragic hero that the Elizabethans found in Seneca, and one of their most popular plots, revenge plays. It's impossible for us when we see *Hamlet* to feel the surprise it must have been to its first audiences when the hero of the revenge play couldn't bring himself to do the killing. It's as if we'd gone for an evening out and found James Bond not doing the killing. But even Atreus starts with doubts as to whether he can manage revenge. Could that have helped Shakespeare get the idea of putting an Elizabethan melancholic into a revenge play?

Again and again in his plays Shakespeare worried away at a problem that worried Seneca – power *v* the quiet life. Thyestes comes out of the Forest of Arden back to Corinth. We can't know if Shakespeare was homesick for Stratford, but we can see why it was so interesting to Seneca. He was born in Spain in about 4BC and came with his family to Rome where he held public office till he was sent into exile in Corsica by the emperor Claudius for eight years, and there he wrote about Stoicism and the pleasures of the simple life. He was called back to be tutor to the boy who soon became the emperor Nero. As Nero's adviser he may have helped the reign to be relatively peaceful for the first few years. Seneca was now rich and powerful and deeply involved in the politics of an increasingly despotic emperor. When Nero had his mother Agrippina murdered, Seneca defended him to the Senate, but by 62AD Seneca had had enough and asked to be allowed to retire. Three years later he was accused by Nero of plotting against him and told to commit suicide, which he did with difficulty and courage.

It's not known if Seneca wrote his plays in exile or if they drew on his experience as Nero's adviser. His whole life was lived in dangerous times, and Greek stories must have given him a way of writing about its horrors without being too direct. All his plays were based on Greek ones – *Phaedra*, *Trojan Women*, *Phoenicians*, *Oedipus*, *Agamemnon*, *Hercules Oetaeus* and *Thyestes*. There's a play called *Octavia*, which may have been by someone copying his style but is extraordinary if it's by Seneca himself. It has Seneca and Nero as characters and is about Nero getting rid of his wife. It's extraordinary anyway, a play about contemporary politics using conventions worked out in rewrites of Greek tragedies. *Thyestes* was presumably based on Greek plays, though we don't have any – Sophocles wrote two about Thyestes, and Euripides another, and there were at least five other Roman versions which haven't survived.

This is the story of Tantalus and his descendants, which gave so many writers their plots:

Tantalus was a rich king, a son of Zeus, friends with the gods. One day when they came to visit he killed his young son Pelops and served him up for dinner. The gods punished him after his death by standing him in a stream while a tree dangled fruit near his mouth – when he tried to eat the tree whisked the fruit away, when he tried to drink the stream dried up. He was being tantalised.

Pelops was brought back to life. He wanted to marry a princess, who would only be given to the man who could beat her father in a chariot race; losers were put to death. Pelops won by having the king's axle damaged so that his chariot crashed and he was killed.

Pelops had two sons, Atreus and Thyestes, who were supposed to take turns ruling the country and keeping the symbol of power, a ram with a golden fleece. While Atreus was king, Thyestes seduced his wife and together they stole the ram. Atreus was driven into exile and there was civil war. He got into power again and drove Thyestes out. The play begins here, with Atreus as king but longing for revenge on Thyestes, who is in exile with his three sons. By the end Thyestes' sons are dead.

Years later Atreus' sons, Agamemnon and Menelaus go to war against Troy to get back Helen, Menelaus' wife. To get a favourable wind, Agamemnon sacrifices his daughter Iphigenia to the gods. When they come back from Troy Agamemnon is murdered by his wife Clytemnestra, avenging Iphigenia, and her lover Aegisthus, another son of Thyestes, avenging his dead brothers. Urged on by his sister Electra, Orestes, Agamemnon's son, kills Aegisthus and Clytemnestra. He is now in terrible difficulties – the revenge code has broken down since he has only been able to avenge his father by killing his mother, whose murder it would have been his duty to avenge. He is pursued by the Furies until the goddess Athene intervenes to quieten them and bring revenge to an end.

I don't think it's just because I've been translating Thyestes that the news seems full of revenge stories. Seneca could have brought a god on at the end of his play, but he's made a world where gods either don't exist or have left. Or he could have had the chorus back at the end saying the kind of generally uplifting and resigned things they do in Greek plays. But he didn't. The play ends bleakly except for our memory of a chorus who'd hoped for something better.

Caryl Churchill, 1995

Characters

GHOST OF TANTALUS, *grandfather of Atreus and Thyestes*
FURY
ATREUS, *king of Argos*
MINISTER
THYESTES, *Atreus' brother*
TANTALUS, *Thyestes' son (called after his great-grandfather)*
    and two other sons who don't speak
MESSENGER
CHORUS

Caryl Churchill's translation of *Thyestes* was first performed at
the Royal Court Theatre Upstairs, London, on 7 June 1994 with
the following cast:

THE FURY/YOUNG TANTALUS   Sebastian Harcombe
CHORUS   Rhys Ifans
MINISTER   James Kennedy
ATREUS   Kevin McMonagle
GHOST OF TANTALUS/THYESTES   Ewan Stewart
THYESTES' TWO YOUNGER SONS
played variously by   Simeon Hartwig
                             Amos Williams
                             Debo Adebayo
                             Rodney Joseph
                             Malachy Rynne
                             Jack Fawcett

Directed by James Macdonald
Designed by Jeremy Herbert
Costumes by Jennifer Cook
Lighting by Jon Linstrum
Sound by Paul Arditti

GHOST OF TANTALUS *and* A FURY

TANTALUS.   Who's dragging me
grabbing avidly
up
from the unlucky underworld?
What god's showing where people live?
It's wrong.
Have you found something worse
than burning thirst in
a stream? worse than gaping
hunger? Is it the
slippery stone now for my
shoulders? or the wheel
to tear me apart? or
lying open a
vast cave of guts dug out
to feed dark birds
renewing by night what
you lose by day so
there's always a full meal
for a fresh monster?
What horror am I
being transferred to? O
whoever, harsh judge
of shades who distributes
new tortures, if there's
anything you can add
to these punishments
which even the jailer
of this dire prison
would shudder at and I'm
trembling to think of,
get hold of it. There's a
mob spawned from me who'll
do things so much worse that
I'll look innocent.
If there's any space
available in hell

we'll take it, and while
my lot last the judge of
sin won't sit about.

FURY.   Go on, detestable
ghost, drive your gods mad.
Let's have a wickedness
competition, swords
out in every street, no
embarrassment at
being very angry –
blind fury. Then let
rage harden and the long
wrong go into the
grandchildren. No time for
anyone to hate
old crimes because here come
plenty of new ones
and the punishments are
even more wicked.
Whichever brother is
triumphant will lose
the kingdom, the exile
get back in. Fortune
will totter back and forth
between them, power
follow misery and
misery power
and waves of disaster
batter the kingdom.
Driven out for their crimes
when god brings them home
they'll come home to more crimes,
everyone hate them
just as they hate themselves.
Then there'll be nothing
anger thinks forbidden,
brother terrifies
brother, father sons and
sons fathers, children's
deaths are vile and their births
even worse. A wife
destroys her husband,
wars cross the sea to Troy,

the earth is watered with
blood and great leaders
are defeated by lust.
Rape's a joke and love and
laws both fade away.
The sky's not exempt. Why
are the stars shining?
do their flames still owe the
world glory? Let night
be something else. Let day
fall out of the sky.
So stir up your gods, call
hatred, carnage and
funerals, and fill the
whole house with Tantalus.

The columns will be
decorated, the doors
made green with laurel,
fires blaze to celebrate
your arrival home.
Now your crime will happen
all over again.
Why is uncle's hand still? –
Thyestes isn't
crying for his sons yet –
when will it strike? Now
see the cauldron bubble
on the fire, pieces
of chopped up flesh dropped in,
the hearth polluted,
and the great feast prepared.
It's not a new crime
to you so be our guest.
We're giving you a
day of freedom to let
your hunger loose on
this dinner. Sate your fast.
Watch them drink wine mixed
with blood. I've found a feast
you'll run away from –
stop, where are you going?

TANTALUS.

Back to the vanishing
pools and streams and the
fruit that escapes my lips.
Let me go back to
my dark lair. If I'm not
wretched enough let me
change streams and stand in the
river of fire.
Listen all of you
punished by fate
if you're lying trembling
under an overhang
fearing the cliff that's
about to fall on you,
if you're shuddering at
the snarling jaws of
lions or tangling with
Furies, if you're half
burnt and fighting off the
flames, listen to
Tantalus.
Believe me. I know.
Love your punishment.
When can I escape the
people who live up here?

FURY.

Not till you've churned them up
to war and the worst
thing for kings, falling in
love with weapons. Now,
shake their wild hearts.

TANTALUS.

I should be punished,
not be a punishment.
I'm being sent like
a poisonous gas seeping
out of the earth or
a virus scattering
plague on my people to
lead my grandchildren to
horrors. Great father
of gods and my father
too even if you're
ashamed of me, my tongue

may be torn out for
speaking but I won't keep
quiet. I'll warn them.
Don't do this murder.
Don't touch the foulness
the Furies make you crave.
I'll stay here and stop –
What? why attack me
with whips and snakes? what? what's
this clawing hunger
you've thrust deep inside me?
My burnt chest blazes
with thirst, flame flickers
in my scorched belly.
I'm going
wherever
it takes me.

FURY.   This this madness rip
through your whole house, like
this like this whirled away
thirsty for blood. Your house
feels you coming and
shudders. What you've done
now is more than enough.
Off to your cave and
stream. The sad land can't bear
you walking on it.
Do you see how water's
driven in away
from the springs, river beds
are empty, how thin
the clouds in the fiery
wind? The trees are all
yellow and bare branches
have lost their fruit, and
where the waves used to roar
now you can hardly
hear them. No more snow on
even the highest
mountain and down below
a terrible drought.
Look, the sun god isn't
sure whether to make

                    day set off and force it
                    out in the chariot
                    to its death.

CHORUS.   If any god loves
                Argos, its chariot races,
            the twin harbours and divided sea,
        the snow seen far away on the mountain peaks,
                    drifted by cold gales,
        melted by summer breezes that sail the boats,
                if any god is moved
                        by our clear streams,
                turn your gentle spirit.

                Stop crime coming back
            and grandsons outdoing their
            famous grandfather in wickedness.
        Why can't they be tired at last and stop?
                    The little son ran
        to his father's kiss and was caught on his sword,
                cut up by Tantalus
                    to make a feast
                for his great guests, the gods.

                Eternal hunger
            followed that meal, eternal
        thirst, and that was a good punishment.
        Tantalus stands tired out with his throat empty.
                Food hangs overhead
        quicker to fly away than a flock of birds.
                A tree heavy with fruit
                        plays with his mouth.
                He turns his head away.

                But the whole orchard
            dangles its riches nearer,
        ripe apples with languid leaves mock him
        till hunger forces him to stretch out his hands –
                the fruit's snatched away.
        Then thirst starts burning his blood, a cool stream flows
                at him then vanishes –
                        he drinks deep from
                the whirling pool, deep dust.

ATREUS *and* HIS MINISTER.

ATREUS.
Not brave. Not clever. Not strong.
What I'm really ashamed of
not avenged. After all that.
My brother's tricks. I trusted –
All these empty words. Am I
acting out angry Atreus?
What do I want? the whole world
roaring with armies, both seas
seething with ships, dark fields
and cities shining with flames,
swords glittering as they slash.
I can hear the thunder of
horses. Forests won't hide him
or little stone fortresses
on mountain tops. My people
swarm out of the city and
sing war. If anyone takes
him in and watches over
that head I hate, smash him down
in cataclysmic . . . I
wouldn't care if this palace
fell on me, if it fell on
him too. Do something . . . come on
come on . . . that no one in the
future's going to admire
but no one can stop talking – yes,
I must dare something so bad
so extreme my brother will
wish he'd done it himself. You
don't avenge unless you do
something much worse. And what
could beat what he's done? Is he
ever beaten? Does he stop
at anything when things go
well, and when they go badly
does he stop? I do know the
unteachable spirit of

the man. It can't be bent, but
it can be broken. So. Now.
Before he gets organised
he must be attacked without
warning or while I'm sitting
quietly he'll attack. He'll
kill or die. There's the crime just
there between us waiting for
whoever seizes it first.

MINISTER.   But what the people will think.

ATREUS.   The best thing about being a king,
              people don't just endure
              what you do, they praise it.

MINISTER.   They praise from fear. Fear makes enemies.
              Wouldn't you like true praise?

ATREUS.   Ordinary people get true praise.
              Only the great get lies.
              Subjects have to want what they don't want.

MINISTER.   But if the king wanted what was right,
              no one wouldn't want the same as you.

ATREUS.   If a ruler's only allowed what's
              right it's quite a precarious rule.

MINISTER.   Where there's no shame or kindness or trust
              I think that's very precarious.

ATREUS.   Shame, kindness and trust are qualities
              for private individuals. The
              king can do what he likes.

MINISTER.   But you would think it wrong to hurt your
                                        brother.

ATREUS.   Whatever's wrong for
              a brother is right
              for him. Because what's
              he ever stopped at?
              Wife and kingdom, he

took both. Our ancient
symbol of power
he took by deceit,
by deceit he brought
our family to
confusion. In our
famous flocks there's a
ram whose wool is gold
so all our kings have
gold on their sceptres.
His owner rules. The
future of our house
follows him. He's safe
shut up in a field,
shielded by stone walls,
sacred. The traitor
dared something huge, he
took my wife to help,
he took the ram. This
is what started it.
I've wandered about
a trembling exile
in this country that's
mine. No part of the
family is free
from traps. My wife is
corrupted. The deal
we made to share the
kingdom's smashed. House sick.
Children's blood in doubt.
Nothing certain but
brother enemy.
Why this stupor? Start.
Take hold of your soul.
Think of Tantalus.
That's the kind of thing
my hands are being
asked to do. Tell me
a way to honour
my brother's vile head.

MINISTER.   With a sword spit out
his enemy spirit.

ATREUS. You're talking about
the end of punishment.
The punishment itself
is what I want. A
soft king annihilates.
In my kingdom death
is something you beg for.

MINISTER. You feel no respect?

ATREUS. Get out, Respect, if you
ever lived in this house.
Cruel throngs of Furies,
come. Shake your torches.
My heart doesn't burn with
enough fury. It
would help to be filled with
something more monstrous.

MINISTER. What mad novelty then?

ATREUS. Nothing the limits
of normal pain can hold.
There's nothing I won't do
and nothing's enough.

MINISTER. Sword?

ATREUS.   Too small.

MINISTER.   What about
fire?

ATREUS.   Still too small.

MINISTER. Then what weapons's any
use for so much pain?

ATREUS. Thyestes himself.

MINISTER. This is worse than anger.

ATREUS. Yes, I admit it.
There's an uproar beating

my heart and turning
things over deep inside.
I'm rushed away and
where to I don't know but
I am being rushed
away. The ground bellows,
the clear day thunders,
the whole house creaks as if
the roof were breaking
and the spirits hide their
faces. Let it be
like this. Let it be an
evil you gods are
frightened of.

MINISTER.   But what?

ATREUS.   I don't know what but
greater than soul and
deeper than custom
and beyond the edge
of what people do
something is swelling
and urging on my
unwilling hands. It's
not that I know what
but it is something
great. All right then. This.
My soul, take it on.
It fits Thyestes,
it fits Atreus,
so we'll both do it
together. This house
long ago saw an
unspeakable feast.
I admit it's a
monstrous sin but it
has been taken on
before. Can my pain
find anything worse?
Stand by me, Procne
and Philomela,
my cause is like yours,
steady my hand. The

greedy father will
happily tear his
children to pieces
and eat his own joints.
It's fine. It's too much.
This is the kind of
punishment I like.
Meanwhile, where is he?
Why is Atreus
harmless for so long?
The whole picture of
slaughter is dancing
in front of my eyes,
bereavement heaped up
in the father's mouth.
My soul, why fall back
in fear? why collapse
before the real thing?
It has to be dared.
Do it. After all
the thing in all this
evil that's really
worst, he'll do himself.

MINISTER.   But how will we get him
to step in a trap?
He knows we're enemies.

ATREUS.   He couldn't be caught
unless he wanted to
catch us. He's hoping
to get my kingdom. In
this hope he'd run to meet Jove
threatening him with a
thunderbolt, in this hope he'd
dive into the threat of
boiling whirlpools or sail
into straits of treacherous
quicksands, in this hope,
what he thinks the greatest
danger, he'll see his
brother.

MINISTER.   Who'll make him trust
                 in peace? who'd he believe?

ATREUS.   With desperate hope
                 you believe anything.
                 But my sons can take
                 a message for uncle.
                 Come home, wandering
                 exile, change misery
                 for power and share
                 the rule of Argos. If
                 Thyestes is too
                 hard and spurns my offer
                 his raw sons are tired
                 of pain, easy to catch,
                 they'll be moved by it.
                 His old rage to be king,
                 hunger and hard work,
                 the pain will soften him.

MINISTER.   Time will have made his
                 hardship easy.

ATREUS   You're wrong.
                 The sense of pain grows
                 every day. Misery's
                 light. But to go on
                 bearing it gets heavy.

MINISTER.   Choose different helpers.

ATREUS.   Youth likes to listen to
                 worse lessons than this.

MINISTER.   They'll treat their father as
                 you say treat uncle.
                 Wickedness turns on you.

ATREUS.   If no one taught them
                 deceit and wickedness
                 power would teach them.
                 Are you frightened they
                 might get bad? They were
                 born to it. You call me

savage and harsh and
think I'm acting cruelly
and with no respect –
don't you think that might be
just what he's doing?

MINISTER.   Will your sons know the plot?

ATREUS.   You can't trust the young.
They might give us away.
You learn silence from
a lifetime of trouble.

MINISTER.   They'll deceive for you
and you'll deceive them?

ATREUS.   So they'll be safe from
blame and even from guilt.
Why mix my sons up
in a crime? It's our hate,
let it work through us.
No, you're doing it wrong,
you're shrinking away.
If you spare your own sons
you'll spare his too. Let
Agamemnon know the
plan, Menelaus
know how he helps father.
I can test if I'm
really their father by
how they do this crime.
If they refuse war and
won't wage my hatred,
if they call him uncle,
then he's their father.
All right then, off they go.
But an anxious face
can give a lot away,
great plans betray you
against your will. Better
they don't know how much
of a thing it is. You
hide what we're doing.

MINISTER.   I don't need telling.
It's locked deep in my heart
by loyalty and
fear, mainly loyalty.

CHORUS.   What fury's driving you
to keep hurting each other
and get the throne by crime?
You're so greedy for power
you don't know what king means.

Riches don't make king
purple robes don't
nor a crown,
it's not having golden doors.

King puts aside fear
and a cruel heart,
ambition
and being loved by the mob,

doesn't want treasure
dug in the west
or the grain
from Libya's threshing floors.

He's never shaken
by thunderbolt
or gales or
rough seas or soldiers' lances.

He's in a safe place,
looking at things,
he meets fate
and doesn't complain at death.

Though kings gather who
rule the Red Sea
and fight those
who walk on frozen rivers,

the good mind has a
kingdom. No need

for horses,
or machines hurling great rocks.

King means fear nothing,
desire nothing.
This kingdom
everyone gives himself.

Let whoever wants
stand powerful
on a peak –
I'd like sweet quiet to fill me.

In an obscure place,
with time for things,
unheard of,
my life will flow through silence.

When my days have passed
without clatter,
may I die
old and ordinary.

Death lies heavily
on someone who
known to all
dies unknown to himself.

THYESTES *and his three sons, the eldest is* TANTALUS.

THYESTES.   The roofs of the houses, I've
                   longed – the riches of Argos,
                   best of all for an exile,
                   earth and our own gods (if there
                   are in fact gods), there it is,
                   the towers the Cyclops built,
                   humans can't make such glory,
                   the crowd at the racecourse, look,
                   I used to be famous for
                   winning in father's chariot.

Argos will run to meet me,
crowds of people will run – but
so will Atreus. Go back
and hide in the thick forest,
a life among animals
and just like theirs. This shining
kingdom shouldn't seduce me
with false glitter. Look at the
gift but look at the giver.
Just now when things were all what
everyone calls harsh I was
strong and happy, and now I'm
being rolled round into fear.
My soul stands still and wants to
carry my body backwards,
each step is against my will.

TANTALUS. What is this? he's in a daze,
and looking back and stumbling.

THYESTES. Why are you hanging about
going over and over
something that should be simple?
Do you trust what you know you
can't, brother and power? fear
pain you've already beaten
and tamed, and run away from
hardship you've made good use of?
It's nice now being wretched.
Turn back while you can, get out.

TANTALUS. What's making you turn from our
country now you've seen it? Why
take your love away from such
good things? Your brother throws off
anger, comes back and gives you
half the kingdom, joins up the
dismembered limbs of our house
and restores you to yourself.

THYESTES. You're asking why I'm frightened.
The thing is I don't know.
I can't see anything to
be frightened of but I am

still frightened. I'd like to go
on but my knees give way and
my legs shake so I'm taken
somewhere other than where I'm
trying to get to – kidnapped.
Like a ship using oar and
sail, swept back by a current
that's stronger than oar and sail.

TANTALUS.   Wipe out whatever's blocking
your mind and see what prizes
are waiting for you. Father,
you can have the power.

THYESTES.   I have the power to die.

TANTALUS.   But the highest power is –

THYESTES.   Nothing, if you want nothing.

TANTALUS.   And you'll leave that to your sons.

THYESTES.   The throne doesn't hold two.

TANTALUS.   Would anyone want to be
wretched who could be happy?

THYESTES.   Listen, that great things make you
happy and harsh ones sad is
lies. When I was high up I
never put panic down, my
own sword on my thigh frightened
me. Oh it's so good to stand
in no one's way, eat dinner
lying on the ground. Killers
don't break into huts, you get
safe food at a plain table,
you drink poison from gold. I
know what I'm talking about.
Bad luck is better than good.
I don't have a house stuck up
on a mountain top to make
people gasp, no high ceilings
gleaming with ivory, no

bodyguards watching me sleep.
I don't fish with a whole fleet
or control the sea with a
massive breakwater. I don't
stuff my stomach with tributes
from tribes, I don't have fields
from the Danube river to
the Caspian sea harvested
for me. I'm not worshipped with
incense and flowers instead
of Jove. I don't have a garden
on my roof or a steam bath.
I don't sleep all day or join
night to night with drink.
I'm not feared. My house is safe
without weapons. And from small things
there comes a great quietness.
You have vast power if you
can manage without power.

TANTALUS.   It shouldn't be desired, but
if god gives it, surely it
shouldn't be refused either.
Your brother begs you to rule.

THYESTES.   Begs is frightening. There's a
trick in it.

TANTALUS.   But brothers can
feel what they used to, and love
can –

THYESTES.   Brother love Thyestes?
Oceans will wash the Great Bear,
whirlpools keep still, ripe corn
grow out of the sea, black night
light up the earth. Water and
fire, life and death, wind and sea
are more likely to make peace.

TANTALUS.   But what's going to go wrong?

THYESTES.   Everything. I don't know what
limit to put to my fear.

He can do as much as he
hates.

TANTALUS.   What can he do to you?

THYESTES.   I'm not afraid for myself
any more. It's you who make
me frightened of Atreus.

TANTALUS.   If you're already on guard
why be afraid of a trick?

THYESTES.   It's too late to be on guard
if you've just stepped in the trap.
Let it go.
But get one thing clear:
I'm following you.
I'm not leading you.

TANTALUS.   God protects good plans.
Go on. Walk steadily now.

ATREUS.   I see him, it's him
and the children too.
At last my hate's safe.
He's coming into
my hand, Thyestes
is coming, the whole
thing. I can hardly
control my soul, my
anguish is hardly
holding the reins. Like
a hound on a leash
slowly tracking prey,
it gets a scent of
pig far away and
follows it quietly,
but when the prey's near
it struggles and bays

and tears itself free.
When rage smells blood it
doesn't know how to
hide but still it must.
Look at his filthy
hair all over his
face and his foul beard.
Now to keep my word.

How wonderful it is to
see my brother. Give me the
embraces I've longed for.
Whatever anger there's been,
let it go. And from today
nourish the love due to blood
and weed hate out of our hearts.

THYESTES.   I could deny the whole thing
if you weren't like this.
But I confess, Atreus,
I confess. I have
done everything you thought.
Your love and duty
have made my case as bad as
possible. A real
villain to be a villain
to such a brother.
I've no advocate but tears.
You're the first person
to see me saying sorry.
These hands which never
touched feet before beseech you,
let our anger go
and let this raging tumour
be cut from our hearts.
As pledge of faith accept these
innocents, brother.

ATREUS.   Take your hands off my knees,
come into my arms.
Boys too, arms round my neck,
comforting the old.
Take off your filthy coat
and spare my eyes, take

clothes as good as mine and
be happy sharing
your brother's power. I
get greater glory
by leaving my brother
unharmed and giving
you back father's honour:
having power's luck,
what's good is to give it.

THYESTES.   The gods will pay you.
My filthy head refuses
the crown and my unlucky
hand drops the sceptre.
Let me hide in the crowd.

ATREUS.   This throne can hold two.

THYESTES.   Whatever's yours brother
I'll consider mine.

ATREUS.   Who refuses gifts from
fortune when they flow?

THYESTES.   Anyone who knows how
easily they ebb.

ATREUS.   Can't I have my glory?

THYESTES.   You've got your glory
already. Mine's waiting.
To refuse power
is my firm decision.

ATREUS.   If you won't accept
your share, I'll give up mine.

THYESTES.   I accept. I'll bear
the name of power you're
putting on me but
laws and arms will still serve
you and so will I.

ATREUS.

Wear these chains I'm putting
on your head and be
honoured. And I'll make the
sacrifice to the
gods of the victims I've
already chosen.

CHORUS.

Will anyone believe this?
Atreus, who can't control his mind,
   stood amazed at his brother.
      No force is stronger
than what you feel for your family.
      Strangers' quarrels last
but if you're joined by love you're joined forever.

When both sides have good cause
   to make them angry,
and Mars keeps the swords striking
   in his thirst for blood,
love forces you into peace.

What god's made this sudden quiet?
Civil war was wrecking the city.
   Pale mothers clung to their sons.
      We mended the walls
and mouldy towers, and barred the gates.
      Pale watchmen stared at
anxious night: worse than war is the fear of war.

Now it's swords that have fallen,
   the trumpets are still,
clashing clarions are silent.
   Deep peace has come back
to the delighted city.

When a north wind churns the waves
sailors are afraid to put to sea
   as Charybdis gulps it in
      and vomits it out,

and Cyclops is afraid Etna's fire
   that roars in his forge
may be put out by a great surge of water.

But when the wind drops the sea's
   gentle as a pool.
Ships were afraid but now
   small boats are playing.
There's time to count the fishes.

No luck lasts, pain and delight
take it in turn – delight's turn's shorter.
   Time flings you from low to high.
      If you wear a crown
   and tribes lay down their arms when you nod,
      soon everything shifts
and you fear how things move and the tricks
                                                    of time.

Power over life and death –
   don't be proud of it.
Whatever they fear from you,
   you'll be threatened with.
All power is under a greater power.

You can be great at sunrise,
   ruined by sunset.
Don't trust good times too much or
   despair in bad times.
The old women mix things up
   and spin every fate.
No one has gods so friendly
he can promise himself tomorrow.
   God turns our quick things over
      in a fast whirlwind.

MESSENGER. A whirlwind to fly me
       headlong through the air
       and roll me in a black cloud
       so the horror's ripped out of my eyes.
       O house even Tantalus
       would be ashamed of.

CHORUS.   What news do you bring?

MESSENGER. So where are we now? Argos?
       Sparta, whose brothers
       love each other? Corinth with
       twin seas? no maybe
       on the wild frozen Danube,
       with Caspian tribes
       under eternal snow or
       with the Scythians
       who just wander anywhere?
       what is this place that's
       in on this unspeakable...

CHORUS.   Speak and open up
       whatever it is.

MESSENGER. If my soul would keep still.
       If my rigid body
       would let go of my limbs.
       The violence sticks to my eyes.
       Take me far away,
       senseless tempests, take me where
       day is taken when it's snatched.

CHORUS.   You're keeping my soul
       in suspense that's worse.
       Say why you shudder
       and say who did it.
       Not who but which one.
       Just say it quickly.

MESSENGER. On top of the citadel
       part of the palace faces
       the south winds. It's high as a
       mountain and presses on the
       city, the people kick at

kings – it's got them where it can
strike. There's a huge glowing hall
that can hold a crowd, columns
brightly painted, golden beams,
but behind what everyone
knows about and can visit
the rich house divides into
more and more spaces – furthest
in, a secret place, a deep
hollow with old woods, the most
inward bit of the kingdom.
No cheery fruit trees here, just
yew and cypress and groves of
black ilex shifting about
and above them one tall oak
sticks up and masters the wood.
From here kings start their new reigns,
here they ask for help when it
all goes wrong. They stick up their
gifts here – noisy war trumpets
and broken chariots, wheels whose
axles were tampered with so
they'd win – all the things they've done,
Pelops' turban, all their
loot, a decorated shirt,
triumph over barbarians.
In the shadows there's a
sad spring that seeps through
black mud, like the ugly
water of Styx that
heaven swears by. They say
gods who deal with death
groan here in the blind night,
chains clank and ghosts howl.
Whatever you're frightened
to hear of, you see.
Wandering about, out of
their graves, turbulent
gangs who lived long ago,
and monstrosities
worse than you've ever seen
jump out. Even worse
the woods glitter with flames,
trees blaze without fire.

Something keeps bellowing
and the house is struck
with terror at huge shapes.
Day doesn't calm fear,
the grove is its own night,
at noon you still feel
this horror of spirits.
Seek an oracle,
with a huge din the fates
are loosed from the shrine,
the cave bellows a voice
as god is released.

When Atreus arrived
in a rage dragging
his brother's children, the
altars were decorated . . .
who can describe it
as it really was?
He ties the princes' hands
behind their backs, ties purple
ribbon on their sad heads;
no shortage of incense
or holy wine or salty
flour to sprinkle on the
sacrifice. The ritual's kept
in case evil's not done right.

CHORUS.   Who takes hold of the knife?

MESSENGER.   He's the priest himself.
He sings the death song,
prays violently,
stands at the altar,
the consecrated
sacrifices he
handles himself and
arranges them and
takes hold of the knife.
He pays attention,
nothing sacred's lost.
The grove's trembling, the
whole palace is shaken
from below, and it

totters, unsure where to put
its weight, and seems to move
up and down in waves.
From the left of the sky
a star runs dragging
a dark trail. The wine turns
bloody in the fire,
his crown keeps falling off,
ivory statues weep.
Everyone's moved by these
monstrous portents but
Atreus stands unmoved
and frightens the gods
who thought they'd frighten him.
And now he's standing
at the altar with a
savage sideways look.
Like a tiger in the
jungle between two
bulls, greedy but not sure
which to bite, turning
her jaws to this one then
looking back, keeping
her hunger waiting, he
eyes the victims and
wonders which to kill first.
It doesn't matter
but he enjoys putting
murder in order.

CHORUS.   So which does he attack?

MESSENGER.   First place (no lack of
respect) dedicated
to grandfather, so
Tantalus goes first.

CHORUS.   How did the boy look,
how did he face his death?

MESSENGER.   He looked unconcerned, there's
no point pleading, then
the savage buried the
knife in the wound and

pressed it in so deep
the hand reached the throat.
When he pulled the blade out
the corpse still stood there
not sure which way to fall,
then fell on uncle.
He dragged Plisthenes
to the altar and
put him by his brother.
He struck his neck and
cut through the nape so the
body crashed forward
and the head rolled away
with a querulous
sort of gasp or growl.

CHORUS.

When he'd carried out two
killings what did he do?
Did he spare the boy
or heap crime on crime?

MESSENGER.

You know what a lion's
like killing cattle,
its jaws are wet with blood
and its hunger's gone
but it can't let go of
its anger, it keeps
running at the bulls and
threatening the calves, but
it's tired and lethargic –
that's how Atreus was,
swollen with anger,
holding the bloodstained knife,
forgetting who he's
angry with, he drove right
through the body with
his murdering hand. The
knife's gone through the chest,
it's sticking out the back,
the boy falls, he'd have
died from either wound.

CHORUS.

Crime of a savage.

MESSENGER.   Does it make you shudder?
              If the evil stopped here
              we'd think it was good.

CHORUS.   Does nature allow
              anything more cruel?

MESSENGER.   You think this is the
              extreme limit of crime?
              It's the first step.

CHORUS.   What more could he do?
              Maybe he threw the
              bodies to wild beasts
              and refused them fire.

MESSENGER.   I wish he had. I
              don't want earth covering
              them or fire burning.
              He can give them to birds
              or drag them off as
              food for wild animals.
              After what happened
              you'd pray for things that are
              usually torture.
              I wish their father could
              see them unburied.
              Unbelievable crime,
              people will say it
              could never have happened.
              Vitals tremble, torn
              from living breasts and
              veins breathe and hearts still leap.
              But he handles them
              and tells fortunes from the
              veins on the entrails.
              When the animals are
              satisfactory, he's
              free for his brother's feast.
              He cuts the body in
              chunks, severs shoulders
              and difficult muscles
              of the upper arms,
              lays open the hard joints
              and cuts through the bones.

He keeps their faces
and the hands they gave him.
Offal stuck on spits
dripping over slow fires,
or bubbling in water.
Fire jumps over the feast
and two or three times
it's carried back to the
hearth and forced to burn.
The liver's hissing – it's
hard to say if fire
or flesh protested most.
The fire goes out in
pitch black smoke, and the smoke,
a thick fog, doesn't
go straight up to the sky,
it settles all around
in an ugly cloud.

Phoebus, god of the sun,
who suffers so much,
even though you've fled back
and plunged the broken
day out of the sky, still
you've set too late. The
father's tearing up his
sons and chewing his
own flesh, he looks splendid
his hair wet with oil
heavy with wine, sometimes
his throat closes and
holds back the food.
In all this evil, one
good thing, Thyestes,
you don't know the evil,
but that'll pass too.
Even though the sun god
turned his chariot back,
and sent night from the east
at a strange time to
bury the foul horror
in a new darkness, still
it must be seen. All
evils get laid open.

CHORUS.

Sun, where have you gone?
how could you get lost
half way through the sky?
The evening star's not here yet,
the chariot hasn't turned in the west
and freed the horses,
the ploughman whose oxen still aren't tired
can't believe it's suppertime.

The way things take turns
in the world has stopped.
There'll be no setting
any more and no rising.
Dawn usually gives the god the reins,
she doesn't know how
to sponge down the tired sweating horses
and plunge them into the sea.

Whatever this is
I hope it is night.
I'm struck with terror
in case it's all collapsing,
shapeless chaos crushing gods and men.
No winter, no spring,
no moon racing her brother, planets
piled together in a pit.

The zodiac's falling.
The ram's in the sea,
the bull's bright horns drag
twins and crab, burning lion
brings back the virgin, the scales pull down
the sharp scorpion,
the archer's bow's broken, the cold goat
breaks the urn, there go the fish.

Have we been chosen
out of everyone
somehow deserving
to have the world smash up and
fall on us? or have the last days come
in our lifetime? It's
a hard fate, whether we've lost the sun
or driven it away.

Let's stop lamenting.
Let's not be frightened.
You'd have to be really
greedy for life
if you didn't want to die when the whole world's
dying with you.

ATREUS.

I'm striding as high as the
stars, I'm above everyone,
my head's touching heaven. Now
I've the kingdom's glory and
father's throne. I'm letting the
gods go, I've got all my prayers.
It's fine, it's too much, it's
enough even for me.
But why should it be enough?
I'll keep going and cram him
full of his sons' death. Day's left
so shame won't get in my way.
On, while the sky's empty. I
do wish I could stop the gods
escaping and drag them all
to see my revenge. But no,
it's enough if the father
sees it. Without daylight I'll
scatter the darkness for you.
You've been lying there too long
having a nice feast, enough
food, enough wine, Thyestes
needs to be sober for this.

Open the temple doors.

I look forward to seeing
what colour he'll go when he
sees his children's heads, what words
his first pain will break out in,
how his body will stiffen.
This is what I've worked for. I

don't want to see him wretched,
just when he's getting wretched.

The hall's gleaming with torches.
He's lying on purple and
gold, heavy head on his hand.
He belches. O wonderful
me, I'm a god, I'm king of
kings. I've done more than my prayers.
He's had enough to eat. He's
drinking unmixed wine from the
silver cup – don't hold back on
the drink. There's still the blood, the
colour of wine will hide it.
With this this cup the meal ends.
I want the father to drink
his children's blood – he would have
drunk mine. Look, he's singing now,
and can't control what he thinks.

THYESTES.

Heart dulled so long
with terrible wrong
put away care
get rid of despair
no more the shame
of losing your name
It's more important where you
fall from than where you fall to.
It really is great
if you fall from a height
to stand on the plain
and walk on again.
It really is great
to bear all the weight –
But the bad times are over
so we'll forget all that.
The good are happy again, let good times roll,
and send the old Thyestes out of my soul.

A weakness of the
wretched, you never
believe you're happy.
Good luck comes back but
it's still hard for the

damaged to smile. Why
do you call me back
and stop me celebrating?
why make me cry, pain
surging up out of nowhere?
why not let me put
flowers in my hair?
It won't it won't let me. The
roses have fallen
off my head, my hair's
sleek with oil but it's
standing on end with
horror, I can't help
tears on my face and
groans get in my words.
Grief loves the tears it's used to
and the wretched get a
terrible desire to cry.
It's nice complaining,
it's nice tearing your
clothes, it's nice howling.
My mind's warning me
something bad's coming.
With no wind, smooth waters swell,
and that means a storm.
But what could it be?
Are you crazy? Trust
your trusting brother.
By now, whatever it is,
it's nothing or it's too late.
I don't want to be
unhappy. But inside
I've aimless terror
wandering about, I
burst into tears
and there's no reason.
Is it grief or fear?
Or does great joy make you cry?

ATREUS.　　　We'll always celebrate this
day with a feast, brother,
it makes my sceptre strong and
binds us in certain peace.

THYESTES.   Enough food and even
                 enough wine. The one thing
                 that could add to my pleasure –
                 share my joy with my children.

ATREUS.   Think of your sons as here
                 held tight by their father.
                 Here they are and always
                 shall be. No one's going
                 to take your children
                 away from you. I'll
                 bring you the faces
                 you're longing to see
                 and give father his
                 fill of family.
                 You'll have enough of them.
                 They're mixing, taking
                 part in the feast, a
                 young dinner, good fun,
                 but I'll get them. Take this cup,
                 it's an old family wine.

THYESTES.   I take this gift from my
                 brother, we'll pour wines to our
                 father's gods, then drain them –
                 but what's this? my hands
                 won't do it, weight's growing
                 making my right hand
                 heavy; when I lift the
                 wine it gets away
                 from my lips, it's spilling
                 round my jaw cheating
                 my mouth, and the table's
                 jumping up from the
                 floor. The lights hardly shine.
                 And now the heavy
                 sky's deserted, between
                 day and night, it's stunned.
                 Now what? more and more its
                 arch is shaken, it's
                 tottering, a thicker
                 fog's gathering with
                 dense shadows and night is
                 added to night. The

stars have all run away.
Whatever it is
I pray it spares my
brother and children
and the whole storm breaks
on this vile head. Now
give me back my sons.

ATREUS.   I'll give you them and
the day shall never come
to take them away.

THYESTES.   What's this uproar churning
my stomach? what's this
shaking inside? I can't
bear the load I feel
and my chest groans with a
groaning that's not mine.
Children, come here, your
unhappy father's
calling you, come here. This
pain will go when I
see your faces. Do I
hear their voices? where?

ATREUS.   Open your arms, father,
they're coming now.
Do you by any chance
recognise your sons?

ATREUS *shows* THYESTES *their heads.*

THYESTES.   I recognise my
brother. Earth how can you
bear all this evil?
Aren't you bursting open
and plunging to the
underworld and snatching
kingdom and king down
a vast road to chaos?
smashing the palace
and turning Mycenae
upside down? By now
both of us should be with

Tantalus. And there
and there break it open,
if there's anything
lower than hell and our
grandfather make a
huge chasm and hide us,
buried under the
river. Guilty souls can
wander over our
heads and the fiery flood
pour lava over
our exile. But earth is
unmoved. Heavy and
still. The gods have left.

ATREUS.   You should be happy
to see them, you kept on
asking for them. Your
brother's not stopping you.
Enjoy, kiss, embrace.

THYESTES.   Was our treaty this?
Is this your friendship,
is this a brother's love?
Let our hate go? I'm
not asking to be a
father with his sons
back unharmed. Just what
can be given with
crime and hate still whole,
I ask as a brother.
Let me bury them.
Give what you'll see burnt.
I'm not asking for
what I'll keep, just
what I'll lose.

ATREUS.   Whatever's left of
your sons, you've got it.
Whatever's not left,
you've got that too.

THYESTES.   Are they lying out as
food for fierce birds or

thrown to dogs or to
feed wild animals?

ATREUS.   You've eaten your sons yourself.

THYESTES.   This is what shamed the
gods and drove day back.
What voice can I give
to my misery? what
lament? what words will
be enough for me?
I can make out the
heads that were cut off,
hands ripped away, feet
wrenched from broken legs –
what even greedy
father couldn't eat.
Their flesh is heaving
inside me and the
evil shut in is struggling
with no way out and
trying to escape.
Your sword, brother, the
one with my blood on.
I'll make the children
a way out with steel.
You won't? I'll break my
chest by beating it.
No, hold back your hand,
leave their souls in peace.
Whoever saw such
evil? Do wild tribes
on the rocks of the
Caucasus do this?
Was Procrustes worse,
terrorising . . .? Look
I'm crushing my sons
and they're crushing me.
Is there any
limit to crime?

ATREUS.   Crime should have a limit
when you commit a crime,
not when you avenge it.

Even this is too
little for me. Hot blood
straight out of the wound
into your mouth while they
were still alive, yes,
my anger was cheated
because I hurried.
I attacked them with a
sword, brought them down at
the altar, fed the fire
with their blood, hacked the
bodies and tore them to
small chunks that I plunged
into boiling water
or grilled on slow fires.
I cut still living flesh,
I fixed the offal
on thin spits and watched it
hissing and fed the
flames with my own hands. And
all this the father
could have done much better.
This pain is no use.
He tore his sons apart
but he didn't know
and they didn't know.

THYESTES.   Shut in by shifting shores,
hear me, seas, and you hear this
crime, gods, wherever you've run;
hear, underworld, hear, lands, and
night, heavy with hell's black clouds,
have time for my cries, (I've been
left to you, only you see my
misery, you who've been left
by the stars) I won't pray for
anything wicked, I can't
ask anything for myself,
what could there be for me now?
It's you I'm praying for.
Whoever's in charge of the
sky and is lord of the air,
wrap the whole earth in rough clouds,
from every side at once send

wars of winds, and thunder. And
not with the hand that seeks out
ordinary houses that
don't deserve any harm, but
the one by which the massive
mountains fell and the Giants
who stood as tall as mountains –
send those weapons. Twist your fires.
Make up for the lost day, launch
flames, give us lightning instead
of the light snatched from the sky.
Don't waste time on a judgment –
call both our causes bad. Or
anyway let mine be bad.
Aim at me, send a flaming
brand forked like an arrow through
this body. To bury my
sons as a father should and
give them to the last fire, I
must be cremated.
But if nothing moves the gods
and no spirit punishes
the wicked, then I'd like the
night to last forever and
cover the vast crime
with endless dark. I've nothing
to complain about if the
sun stays gone.

ATREUS.   Now I can praise my hands.
Now I've really won.
I would have wasted my
wickedness if you
didn't suffer like this.
Now I believe my
children are really mine,
now I get back my
faith in my marriage.

THYESTES.   How did my children deserve . . . ?

ATREUS.   Because they were yours.

THYESTES.   Sons killed for the father –

ATREUS.   Yes, and what makes me happy
                     mine are mine and yours are yours.

THYESTES.   Where were the gods who
                     protect the innocent?

ATREUS.   Where were the marriage gods?

THYESTES.   But who'd try to balance
                     a crime with a crime?

ATREUS.   I know what it is
                     you're complaining about.
                     You're suffering because
                     I snatched the crime away,
                     you're not grieving at
                     gorging forbidden food
                     but because you weren't
                     the one to prepare it.
                     You'd have liked to set up
                     just this sort of feast
                     for your brother who
                     wouldn't have known what
                     was going on and
                     get their mother to
                     help you attack my
                     children and throw them
                     down to the same death.
                     Just one thing stopped you –
                     you thought they were yours.

THYESTES.   Avenging gods will come.
                     I leave you to them
                     for punishment.

ATREUS.   For punishment
                     I leave you to your children.